Middle East Today

Series Editors
Fawaz A. Gerges
Department of International Relations
London School of Economics
London, UK

Nader Hashemi
Center for Middle East Studies
Josef Korbel School of International Studies
University of Denver
Denver, CO, USA

The Iranian Revolution of 1979, the Iran-Iraq War, the Gulf War, and the US invasion and occupation of Iraq have dramatically altered the geopolitical landscape of the contemporary Middle East. The Arab Spring uprisings have complicated this picture. This series puts forward a critical body of first-rate scholarship that reflects the current political and social realities of the region, focusing on original research about contentious politics and social movements; political institutions; the role played by non-governmental organizations such as Hamas, Hezbollah, and the Muslim Brotherhood; and the Israeli-Palestine conflict. Other themes of interest include Iran and Turkey as emerging pre-eminent powers in the region, the former an 'Islamic Republic' and the latter an emerging democracy currently governed by a party with Islamic roots; the Gulf monarchies, their petrol economies and regional ambitions; potential problems of nuclear proliferation in the region; and the challenges confronting the United States, Europe, and the United Nations in the greater Middle East. The focus of the series is on general topics such as social turmoil, war and revolution, international relations, occupation, radicalism, democracy, human rights, and Islam as a political force in the context of the modern Middle East.

More information about this series at
http://www.palgrave.com/gp/series/14803

Irene Weipert-Fenner • Jonas Wolff
Editors

Socioeconomic Protests in MENA and Latin America

Egypt and Tunisia in Interregional Comparison

Editors
Irene Weipert-Fenner
Peace Research Institute Frankfurt
Frankfurt am Main, Hessen, Germany

Jonas Wolff
Peace Research Institute Frankfurt
Frankfurt am Main, Hessen, Germany

Middle East Today
ISBN 978-3-030-19620-2   ISBN 978-3-030-19621-9 (eBook)
https://doi.org/10.1007/978-3-030-19621-9

© The Editor(s) (if applicable) and The Author(s), under exclusive licence to Springer Nature Switzerland AG 2020
The chapter "From North Africa to Latin America and back: Comparative findings and theoretical reflections" is licensed under the terms of the Creative Commons Attribution 4.0 International License (http://creativecommons.org/licenses/by/4.0/). For further details see licence information in the chapter.
This work is subject to copyright. All rights are solely and exclusively licensed by the Publisher, whether the whole or part of the material is concerned, specifically the rights of translation, reprinting, reuse of illustrations, recitation, broadcasting, reproduction on microfilms or in any other physical way, and transmission or information storage and retrieval, electronic adaptation, computer software, or by similar or dissimilar methodology now known or hereafter developed.
The use of general descriptive names, registered names, trademarks, service marks, etc. in this publication does not imply, even in the absence of a specific statement, that such names are exempt from the relevant protective laws and regulations and therefore free for general use.
The publisher, the authors and the editors are safe to assume that the advice and information in this book are believed to be true and accurate at the date of publication. Neither the publisher nor the authors or the editors give a warranty, express or implied, with respect to the material contained herein or for any errors or omissions that may have been made. The publisher remains neutral with regard to jurisdictional claims in published maps and institutional affiliations.

Cover illustration: © Aanas Lahoui / shutterstock.com

This Palgrave Macmillan imprint is published by the registered company Springer Nature Switzerland AG
The registered company address is: Gewerbestrasse 11, 6330 Cham, Switzerland

Preface

This book is the result of a collaborative research project that was carried out by the Arab Forum for Alternatives (AFA—Egypt), the Peace Research Institute Frankfurt (PRIF—Germany), and the University of Sfax (Tunisia) between 2013 and 2018. During this period, the core group consisted of eight scholars: Nadine Abdalla, Nayera Abdelrahman Soliman, and Amr El Shobaki at AFA; Samiha Hamdi and Bassem Karray at Sfax University; and Jan-Philipp Vatthauer, Irene Weipert-Fenner, and Jonas Wolff at PRIF. The project was entitled "Socioeconomic protests and political transformation: dynamics of contentious politics in Egypt and Tunisia against the background of South American experiences." Between 2013 and 2018, we met at least once a year to discuss our empirical research, theoretical interpretations, and political implications. In addition to our project workshops, we also organized panels at international conferences to discuss our findings with other scholars. Visiting fellowships offered further opportunity for cooperation. The group grew closer, bringing up new ideas such as joint field research. Inter-institutional ties developed, too, and paved the way for a new joint research project that has just started and will continue our research on the social question in the Middle East and North Africa (MENA) and beyond.

None of this would have been possible without the generous funding of the Volkswagen Foundation. We are particularly indebted for the funds specifically targeted at young researchers, which enabled us to provide important support to the Ph.D. candidates in our team. We would also like to express our gratitude for the helpful guidance in handling administrative procedures and for keen sensitivity to challenges arising from changing political contexts. The Volkswagen Foundation has been impressively supportive throughout this project, in particular Dr. Anika Haverig.

We toured the world (at least parts of it) to present and discuss our work at the Middle East Studies Association (MESA), the International Political Science Association (IPSA), the German Middle East Studies Association (DAVO), the German Political Science Association (DVPW), the Arab Council for the Social Sciences (ACSS), and the Latin American Studies Association (LASA), to name but a few. On these occasions, as well as during various events we organized at PRIF, we were lucky enough to receive an astonishing amount of input from great scholars, from experts on MENA and Latin America, as well as from scholars whose work generally focuses on the socioeconomic dimension of political change in the Global South. We gained fascinating insights and a great deal of food for thought. In particular, we would like to thank Amr Adly and Hamza Meddeb, who eventually became a part of the team (as their chapter in this book testifies), as well as Federico Rossi and Eduardo Silva, who shared their insights and thoughts about many things with us during our final conference including the question of popular sector incorporation, and provided helpful comments on several draft chapters of this volume. In addition, several colleagues contributed with critical questions and thought-provoking ideas: Naoual Belakhdar, Chantel Berman, Dina Bishara, Melanie Cammett, Didier Chabanet, Janine Clark, Carine Clert, Ruth Collier, Emmanuela Dalmasso, Thomas Demmelhuber, James M. Dorsey, Kristina Dietz, Marie Duboc, Bettina Engels, Lorenza Fontana, Carmen Geha, Doaa Kaddah, Markus Loewe, Chiara Loschi, Ellen Lust, Rania Masri, Katia Pilati, Hans-Jürgen Puhle, Jillian Schwedler, Yann Philippe Tastevin, Zafiris Tzannatos, and Fréderic Volpi as well as several people from the Egyptian Center for Economic and Social Rights, the Forum Tunisien de Droits Économiques et Sociaux, and the Friedrich-Ebert Foundation.

The project was carried out in close cooperation with the research network "Re-configurations" at the Centre for Near and Middle East Studies (CNMS) at Marburg University. We owe particular gratitude to Thorsten Bonacker, Susanne Buckley-Zistel, Anika Oettler, Rachid Ouaissa, Achim Rohde, Laura Ruiz de Elvira, Mariam Salehi, and Christoph Schwarz. At AFA, we also thank Mohamed El Agati. At Sfax, Amour Boubakri, who was a team member during the very first stages of the project before he left Tunisia for Afghanistan, provided important ideas and helped set up the cooperation between our institutions. At PRIF, we owe crucial observations and suggestions to several of our colleagues. In the early phase of drafting the project, Achim Spanger was particularly important in critically challenging our ideas. During the final stages, Cornelia Hess, supported by Nadine Benedix, was indispensable in preparing the manuscript. Several interns and student research assistants also contributed with literature research, data collection, and critical comments, including Matteo Barutzki, Giuseppe Campisi, Johanna Faulstich, Francy Koellner, Ouassima Laabich, Janne Rossen, Isabel Ruckelshauss, Yannick Schimbera, Jonas Schröder, Clara Süß, Babette Ullemeyer, and, most notably, Prisca Jöst, who eventually became a co-author of one of the contributions to this volume. At Palgrave, we would like to thank Alina Yurova and Mary Fata for the excellent management of our book project. We also highly appreciate the valuable comments and suggestions of an anonymous reviewer. Finally, Matthew Harris greatly improved the language of all the chapters that follow.

Last but not least, we also would like to express our gratitude to all the activists in Egypt and Tunisia who were kind enough to talk to us, take us to their field of contention, and explain their situation and challenges to us.

Frankfurt, Germany Irene Weipert-Fenner
Frankfurt, Germany Jonas Wolff
January 2019

Praise for *Socioeconomic Protests in MENA and Latin America*

"This book breaks new ground in its approach to comparison and theory building. It presents original analyses of socio-economic protest in the little studied cases of Egypt and Tunisia in light of theory generated in more extensively studied cases across Latin America. The result is at once a major intra-regional study of socio-economic grievance in the MENA region and how it opens space for larger uprisings that make demands for major regime change, at the same time that it builds cross-regional theory about dilemmas of different movement strategies concerning autonomy, politicization, and decentralization. The result is a new model of comparative analysis as well as a novel analysis of the Arab spring."
—Ruth B. Collier, *Professor, University of California, Berkeley, USA*

"In *Socioeconomic Protests in MENA and Latin America*, Irene Weipert-Fenner and Jonas Wolff made a unique in its kind double comparative effort. They put together a group of stellar scholars to comparatively analyze the revolts for democratization in Tunisia and Egypt through the lenses of the Latin American literature. The role of trade unions and popular movements in South America's dynamics of democratization and the struggles for reincorporation are interconnected with the cross-national comparative analysis of Tunisia and Egypt to understand the political economy of these dynamics. This thought provoking volume offers a new inter-regional research agenda that will certainly redefine the current debates in the MENA."
—Federico M. Rossi, *Professor, CONICET-National University of San Martín, Argentina, and author of* The Poor's Struggle for Political Incorporation

"*Socioeconomic Protests in MENA and Latin America* stands out among a crowded field of books on the 2011 uprisings in Tunisia and Egypt. Easily one of the most theoretically rich frameworks to date, Weipert-Fenner and Wolff led a collection of scholars through a multi-year project that examined not the uprisings per se but protests dealing with economic grievances and inequalities that began well before the uprisings and continued after the largest crowds went home. The result is an empirically and theoretically rich set of contributions that, unlike most edited volumes, cohere into a whole that is greater than even its excellent parts. This book is a must read for its substantive engagement with the contentious politics literature and its rich original empirical material. The shadow comparison with socioeconomic protests in Latin American further extends the reach of this collection well beyond those interested primarily in the MENA region."

—Jillian Schwedler, *Professor, City University of New York, USA*

"This groundbreaking volume offers a theoretically persuasive and empirically rich account of the role of socioeconomically motivated contentious action against the politics of austerity during the Arab Spring and its aftermath. In a tightly crafted, flexible analytical framework that combines structure, agency, and contingency, a comparison to broadly similar cycles of protest in Latin America drives home a crucial the point. The dynamics of contention of the Arab Spring and its political consequences were not just the product of distinctive culture or the diffusion of democratic norms but decisively linked to world historical political-economic trends—a brilliant synthesis of social movement theorizing and comparative political economy."

—Eduardo Silva, *Professor, Tulane University, New Orleans, USA*

Contents

1 Introduction: Socioeconomic Protests in Times of
   Political Change—Studying Egypt and Tunisia from a
   Comparative Perspective   1
   Irene Weipert-Fenner and Jonas Wolff

Part I   General Trends   41

2 Beyond Regime Change: The State and the Crisis of
   Governance in Post-2011 Egypt and Tunisia   43
   Amr Adly and Hamza Meddeb

3 Socioeconomic Contention in Post-2011 Egypt and
   Tunisia: A Comparison   71
   Prisca Jöst and Jan-Philipp Vatthauer

Part II Organized Labor   105

4 Organized Labor and Political Change in Latin America:
   An Overview   107
   Jonas Wolff

5 Proposals, Intermediation, and Pressure: The Three Roles of the UGTT in Tunisia's Post-revolutionary Constitutional Process   123
Bassem Karray

6 From the Dream of Change to the Nightmare of Structural Weakness: The Trajectory of Egypt's Independent Trade Union Movement After 2011   145
Nadine Abdalla

Part III Marginalized Groups   169

7 Contention by Marginalized Groups and Political Change in Latin America: An Overview   171
Jonas Wolff

8 Unemployed Protests in Tunisia: Between Grassroots Activism and Formal Organization   195
Samiha Hamdi and Irene Weipert-Fenner

9 Mobilized Along the Margins: Survival Strategies of Tuktuk Drivers in Egypt   221
Nayera Abdelrahman Soliman

Part IV Conclusion   249

10 From North Africa to Latin America and Back: Comparative Findings and Theoretical Reflections   251
Irene Weipert-Fenner and Jonas Wolff

Notes on Contributors

Nadine Abdalla is visiting assistant professor of Sociology at the American University in Cairo (AUC) and research associate at the Arab Forum for Alternatives (AFA), Beirut. She holds a Ph.D. from Sciences-Po Grenoble. Her areas of expertise are labor and youth movements, the socio-political transformation in Egypt, as well as the European Neighborhood Policy. Her work was published in academic journals such as *Mediterranean Politics* as well as by many think tanks and research centers such as The European Institute of the Mediterranean (IEMed) in Barcelona, the Arab Reform Initiative (ARI) in Paris, and The Middle East Institute (MEI) in Washington.

Nayera Abdelrahman Soliman is a Ph.D. fellow at the Berlin Graduate School for Muslim Cultures and Societies, Freie Universität Berlin. She also worked as a fellow researcher at the Arab Forum for Alternatives (AFA), Beirut.

Amr Adly is an assistant professor in the Department of Political Science at the American University in Cairo (AUC). Previously, he worked at Stanford University, at the Middle East Directions Programme at the European University Institute (EUI) and as a non-resident scholar at the Carnegie Middle East Center. His research centers on political economy, development studies, and economic sociology of the Middle East. He is the author of *State Reform and Development in the Middle East: The Cases of Turkey and Egypt* (2012), and his articles have appeared in a number of peer-reviewed journals, including *Business and Politics*, the *Journal of Turkish Studies*, and *Middle Eastern Studies*.

Samiha Hamdi holds a Ph.D. of Sociology from the Faculty of Arts and Humanities, University of Sfax, and is a member of the research unit Etat, Culture et Mutations de Société (ECUMUS) at this university.

Prisca Jöst is a Ph.D. candidate at the Department of Political Science, University of Gothenburg, affiliated with the Program on Governance and Local Development (GLD). Previously, she was a student research assistant at the Peace Research Institute Frankfurt (PRIF). Her work focuses on political participation and social movements in Africa and the Middle East.

Bassem Karray is professor in Public Law at the Faculty of Law of the University of Sfax. He is also a member of the Fiscal Studies Center and Doctoral School of the Sfax Faculty of Law as well as an associated member of the European Law Laboratory of the Faculty of Legal, Political and Social Science of Tunis. He has worked as a consultant for Tunisian and international NGOs and organizations as well as Tunisian authorities on manifold topics such as constitutional law, decentralization, Euro-Mediterranean relations, as well as customs law and international trade.

Hamza Meddeb is assistant professor at the Mediterranean School of Business, South Mediterranean University in Tunis and non-resident scholar at the Carnegie Middle East Centre. His research interests focus on the intersection of political economy, security studies, and state-society relations in Tunisia. He is the co-author of *L'État d'injustice au Maghreb. Maroc et Tunisie* (2015, together with Irene Bono, Béatrice Hibou and Mohamed Tozy). His work has been widely published, such as in *Middle East Law and Governance*.

Jan-Philipp Vatthauer is deputy spokesman of the parliamentary group of Die Linke in the German Bundestag and associate fellow at the Peace Research Institute Frankfurt (PRIF). Between 2014 and 2017, he worked as a doctoral researcher at PRIF.

Irene Weipert-Fenner is a senior research fellow at the Peace Research Institute Frankfurt (PRIF). She holds a Ph.D. in political science from Goethe University Frankfurt. She works on authoritarian regimes, democratization, and social movements in Egypt and Tunisia. Her articles have appeared in peer-reviewed journals such as the *Journal of North African Studies* and *Politische Vierteljahresschrift* (PVS). She is the co-editor of

Clientelism and Patronage in the Middle East and North Africa: Networks of Dependency (2018, together with Laura Ruiz de Elvira and Christoph Schwarz).

Jonas Wolff is head of the research department "Intrastate Conflict" and executive board member of the Peace Research Institute Frankfurt (PRIF). His research focuses on the transformation of political orders, contentious politics, international democracy promotion, and Latin American politics. Recent publications include *The Negotiation of Democracy Promotion: Issues, parameters and consequences* (*Democratization* Special Issue, 2019, co-edited with Annika E. Poppe and Julia Leininger) and *Justice and Peace: The role of justice claims in international cooperation and conflict* (Springer, 2019, co-edited with Caroline Fehl, Dirk Peters, and Simone Wisotzki).

List of Figures

Fig. 3.1	Protests in Tunisia. Source: Authors' data collection based on the ACLED data set	77
Fig. 3.2	Socioeconomic protesters in Tunisia. Source: Authors' data collection based on the ACLED data set	81
Fig. 3.3	Protesters' demands in Tunisia. Source: Authors' data collection based on the ACLED data set	83
Fig. 3.4	The types of protest in Tunisia. Source: Authors' data collection based on the ACLED data set	84
Fig. 3.5	Protests in Egypt. Source: Authors' data collection based on the ACLED data set	87
Fig. 3.6	Socioeconomic protesters in Egypt. Source: Authors' data collection based on the ACLED data set	92
Fig. 3.7	Protesters' demands in Egypt. Source: Authors' data collection based on the ACLED data set	93
Fig. 3.8	Types of protests in Egypt. Source: Authors' data collection based on the ACLED data set	94
Fig. 9.1	Belqas, Egypt; October 18, 2017; taken by researcher	223
Fig. 9.2	The view after crossing the bridge over the railway "Mazlaa'an," taken by the researcher, June 29, 2015	239
Fig. 9.3	Picture taken from a tuktuk in Belqas by the researcher, June 22, 2015	244

List of Tables

Table 1.1	Dynamics of socioeconomic contention	14
Table 3.1	Protest numbers in Tunisia and Egypt (in brackets: per million inhabitants)	76
Table 3.2	Socioeconomic protests by region in Tunisia	86
Table 3.3	Socioeconomic protests by region in Egypt	95
Table 9.1	Laws and protests related to tuktuks from 2008 to 2016	226

CHAPTER 1

Introduction: Socioeconomic Protests in Times of Political Change—Studying Egypt and Tunisia from a Comparative Perspective

Irene Weipert-Fenner and Jonas Wolff

1.1 INTRODUCTION

When millions of people took to the streets in late 2010 and early 2011, first in Tunisia, then in Egypt, they shouted slogans such as *khubz wa ma', Ben 'Ali la* (bread and water, no to Ben Ali), *shughl, hurriyya, karama wataniyya* (employment, freedom, national dignity), and *'aysh, hurriyya, 'adala ijtima'iyya* (bread, freedom, social justice). In the very moment when the two uprisings successfully brought down the respective dictators, it became undeniable that socioeconomic grievances had played an important role in motivating people to dare the—until then—unthinkable: to directly and openly challenge the rule of two repressive authoritarian regimes. Yet, shortly after the toppling of Ben Ali and Hosni Mubarak,

I. Weipert-Fenner (✉) • J. Wolff
Peace Research Institute Frankfurt, Frankfurt am Main, Hessen, Germany
e-mail: weipert-fenner@hsfk.de; wolff@hsfk.de

© The Author(s) 2020
I. Weipert-Fenner, J. Wolff (eds.), *Socioeconomic Protests in MENA and Latin America*, Middle East Today,
https://doi.org/10.1007/978-3-030-19621-9_1

this seemed to have been forgotten: rapidly, the reform of political institutions and conflicts over (religious) identity and civil-military relations began to dominate the political agenda—and academic debates too (Al-Anani 2012; Albrecht and Bishara 2011; Albrecht and Ohl 2016; Brumberg 2013; Zeghal 2013).[1]

In terms of political developments, Egypt and Tunisia have taken different paths since polarization between Islamists and secular forces reached its height in the summer of 2013 in both countries. In Egypt, the military used the mass demonstrations to oust the then president Muhammad Morsi, to reassume power, and to openly oppose first the Muslim Brotherhood and soon afterwards all kinds of oppositional groups (Pioppi 2013; Roll 2016). Tunisia took another direction: a compromise was brokered between the Islamist al-Nahda Party and the anti-Islamist groups with the help of four civil society organizations referred to as the National Dialogue Quartet. Additional external pressure from international financial institutions contributed to the emergence of an elite consensus, which was long portrayed as a success story, but was also criticized for not moving in any direction apart from re-establishing old power structures and suppressing dissent (Boubekeur 2016; Marzouki and Meddeb 2016). Since 2018, cracks in this consensus have become visible, yet the democratic order seems to be firmly established (Dihstelhoff 2018).

In spite of the different political trajectories, both countries saw the introduction of a new constitution as well as presidential and parliamentary elections in 2014. Frequent government reshuffles, including changes of prime minister, notwithstanding, it seems that in the course of 2015 the political transition phase—to democracy in one case and to a reconfigured authoritarian regime in the other—gave way to a period of relative politico-institutional stability. Also, when it comes to questions of socioeconomic development and economic policies, the post-revolutionary trajectories in the two countries have been remarkably similar. The predominant state response during the first years after the revolutions was marked by pragmatic muddling through that refrained from pursuing structural and/or redistributive reforms. Post-revolutionary governments in Egypt and Tunisia were unable and/or unwilling to improve the socioeconomic situation of the general population, and as a result, the socioeconomic grievances

---

[1] For an overview of the first wave of publications on the transformations in the Arab World of 2011, see Weipert-Fenner (2014). For the second wave, see Grimm (2015), and for further consolidated overviews, see Valbjørn (2015) and Bank (2018).

that were key drivers of the 2010–2011 uprisings remained unaddressed. This state of affairs was reflected in the surveys of the Arab Barometer, which showed a clear continuity in this regard: no matter whether people were asked in 2007, 2011, 2013, or 2015 (Tunisia) and 2016 (Egypt), "the economic situation" was cited as the most important challenge of the respective country by more than 60%.[2] This is remarkable, given that scholars generally acknowledged that socioeconomic concerns were important drivers of the uprisings in Tunisia, Egypt, and beyond, and they speculated that addressing "citizen demands for material improvement and social justice" would be crucial for the future of the political transformations (Burnell 2013, p. 846; see also Bayat 2013; Costello et al. 2015, p. 97; Dupont and Passy 2012, p. 101; Schlumberger and Matzke 2012, pp. 107–108).

Against this background, the present book addresses a set of key questions: What has happened to the socioeconomic discontent voiced in the mass mobilizations of 2010 and 2011 in Egypt and Tunisia? How did socioeconomic protests, understood here as contentious collective actions in which socioeconomic demands are raised, develop after the fall of Ben Ali and Mubarak, including the issues being contested and the actors involved? How did the political actors of the transition period react to socioeconomic contention, including the ways in which they dealt with contentious actors and eventually modified their economic policies? What were the resulting dynamics of contentious politics, that is, the patterns of interaction between state and contentious actors? This is all the more important as socioeconomic grievances not only fueled the general frustration voiced in the uprisings of 2011 but also found expression prior to 2011 in socioeconomic protests. More specifically, in both countries the 2000s were marked by a general (re-)emergence of socioeconomic protests and by particular protest events and cycles of contention that gained nationwide attention.

With hindsight, these pre-revolutionary dynamics of socioeconomic contention have been interpreted as having sowed the seeds for the uprisings. In Egypt, these were mainly labor protests. As Nadine Abdalla's contribution elaborates in detail, starting in 2004, a wave of strikes both among blue- and white-collar workers led to the mobilization of around two million people by 2010. As Joel Beinin has argued, these strikes played

---

[2] The Arab Barometer survey data is available for all four waves on arabbaromter.org. Also, Teti et al. (2018) confirm the importance of socioeconomic grievances for 2011 based on different survey data.

a major role in delegitimizing the regime and popularizing a culture of protest (Beinin 2012). While very few and small political movements and organizations such as Kifaya reconquered the public space by raising domestic political claims, it was the workers' movement that expanded the scope and the repertoire of contention (Duboc 2015; El-Mahdi 2011; Weipert-Fenner 2013). Through this, the movement "began to weaken the barrier of fear" (Allinson 2015, p. 305). But important incidents such as the bread shortage in 2008, which led to spontaneous protests in front of bakeries, were also crucial, as they evoked the powerful collective memory of the so-called bread riots of 1977. Not least important for this sensitive parallel, the army intervened and distributed bread (produced in army-owned companies) in the streets in order to resolve the crisis (Kamal 2015, 43). Socioeconomic protests made it clearly visible that welfare, one pillar of regime legitimation, had ceased to exist for many social groups. At the same time, they opened the public space for contentious actions.

In Tunisia, protests started to spread from 2008 on in the marginalized interior regions of the country (Allal 2013). The most important one was the six-month-long uprising in the Gafsa mining basin. Starting as a small-scale protest by unemployed people, who had expected to be on new hiring lists of the public sector mining company, mobilization spread and turned into a general outcry against the socioeconomic marginalization of the region, including a lack of jobs, miserable infrastructure, and unfair distribution of wealth within the country (Allal 2010; Gobe 2010). Only massive state repression brought the regional uprising to an end. Another example of a symbolically important socioeconomic protest was the contentious actions in August 2010 in Ben Guerdane, a town on the border with Libya that lives off informal transnational trade. Attempts to divert the gains of this lucrative business into the pockets of the clan of Ben Ali's wife Layla Trabelsi were met with heavy resistance by the local population (Allal 2013). Similar to workers' protests in Egypt, the importance of socioeconomic contention did not lie in directly calling for the end of autocracy; instead, the protests "revealed cracks in the edifice of party-state influence and control" (Allal 2013, p. 191), and thus undermined the power of the authoritarian regime.

In contrast to Egypt, where labor activism developed outside a completely state-controlled trade union federation, the situation in Tunisia was more complex. Today, the Tunisian General Labor Union (Union Générale Tunisienne du Travail, or UGTT) is hailed for its mediator role within the National Dialogue Quartet that won the Nobel Peace Prize in 2015 for ending the deadlock between secular and Islamist politicians and bringing the constitutional process to a successful end. Before the uprising, however, the national level of the UGTT did not play any supportive role in democracy, nor did it support socioeconomic protests. This pro-regime stance of the national leadership dates back to the general strike in 1978 and the bread riots in 1983–1984, when the UGTT had still played a crucial role in mass mobilizations and had made use of its high legitimacy stemming from its active role in the struggle for independence (Beinin 2016). Yet, the state response at that time was brutal, and high levels of repression made the national level of the UGTT more obedient to the authoritarian elites. Only local cadres remained autonomous; the regional level was already (perceived as being) part of the regime. In the Gafsa revolt mentioned earlier, for instance, regional UGTT leaders and their clientelist recruitment practices were a trigger for protests that, unlike their national counterparts, local UGTT cadres supported (Beinin 2016, p. 103; Netterstrøm 2016, pp. 384, 388, 393). This means that, before 2011, local activism was the backbone of socioeconomic protests, inside and outside the UGTT, which did not call for regime change but gradually undermined authoritarian power by reviving contention in the public space. By establishing networks of mobilization, this activism also made it possible for protests to spread and, in this sense, paved the way for the revolution of 2011.

In both cases, Egypt and Tunisia, the dictators were brought down by a cross-class mobilization and no revolutionary power directly acclaimed rule for itself. Although they did not take the steering wheel, not even the center stage, the major socioeconomic protest actors prior to 2011 played an important role during the uprisings. In both countries, their major contribution—though manifested in different forms—was, first, to help the protests to start and spread and, second, in augmenting the pressure on the ruling elites to let their former head fall. Regarding the role of Egyptian labor, Abdalla elaborates in Chap. 6 that, although the entirely co-opted Egyptian Trade Union Federation (ETUF) opposed any protest, individual workers as well as independent labor organizations were present from the first days of the uprising on January 25 and 28, both at Cairo's Tahrir Square and across the country. In early February, a nationwide strike wave brought the country to a standstill, creating massive civil disobedience that spread across 20 out of 29 governorates and even encompassed military-owned companies—one indication "that sustained workers' mobilization was a cause for concern for the SCAF [Supreme

Council of the Armed Forces], which intervened to force Mubarak to step down on February 11, 2011" (Bishara 2018, pp. 135–136).

In contrast to Egypt, where the uprising started and ended in the capital Cairo, the Tunisian revolution began in the marginalized interior regions. Triggered by the self-immolation of Muhammad Bouazizi in December 2010, socioeconomic protests demanding jobs and development quickly spread from Sidi Bouzid to similarly marginalized regions, among them the protest-prone Gafsa mining basin. Only after three weeks, the protest wave reached the capital Tunis and included more politically oriented demands such as the fall of the regime. Also, in Tunisia, the behavior of the national trade union federation was more nuanced than in Egypt. Following the pre-revolutionary pattern described earlier, local UGTT members were the first to interpret Bouazizi's self-immolation "not as a suicide … but rather as a political assassination; they cast Bouazizi as a victim of [the] regime" (Angrist 2011, quoted in Langhohr 2014, p. 181). With the escalation of protests and violence, more and more local UGTT bureaus, first in Gafsa and Kasserine, later in Sfax and Sousse, and finally in Tunis, went on strike and, thereby, helped spread protests across the whole country (Langohr 2014, p. 183; Omri 2016; Zemni 2013). During the last days of the revolution, even members of the trade union federation's national executive office withdrew their support for the regime and called for a national strike on January 13—a day later, Ben Ali gave up power and fled the country (Chomiak 2014, pp. 38–39).

Considering this important role of socioeconomic protests in preparing and helping spread the mass uprisings of 2010 and 2011 as well as in building up pressure that contributed to tipping the scales in favor of the dictators' ouster, it is even more surprising that socioeconomic issues did not play an important role in the political debates that immediately followed the dictators' fall. Furthermore, this observation requires explanation, because it apparently applies to both regimes, democratic Tunisia and Egypt's reconfigured autocracy. Given the continuity and even aggravation of socioeconomic grievances after 2011, this edited volume explores whether and how socioeconomic discontent was voiced publicly during the first five years after the revolutions (2011–2016). In combining comparative macro-studies, including a quantitative protest-event analysis, with detailed qualitative case studies on key protagonists in socioeconomic protests, the contributions offer a systematic account of the post-revolutionary dynamics of socioeconomic contention in Egypt and Tunisia. In-depth case studies cover the two most important types of socioeconomic contention found in the quantitative analysis: labor protests and protests by marginalized groups, that is, socioeconomically disadvantaged people outside or at the margins of the formal economy.[3] Finally, we engage in an interregional comparison with Latin America, focusing on experiences in this region with the interrelated dynamics of socioeconomic contention and political change since the late 1970s. In the democratic transitions in Latin America during "the long 1980s,"[4] socioeconomic grievances had also contributed to the mobilization of dissent that undermined authoritarian rule. Yet, much like what happened in Egypt and Tunisia, during the political transition processes themselves, socioeconomic demands were generally sidelined (see Chaps. 4 and 7).

In the following four sections, we present and critically reflect upon the contentious politics approach as applied in this study (see Sect. 1.2), elaborate the analytical framework that was used to systematically study socioeconomic contention in Egypt and Tunisia (see Sect. 1.3), give a brief overview of socioeconomic contention in the Middle East and North Africa (MENA) beyond Egypt and Tunisia (see Sect. 1.4), and lay out the rationale and the limitations of the interregional comparison with Latin America (see Sect. 1.5). The chapter concludes with an overview of the contributions compiled in this book (see Sect. 1.6).

1.2 Contentious Politics as a Conceptual Toolbox: A Critical Reflection

The focus of this book is on contentious politics, understood here as non-routinized interactions between the state and recognizable sets of people who engage in collective claim-making.[5] The latter include a wide range of

---

[3] We define marginalized groups as socioeconomically disadvantaged groups that are either unemployed or employed in precarious conditions and/or outside the structures of the formal economy. Marginalized groups are marginalized in at least one of the following regards (but frequently in more than one): general socioeconomic marginalization (poor people); marginalization from the official labor market (informal sector, unemployed); socio-geographical marginalization (rural areas, remote regions, urban shantytowns).

[4] The "long 1980s" include the years between the transitions to democracy in the Dominican Republic and Ecuador in 1978/1979 that started the 1980s wave of democratization in Latin America and the return to democracy in Chile in 1989/1990. During these years, the majority of Latin American countries underwent transition from non-democratic to democratic regimes.

[5] Given the focus on non-routine politics, the (increasingly sectoral) strikes of the UGTT that were staged according to formal procedures demanding better working conditions were

social actors who can be more or less formalized and more or less stable (from business associations and trade unions to social movements and spontaneous protests). "The state" encompasses governments, agents of governments, and polity members in a broader sense (judiciaries, parliaments, political parties). The book draws on the refined version of the contentious politics approach in which Charles Tilly, Sidney Tarrow, and colleagues have modified their all too structuralist and rationalist framework by recognizing the crucial roles of agency, ideas, and interactions. However, because their approach can still not be expected to simply "fit" the specific dynamics of contentious politics in the countries at hand, we use the approach neither as a fixed template for "pigeonholing" actors and events nor as an explanatory framework to be "applied" to our cases. In a much more modest—but still very useful—way, the contentious politics approach basically helped us to define and clarify some of our core concepts and typologies. At the same time, the approach served as one important source of our analytical framework—a framework that is descriptive and inductive rather than explanatory and deductive.

The contentious politics approach developed by Tilly, Tarrow, and colleagues is part of a broader research program that deals with social movements and related aspects of unconventional collective action.[6] It has emerged, in particular, from the polity model introduced by Tilly (1979), which emphasized the crucial role of political opportunities and constraints in shaping processes of mobilization and demobilization (see Tarrow 1998). What became known as the "political opportunity approach" or "political process theory" essentially explained the dynamics of contentious politics by focusing on changes in political opportunities and constraints that incentivize or deter collective action.[7] This emphasis on the (changing) political context in which contentious collective action takes place constitutes an important correction to those theories that, in

---

not analyzed in a separate case study. In their chapter on the political economy of both countries, Adly and Meddeb reflect on the power of the public sector, mainly represented in the UGTT. Two general strikes by the UGTT that can be considered non-routinized actions were staged for political reasons, and thus do not represent socioeconomic protests (see Vatthauer and Weipert-Fenner 2017, p. 28).

[6] The literature on the contentious politics approach is vast. For key contributions, see McAdam et al. (2001) and Tilly and Tarrow (2007).

[7] "When institutional access opens, rifts appear within elites, allies become available, and state capacity for repression declines, challengers find opportunities to advance their claims" (Tarrow 1998, p. 71).

the tradition of Ted Robert Gurr (1970), regard perceived discontent, grievances, or "relative deprivation" as the core drivers of contentious action (see Schock 1996, pp. 98–105). In fact, there is little doubt that it is of crucial relevance for the dynamics of contentious politics whether protest actors who challenge a given political regime are confronted with institutional access or with extensive repression, whether rifts among elites create potential allies, or whether political, economic, and military elites are unified in rejecting the challenge. Yet, the approach originally put forward by Tilly and colleagues had a clear structuralist and rationalist bias, which also made it rather static.[8] Competing approaches to social movements highlighted the relevance of agency, of ideas and ideologies, as well as of the dynamic and creative nature of mobilization and interaction processes. From a constructivist perspective, for instance, scholars have drawn attention to the need to analyze framing processes and, in particular, collective action frames (Benford and Snow 2000). From an actor-centered, rationalist perspective, resource mobilization theory has emphasized the role of economic, communication, and human resources, of preexisting organizational structures, and of "movement entrepreneurs" (McCarthy and Zald 1977).[9]

In taking up at least part of this criticism, in their more recent theoretical conceptualizations, Tarrow, Tilly, and colleagues have integrated the dynamic role of agency and actors, social interaction and communication:

> But in the course of our work on a variety of contentious politics in Europe and North America, we discovered the necessity of taking strategic interaction, consciousness, and historically accumulated culture into account. We treat social interaction, social ties, communication, and conversation not merely as expressions of structure, rationality, consciousness, or culture but as active sites of creation and change. We have come to think of interpersonal networks, interpersonal communication, and various forms of continuous negotiation—including the negotiation of identities—as figuring centrally in the dynamics of contention. (McAdam et al. 2001, p. 22)

---

[8] See, for instance, the harsh criticism by Goodwin and Jasper (1999), the sympathetic discussion of the evolution of Tilly's work by Tarrow (2008), and the self-critical reflections and theoretical modifications in McAdam et al. (2001, chap. 1).

[9] These two are, of course, only the most prominent "competitors." For overviews of the state of social movement research, see Della Porta and Diani (2015), Goodwin and Jasper (2004), Morris and McClurg Mueller (1992), McAdam et al. (1996), and Rucht et al. (1999). For a recent reformulation of grievance theory, see Simmons (2014).

As a consequence, in their 2007 book, Tarrow and Tilly included mechanisms such as "social appropriation" (the transformation of nonpolitical into political actors) or "identity shift" (the formation of new identities within challenging groups) in their analytical framework (Tilly and Tarrow 2007, p. 34).

These modifications make it possible to apply the contentious politics approach without downplaying the significance of agency, ideas, or the dynamic (and contingent) nature of interaction processes. But, still, certain blind spots remain, as does the structuralist legacy. These limitations of the approach become particularly clear when research dealing with societies outside the rather specific part of the world—"Europe and North America" (McAdam et al. 2001, p. 22)—on which the contentious politics approach is largely built is taken into account. It was only in the late 1990s that the approach was applied to and further developed in other regions.[10] Major contextual differences such as the autocratic nature of many political regimes and different socioeconomic challenges in developing countries were generally identified as factors that shape state-society relations and thus affect the dynamics of contentious politics (Shigetomi 2009, p. 6). In what follows, we highlight a number of insights from the two regions this book is concerned with: Latin America and, of course, Middle East and North Africa (MENA).

In a review of studies on social movements and political change in Latin America, for instance, Kenneth Roberts argued that democratization "may provide social actors with new channels of access to public institutions, but it can also remove authoritarian rulers against which opposition forces unified and mobilized, inject divisive forms of partisan competition into social organizations, and resurrect political parties and electoral activities that can siphon off energy from social networks" (Roberts 1997, p. 139). In this sense, political opportunity structures that, according to the contentious politics approach, should facilitate contentious collective action had, in fact, demobilizing effects in a series of Latin American countries. At the same time, however, in later years this same structural political context enabled a remarkable re-emergence of social protest and social movements (see Chaps. 4 and 7). The combination of relatively open political opportunity structures with the

---

[10] For overviews of social movement studies on different regions of the Global South, see Brandes and Engels (2011) on Africa, Rossi and Bülow (2015) on Latin America, and Beinin and Vairel (2013) on MENA.

social hardships associated with neoliberal reforms certainly constituted the overall structural background that enabled this new cycle of contention; still, in explaining dynamics and differences in contentious mobilization across the region, scholars have emphasized the creative agency of individual and collective actors, associational networks that could be used, appropriated, and transformed by such actors, as well as the relevance of collective action frames (for instance, in the case of indigenous movements).[11] Another specific issue that has emerged from studies of Latin America involves the issue of clientelism, patronage, and, more generally, informal institutions which have been shown to be crucial in shaping interactions between contentious actors and "the state" and are, thus, important to consider if we are to understand cycles of contention in this region (see Auyero 2000; Lapegna 2013; Wolff 2007, 2008).

With a view to the MENA region, the concept of contentious politics was first and foremost applied to the study of Islamist movements (Bennani-Chraïbi and Fillieule 2003; Clark 2004; Wickham 2002; Wiktorowicz 2004). Underlying this was the attempt to show that Islamist activism was "not unique" but a normal social phenomenon that "has elements common to all social movements" (Singerman 2004, p. 13). Yet, in some cases, the contentious politics approach was simply applied in order to prove that the MENA region fitted the concept instead of critically reflecting on its limitations and blind spots (see Bayat 2005). Furthermore, while the approach was already further developed in the 2000s, as explained earlier, these innovations were only selectively integrated into studies on the MENA region (see Meijer 2005, p. 289). As a result, Beinin and Vairel (2013b, p. 6) argued that structural determinism continues to shape research on social movements in the region.

Several studies shortly before or shortly after the Arab uprisings included different kinds of social contentions such as the workers' and civil rights movements (Beinin and Vairel 2013a; El-Mahdi 2009; Weipert-Fenner 2013). These studies showed that the contentious politics approach can indeed be helpful for understanding the dynamics of contention in the MENA region by conceptualizing repertoires of contention, formal and informal protest networks, and cycles of contention. What is important

---

[11] See, for instance, the studies by Silva (2009), Van Cott (2005), and Yashar (2005). For broader comparative assessments of social movements in Latin America from different theoretical perspectives, see the edited volumes by Alvarez et al. (1998), Eckstein (2001), Eckstein and Wickham-Crowley (2003), Johnston and Almeida (2006), and Rossi and Bülow (2015).

here is the clear focus on actors' perceptions and relations, which has enabled scholars to avoid assumptions of "structuralism and teleology" (Beinin and Vairel 2013b, p. 19). From this perspective, the different contexts in which contentious politics are embedded in the MENA region do not prevent scholars from applying the approach but, if systematically studied from the actors' perspectives, offer a chance to contribute to the further development of the approach itself. This is even more important as the context in which the cases studied in this book are situated was characterized by dynamic, yet ambivalent transformation processes. Against this background, we agree that

> the Middle East and North Africa can be understood using the tools that social science has developed for the rest of the world. And we argue that the Middle East and North Africa provide a complex and fascinating laboratory, not only to confirm the applicability of SMT [social movement theory] but also to enrich our theoretical knowledge of social movements and other forms of political contestation. (Beinin and Vairel 2013b, p. 2)

A number of studies have recently been published that indeed critically reflect upon and further develop certain elements of the social movement literature. On state responses to public contention for instance, Dina Bishara used the example of the Egyptian tax collectors' protests for a more nuanced understanding of "ignoring" as a government reaction (Bishara 2015). Jannis Grimm and Cilja Harders refined the working of the protest-repression nexus by analyzing the massive violence used by the Egyptian regime against Islamist protests in 2013 (Grimm and Harders 2017). In *Clientelism and Patronage in the Middle East and North Africa* (Ruiz de Elvira et al. 2018), several contributions discuss the connection between clientelism and contentious politics. In a special issue edited by Frédéric Volpi and Janine Clark, case studies from across the MENA region were used to develop the social network approach in social movement studies (Volpi and Clark 2019). In an impressive historical work, John Chalcraft (2016) reconstructs two centuries of MENA history through the lens of popular protests, making pragmatic use of elements of the contentious politics approach in a way similar to the present book (see Chalcraft 2016, pp. 22–29). The majority of publications, however, have focused on social mobilization in the context of the mass upheaval of 2010/2011 (Asseburg and Wimmen 2017; Bayat 2017; Della Porta 2014; Ketchley 2017; Sika 2017; Volpi 2017).

All in all, the events of 2011 and the ensuing processes still unfolding across the MENA region have stimulated lively debates about contentious politics, which have given rise to the development of creative approaches to the study of social movements. In the following section, we lay out our contribution to this debate.

1.3 Socioeconomic Protests and Political Change: The Analytical Framework

Our book seeks to contribute to a better understanding of a particular kind of contentious collective action: socioeconomic contention. Drawing on work on social movements in Latin America (Eckstein and Wickham-Crowley 2003; Johnston and Almeida 2006), we define socioeconomic contention as encompassing all kinds of protest in which claims refer to at least one of the following types of socioeconomic issues: (1) productive activities (e.g., access to land, subsidies, credits, taxes); (2) social consumption (e.g., public services, health, education, water, transportation, price/tariff subsidies); (3) income (e.g., wages, collective contracts, pensions, work, income transfers); and (4) labor rights (e.g., the right to unionize, employment standards) (see Weipert-Fenner and Wolff 2015, pp. 5–6).

In responding to such socioeconomic demands during processes of political transformation, governments need to deal with contradictory claims that, on the one hand, demand protection of economic elite interests, which tend to be threatened by protest-driven processes of political transformation, and, on the other, call for a redistribution of socioeconomic resources ("social justice"), which tend to accompany demands for a redistribution of political power (Wolff 2008, 2009). This challenge may be limited to disputes about specific policy changes with redistributive consequences, but becomes particularly serious when the process of transforming the political order also gives rise to a more fundamental debate about changing the economic order. At the same time, the above-mentioned reference to labor rights, such as the right to unionize, already shows that socioeconomic contention is not only about *policy*-related demands but also about *polity*-related claims. In this polity dimension, the question is how emerging political regimes balance respect for the autonomy of contentious actors and their interest in controlling them, and to what extent they establish institutionalized mechanisms of inclusion or choose strategies of exclusion. Our analytical framework (Table 1.1) therefore distinguishes between (1) the policy

Table 1.1 Dynamics of socioeconomic contention

	Protest demands	*Political responses/consequences* (range of options)
Policy dimension (*substantial*)	Economic and social policies	Continuity vs. policy change
	Economic order	Continuity vs. structural change
Polity dimension (*institutional*)	Political inclusion	Inclusion vs. exclusion
	No repression/co-optation	Autonomy vs. control

dimension, which includes redistributive struggles over economic and social policies as well as the shape of the economic order at large, and (2) the polity dimension, which includes conflicts over bottom-up demands for political inclusion and top-down attempts at repression or co-optation.

As Table 1.1 suggests, the distinction between these two dimensions is relevant to both the claims made by protest actors and the political responses and consequences.[12] In analyzing the dynamics of socioeconomic contention, the studies compiled in this book thus address four key questions: (1) Which types of demand for changes in specific economic policies or in the economic order are made and how far-reaching are they, and (2) to what extent do political authorities promise and actually implement corresponding changes? (3) To what extent do socioeconomic protests refer to issues of political inclusion or control, and (4) to what extent and in what way does "the state" incorporate, co-opt, or repress the corresponding protest actors.[13]

Theoretically, such a perspective on socioeconomic contention does not build on a neo-Marxian approach such as that of Achcar (2013) or Abdelrahman (2014). Rather, it addresses the debates on the dissolution of the authoritarian social contract or pact in the Arab world. In one interpretation, the Arab uprisings were considered a result of the breakdown of a previous kind of social contract in which the autocratic regimes had offered

---

[12] The latter category includes direct governmental responses—such as repression or concessions—that directly respond to a given protest (see Franklin 2009) as well as broader, and usually more indirect, consequences that protests and entire cycles of contention may bring about (see Giugni et al. 1999).

[13] In the polity dimension, the fourfold range of options includes the ideal-type liberal-democratic form of political incorporation (inclusion with autonomy) and its opposite, repression (exclusion with control), but also co-optation (inclusion with control) and marginalization (exclusion with autonomy).

limited socioeconomic benefits in exchange for loyalty (see Guazzone and Pioppi 2009; Zorob 2013). In this reading, the social pact was regarded for a long time as one explanation for autocratic persistence in the MENA region. While the neo-patrimonial states (Eisenstadt 1973) essentially controlled economic, political, and social affairs, the co-optation of corporatist organizations gave them some bargaining power vis-à-vis the state, but without allowing for public dissent or bottom-up participation (Desai et al. 2009). Yet, liberalization and privatization reforms increasingly undermined this arrangement, and the state increasingly withdrew from welfare provision. One result was the increase in informal ways of coping with daily life, a process that Harders called the informalization of the social pact (2003). Another result was the (re-)emergence of the socioeconomic protests before 2011, outlined earlier. Since these protests are interpreted as a symbol of the dissolution of this pact as well as an action actively challenging it, the question arises whether a new (or renewed) social contract would emerge, what it might look like, and what role socioeconomic protest actors might play in it (see Karshenas et al. 2014).

In contrast to the notion of a social contract or pact, which focuses on the emergence, dissolution, and potential renewal of stable and coherent patterns of state-society and state-economy relations, we wanted to be open to fuzzier, more fluid, and rather fragmented configurations, in which old and new mechanisms of societal integration may coexist and in which segmented "subcontracts" incorporate different societal groups in different ways. In terms of our analytical framework, for instance, policy concessions (potentially aimed at specific protest actors) can combine with strategies of repression (aimed at the same or other groups) as attempts at including certain social groups, but can coexist with the marginalization of others.[14] More generally, it is important to emphasize that our framework is applicable across different regime types.

1.4 Socioeconomic Contention in Middle East and North Africa: An Overview

The present study focuses on Egypt and Tunisia as the two MENA countries in which mass protests in the context of the Arab uprisings actually led to the successful toppling of the sitting president and a substantive

---

[14] We return to this overarching question in the concluding chapter, in which we draw on the scholarship on political incorporation (in Latin America) in order to help make sense of recent developments in Egypt and Tunisia (see Chap. 10).

attempt at peacefully transforming the political regime at hand. As such, they are the only two contemporary cases in the region in which we can study the dynamics and consequences of socioeconomic protests in times of political change, that were not subject to foreign intervention and/or civil war. In this sense, too, the initial observation—that socioeconomic grievances were a key element in the Arab uprisings but were then very much sidelined in the post-revolutionary context—is most puzzling for Egypt and Tunisia. Yet, the overall issue of socioeconomic protests is certainly relevant beyond the two countries studied in this book. As the following brief overview of recent episodes of socioeconomic contention in MENA shows, there are quite a few similarities when it comes to protest actors, claims, and dynamics across the region, at least based on the still-limited knowledge we have.

With the exception of the resource-rich countries of the Gulf, which have mostly been able to buy off discontent as a long-term strategy, most countries in the MENA region have witnessed recurring and increasing waves of socioeconomic protest since 2011. One overall feature of these processes is that "while each country has its own specific profile of discontent, the narrative of disaffection with incumbent rulers and the prevailing political economies resonated across the borders of Arab countries, that share a common language and similar but not identical historical experiences of economic and political development" (Cammett and Salti 2018, p. 90). As a result, as Cammett and Salti's (2018) analysis of the 2011 uprisings suggests, grievances were relatively similar across the region, yet in the individual countries, different social groups suffered most. From this perspective, it does not make much sense to try to identify one specific social group—such as the youth, the middle class, or the poor—as the key driving force behind the uprisings.

Starting from the Western border of the MENA region, Morocco has witnessed unemployed activism since the 1990s that started off as clear criticism of the regime and a lack of jobs for university graduates. Yet, in the wake of Morocco's version of the Arab uprising, the February 20 movement, relevant organizations refrained from joining protests critical of the regime and retained their own routinized protest events that the regime tolerates and eventually rewards with public sector jobs (Emperador Badimon 2013). However, a massive wave of protests against its socioeconomic marginalization has recently emerged in the Rif region. Starting in November 2016, with the death of 31-year-old fisherman named Mohsen

Fikri in al-Houceima, a city in the Rif mountains,[15] spontaneous protests developed into sustained mobilization against poverty, unemployment, and corruption. Under the charismatic and efficient leadership of Nasser Zafzafi, organizational structures and social media usage helped sustain the mobilization. In spite of state repression, up to May 2017, more than 700 protest events had been counted under the banner of *Hirak al-Rif* (Masbah 2017, p. 6). In 2018, activists, among them Zafzafi, were detained and received harsh sentences, leading to solidarity protests across the country. Of course, as in the cases studied in this book, resistance did not come out of the blue but had historical roots: the Rif movement dates back to the anti-colonial movement of Abdelkarim Khattabi (1920–1926) and the rebellion of 1958–1959 (Wolf 2018).

Less acknowledged by international observers are socioeconomic protests in Algeria. In 2011, an unemployed movement—organized in the Committee for the Defense of the Rights of the Unemployed—emerged in Southern Algeria, condemning their marginalization in spite of oil wealth, in particular in the Ouargla Province. In 2013, unemployed activists staged an unprecedentedly large demonstration to voice their grievances and oppose neoliberal reforms (Belakhdar 2015, p. 34). Since 2014, however, due to low oil and gas prices, the government has reduced social spending through subsidy cuts and import restrictions, leading to rising food prices. In 2018, the situation worsened and led to increasing socioeconomic protests. A huge number of labor protests were staged by teachers' unions and by employees in the public health sector (Chikhi 2018). Socioeconomic protests also changed their repertoire of contention in the marginalized South. New forms of contention were introduced, such as boycotting government-financed cultural events in order to divert the resources to investment in regional infrastructure and activists "sewing their mouths shut" (Marwane 2018).

Even less attention has been paid to a cycle of labor protests in Jordan starting in 2011 with a sharp increase in workers' protests from 139 in 2010 to 829 in 2011. The protest level remained high in 2012 (901) and 2013 (890) but started to decrease in 2014 (Phenix Centre for Economics and Informatics Studies 2017, p. 8), dropping to 229 in 2017 (Phenix Centre for Economics

---

[15] After confiscating his goods, the police threw his catch into a garbage truck and turned the compactor on when Fikri jumped into the truck to save his fish. The video of the horrible scene that led to Fikri's immediate death was quickly distributed across the MENA region, although its mobilizing effects occurred among the Amazigh population in Morocco.

and Informatics Studies 2018). This can be explained as resulting from government responses to public sector workers, a mix of concessions (higher salaries and improved working conditions) as well as state pressure on workers to stop protesting. However, labor activism in the private sector persisted. In the summer of 2018, more than 30 trade unions began a general strike against an increase in income tax, which turned into cross-class protest against subsidy cuts and a general erosion of welfare in the course of neoliberal policies. Prime Minister Hani Mulki had to step down, and the reforms demanded by the International Monetary Fund (IMF) were put on hold (Ababneh 2018; Francis 2018).

Protests against the state's failure to provide basic services have been recurrently staged in Iraq in recent years, but gained nationwide attention in 2018. In the oil-rich South, people suffered from unemployment and poor living conditions including electricity cuts and water shortages. During the summer, protests, including riots and violent attacks on government buildings, denounced corruption and neglect by politicians (International Crisis Group 2018; Mohammed and Jalabi 2018). Iran has also seen a wave of socioeconomic protests since 2017 against price increases, unemployment (particularly among university graduates), and deteriorating living conditions, which ultimately spread to 85 cities (Asadzade 2018; Bayat 2018). One of the hotbeds was the province of Khuzestan, rich in natural resources yet poorly developed and marginalized from state elites, with the country's highest level of unemployment (Perletta 2018).

While this overview of socioeconomic protests in MENA is by no means comprehensive, the examples still clearly show how widespread the phenomenon is and suggest that there has been a broader trend of expanding socioeconomic protests in terms of numbers and intensity since 2011. Furthermore, the overview indicates that the major protest actors, labor and people in marginalized regions, in particular when the regions are rich in natural resources, are major driving forces of socioeconomic contention beyond Egypt and Tunisia, too. Before drawing hasty conclusions, we need to acknowledge that we still know too little about this sub-phenomenon of contentious action in the MENA. For a thorough understanding, all of these protests need to be studied in detail, including how they are embedded within the national, regional, and local collective memories of resistance. For the two cases studied in this volume, we found memories of the past to be important when it comes to understanding the grievances, framings, perceptions of entitlement, the interplay with the state (or different state actors), and the repertoires of contention. In spite of all specificities, Egypt and Tunisia also show that socioeconomic protest can contribute to undermining entrenched authoritarian regimes. Furthermore, even when socioeconomic protests remain small, locally limited, issue-specific, spontaneous, and beyond formal organization, as observed in Egypt and Tunisia, Latin American experiences tell us that fragmented forms of mobilization can also provide a foundation on which larger dynamics of contentious action can build and ultimately push for far-reaching change, even at the macro-political level.

1.5 Comparing MENA and Latin America: Rationale and Limitations

When the Arab uprisings ushered in processes of political transformation in at least parts of MENA, including attempts to establish democratic regimes, scholars could not draw on comparable experiences from this specific region in order to make sense of what was happening and what might come in the future. Similarly, in connection with our more specific topic, contentious politics in general and socioeconomic contention in particular have only quite recently become topics of scholarly interest. Latin America, by contrast, is a world region that offers a wealth of well-researched insights into the relationship between contentious politics, socioeconomic dynamics, and political change, both in the context of what (with hindsight) can be identified as transitions to democracy and, more recently, in the context of challenges to and transformations of the post-transition model of "neoliberal democracy." Consequently, this book systematically uses empirical experiences from and academic research on Latin America to inspire, orient, and interpret comparative analysis of Egypt and Tunisia.[16]

Within Latin America, we chose to focus on South America because most of Latin America's transitions to democracy during the "long 1980s" occurred in this particular subregion.[17] The countries of Central America

---

[16] We are aware of two studies that have also drawn on Latin American experiences in order to better understand recent developments in the MENA region and in Egypt and Tunisia, in particular (Grand 2014; Kellogg Institute for International Studies and Kroc Institute for International Peace Studies 2012). In contrast to this book, these studies focus on the issue of democratization and reflect the situation immediately following the Arab uprisings. An interregional comparison that includes MENA and Latin America and focuses on workers and organized labor can be found in Lazar (2017).

[17] With the exceptions of Colombia and Venezuela, all South American countries—namely, Argentina, Bolivia, Brazil, Chile, Ecuador, Paraguay, Peru, and Uruguay—experienced a transition to democracy between the late 1970s and 1990 (see, for instance, Hagopian and Mainwaring 2005).

were excluded because democratization there mostly took place in the context of transitions from civil war to peace. Mexico is also mostly ignored because the 71 years of one-party rule (until 2000) meant that democratization took a very particular shape in that country that contrasts with experiences both in South America and in Egypt and Tunisia. Furthermore, the more recent revival of popular protest and the so-called leftist turn in Latin American politics it gave rise to was mainly concentrated in South America.[18] In both episodes, during the transition to democracy as well as in the context of the shift to the left, socioeconomic contention played a relevant role, as Jonas Wolff shows in his overviews of the dynamics and consequences of protests by organized labor (see Chap. 4) and by marginalized people (see Chap. 7) in Latin America.

The reconstruction of what happened to socioeconomic contention during the processes of democratization in Latin America and the analysis of how socioeconomic issues made it back to the top of the political agenda decades later does not aim at producing generalizable knowledge on socioeconomic protests in the context of political transformation that may subsequently simply be applied to the cases of Egypt and Tunisia. Instead, the overall aim of the interregional perspective is to de-essentialize the challenges and backlash faced by the two North African countries, to broaden the horizon of expectations for multiple dynamics of contentious politics in the socioeconomic field beyond "democratization" and "authoritarian resurgence" and to inspire empirical case studies on Egypt and Tunisia that think "outside the MENA box" about alternative routes developments can take. In this sense, this book certainly does not claim to engage in a classic comparison of "most-similar" or "most-different" cases. Yet, as we demonstrate, accumulated knowledge on contentious transformations in Latin America can serve as a source of inspiration for interpreting contemporary dynamics in the MENA region and open up new perspectives on possible future trajectories. At the same time, though, there are a number of challenges and limitations to the comparison that need to be reflected upon.

As MENA is the region that most recently saw a regional wave of anti-autocracy uprisings, any comparison with uprisings and transformations that are somehow similar in other world regions is inevitably a diachronic

---

[18] Starting with Hugo Chávez in Venezuela (1998) and Lula da Silva in Brazil (2002), all South American countries except Colombia experienced the election of left-of-center governments in the early 2000s. The most prominent cases include Argentina, Bolivia, Brazil, Chile, Ecuador, Uruguay, and Venezuela (see Levitsky and Roberts 2011; Silva 2009).

one. This did not prevent cross- and interregional comparative studies from emerging after 2011 (see Bank 2018, pp. 126–127). However, it requires reflection on the repercussions that differences in time have on our findings. First of all, for the Latin American cases, we look at much longer periods under study—and we can do so with hindsight. In the landmark study on *Transitions from Authoritarian Rule* in Latin America from the mid-1980s, for instance, Bolivia was analyzed as a failed democratization and Brazil as a case of liberalization of authoritarian rule (O'Donnell et al. 1986). It was not until the end of the 1980s that it could be concluded that Bolivia between 1979 and 1985 had experienced a turbulent, but eventually successful return to democracy that involved significant political crises and a return to temporary military rule in the process. In the case of Brazil, the process of gradual liberalization initiated in the late 1970s turned into outright democratization only at the end of the 1980s. This serves as a reminder that political transformations are processes not events and that, in the cases of Egypt and Tunisia, we are still talking about processes that were only initiated fairly recently. The experiences of countries like Bolivia or Brazil thus remind us of the need to be cautious about dismissing cases such as Egypt as a failed transformation or to think of the MENA region as having simply returned to stable authoritarianism, as has been argued by some scholars (e.g., Brownlee et al. 2013). There is no deterministic development to democracy, but we need to be open to the "dynamic, ambivalent, and open-ended processes of transformation" in the region (Hoffmann et al. 2013, p. 2; similarly, Asseburg and Wimmen 2017, p. 4; Sadiki 2009). This, of course, includes awareness that we cannot know how the processes in MENA will continue to unfold, making every conclusion based on comparison with Latin America a tentative one.

Second, the comparison is biased to some extent because of the much longer period of scholarship in the Latin American cases (between 30 and 40 years vs. 7 years). Again, given the vast amount of material to be dealt with, we consider this an asset for our endeavor. The rich body of research on Latin America allows us to engage in an interregional comparison where we can combine a comprehensive literature review of one region with original empirical research on the other one. Yet, as scholarship on the uprisings and the aftermath in MENA is currently growing at a rapid pace, it is necessary to keep in mind that new perspectives will certainly emerge that will require rethinking our results, too.

Third, comparing different historical periods and therefore different contexts calls for additional elaboration. There is one fundamental difference between world regions that is of utmost importance to our study: the different sequence of the (attempted) replacement of authoritarian regimes and the implementation of neoliberal reforms. With the exception of Chile, most Latin American countries embarked on an in-depth restructuring of their economy, including of state-economy relations, along the lines of the so-called Washington Consensus after authoritarian rule came to an end in their respective countries. The MENA cases, by contrast, initiated neoliberal reforms quite a few decades before the Arab uprisings, in the late 1970s (Egypt) or early 1980s (Tunisia). These reforms were implemented very slowly, and popular resistance to cuts in social spending, such as the infamous bread riots (1977 in Egypt, 1984 in Tunisia), caused the regimes to be even more careful.[19] At the same time, the slow pace of the privatization of former state companies revealed only incrementally that, instead of a free market economy, these reforms had brought about forms of crony capitalism. From the early 2000s on, however, these crony capitalists had either made inroads into politics, thereby accelerating the speed of reforms (the Nazif government in Egypt), or become less restrained in exercising power in arbitrary ways to accumulate even more wealth (members of the clan of Ben Ali's wife Layla Trabelsi). In this sense, the corrupt and clientelist way in which neoliberal reforms were implemented as well as their repercussions for society in terms of welfare reduction, increasing prices, and deteriorating working conditions contributed to the eruption of socioeconomic protests and their increase during the 2000s, and finally also fueled the general discontent that led to the uprisings of 2010–2011. How these differences in the sequence of economic reforms and political transitions actually affect socioeconomic protests after the ouster of an authoritarian ruler is one question we seek to answer based on our empirical findings.

Comparing different time periods also recognizes that the international context can vary considerably. While our study does not systematically look at external actors and transnational dynamics, we do reflect on the different ways in which these have influenced the domestic processes in MENA and Latin America, respectively (see Chaps. 4, 7, and 10). Very generally speaking, austerity politics and neoliberally guided structural reforms (liberalization

---

[19] In general, the food riots in the 1980s in MENA are an important part of today's collective memory and shape domestic contention and politics.

and deregulation of the economy, downsizing of the public sector, and privatization of state functions) are still seen as the remedy for economic problems promoted by the international financial institutions (IFIs). Interestingly, in this study of the first five years after the revolutions, IFIs were not a central actor or an important subject of socioeconomic contention in Egypt or Tunisia, which contrasts with the so-called IMF riots caused by IMF-promoted austerity programs in Latin America in the 1980s (see, for instance, Walton 1989). Arguably, however, the influence of the IFIs is about to increase in Egypt and Tunisia, because governments to negotiate with have emerged as a result of political re-institutionalization and, probably more important, because the economic situation in both countries has deteriorated, while lenders—the EU, IFIs, and the Gulf countries—have increased pressure to institute austerity measures.

Reflecting on relevant and substantial differences between the two world regions, the role of organized labor deserves particular scrutiny. Labor was arguably still more powerful in Latin America during the 1980s than it is in the MENA region today. Yet, the general loss of influence of trade unions over time notwithstanding, labor still plays an important role globally (see Lazar 2017) as well as in Egypt and—even more—in Tunisia: a whole section of this book deals with the processes that organized labor went through in the first five years after the ouster of the dictators. An additional difference lies in the generally close ties between labor unions and leftist parties in the case of Latin America, which contrasts with a complete separation of unions and parties in the whole MENA region except for Morocco (see Langohr 2014, p. 187). In Egypt, this helps explain the weakness of the independent trade union movement; in Tunisia, it explains the prominent and manifold roles of the UGTT in the constitutional process, as the trade union federation does not feel it needs political allies (see Chaps. 5 and 6).

Another remarkable difference is the constellation of cleavages and the role of identity politics in particular. In some Latin American cases, identity conflicts played a pivotal role in the emergence and rise of indigenous movements, which usually combined claims for specific indigenous rights with traditional class-based claims for "social justice" (see Van Cott 2005; Yashar 2005). Thus, during the wave of mobilization since the mid-1990s that ultimately led to the "leftist turn" in the region, the rejection of "neoliberalism" offered a common motif that enabled broad leftist alliances including both indigenous and non-indigenous social forces. In Egypt and Tunisia, by contrast, the major identity conflict is between Islamist and secular forces.

While the Islamist movements are generally mostly conservative in terms of social values and liberal when it comes to economic policies, the secular camp also includes significant leftist groups. Yet, the dominant groups and parties on both sides are clearly in favor of a free-market economy and are open to, or are actively implementing, austerity politics. This constellation of cleavages explains one general finding on Egypt and Tunisia: Islamists did not play any role in any of the socioeconomic protests and social movements analyzed there. That is why this book is completely silent on the topic of Islamism. Future research, however, will have to look more broadly at debates about socioeconomic reforms in which Islamist actors do play a role. The Tunisian al-Nahda party and its role in the implementation of austerity politics is a case in point. Another field of action that needs to be studied in this context, too, is Islamic charity. Yet, so far the identity conflict cuts across socioeconomic cleavages (Weipert-Fenner 2018). For MENA as a whole, it is important to keep in mind that cases differ greatly in regard to the relationship between social class and identity-based communal cleavages, which in turn affects the dynamics of socioeconomic contention (see Hinnebusch 2015, pp. 210–211). In Morocco, for instance, the identity of being Amazigh overlaps with the perception of socioeconomic marginalization, as does the Sunni-Shia divide in Bahrain. At the same time, socioeconomic protest actors can also deliberately try to overcome identity-based cleavages, such as the explicitly cross-confessional "You Stink" movement in Lebanon or the anti-austerity protests in the summer of 2018 in Jordan.

Having laid out the rationale of the interregional comparison as well as its limitations, it is hoped that the chapters in this book, which are summarized in the following section, will show how a comparative study of Latin America and MENA can produce novel ideas and insights while taking seriously the specificities of each region as well as of the individual countries.

1.6 Outline of the Book

The core of this volume consists of eight empirical chapters, which are grouped into three parts. Following this introduction (Chap. 1), Part I discusses general post-revolutionary trends in Egypt and Tunisia from a comparative perspective (see Chaps. 2 and 3). Part II focuses on organized labor (see Chaps. 4, 5, and 6), while Part III looks at marginalized groups (see Chaps. 7, 8, and 9). Parts II and III start with an overview chapter on Latin America and then present case studies on Tunisia and

Egypt. The conclusion (see Chap. 10) brings the various parts, trends, and cases together from a comparative and theoretical perspective.

In the first part, Amr Adly and Hamza Meddeb analyze macro-political developments in Egypt and Tunisia since the 2011 revolutions, in order to reconstruct the broader political context in which socioeconomic protests have been unfolding. The chapter offers an account of the puzzling observation that incumbent governments in both countries, despite their different regime trajectories, have had limited capacity to adopt economic reforms with distributional implications through authoritative state action. In doing so, the chapter explains why the two diverging regime paths taken by Egypt and Tunisia have led to basically similar policy impasses.

The key argument put forward in the chapter is that the different post-revolutionary governments in Egypt and Tunisia have demonstrated limited political capacity to tackle the structural roots of the economic and fiscal problems the two countries face. This incapacity transcends regime type, because it is caused by more fundamental sociopolitical dynamics related to the sociopolitical coalitions on which social and political stabilization has depended. What explains the limited political capacity in both cases is the incumbent governments' vulnerability vis-à-vis representatives of old distributional coalitions (including elements of both state-dependent labor and private business constituencies) whose support (or at least acquiescence) has been essential for post-revolution stabilization, either on a pluralist or on an authoritarian basis. This persisting vulnerability has undermined the autonomy and capacity of state representatives to shift away from old interests and established patterns of distribution of public resources, even if this has meant prolonged economic crises. Since the beginning of serious attempts at political re-stabilization in Egypt and Tunisia in 2013 and 2014, respectively, state representatives have largely refrained from adopting measures that would have negatively impacted old beneficiaries of state distributional policies in a direct and politically traceable fashion. Facing mounting deficits in their budgets, balances of payments, and foreign currency shortages, their preference has gone to options that are less politically costly such as external aid (cash and in-kind), indirect taxation, accumulating foreign debt, and tolerating higher inflation and currency depreciation.

Against this background of politico-economic dynamics, Jan-Philipp Vatthauer and Prisca Jöst analyze the dynamics of socioeconomic contention in post-2011 Egypt and Tunisia on the basis of data provided by the

Armed Conflict Location & Event Data Project (ACLED), which has been coded and analyzed specifically to encompass socioeconomic protests.

After looking at the protest numbers in both countries and their evolution between 2011 and 2016, the authors assess the protest actors, the claims of the protesters, the different tactics used, and the geographical patterns of socioeconomic protest. The analysis, on the one hand, shows important *quantitative* differences between the two countries. Most importantly, Tunisia has faced significantly higher numbers of socioeconomic protests both relative to its population and as a share of the overall number of protests. In particular, and in contrast to Egypt, since 2014 Tunisia has seen a steady increase in the number of socioeconomically motivated protests, which finally even outnumbered non-socioeconomic protests in 2016. In post-revolutionary Egypt, there have been far fewer socioeconomic protests, both in absolute and in relative terms. However, also in Egypt, socioeconomic protests continued during the years after the 2011 uprisings, even if they did not reach the high level of political and societal relevance of non-socioeconomic contention. On the other hand, a quantitative analysis of protest events also shows important similarities in relation to the *quality* of socioeconomic protests in the two countries. In both Tunisia and Egypt, socioeconomic protests have not been a continuous phenomenon. Instead, the years between 2011 and 2016 in the two countries were characterized by short-lived outbursts of discontent, most notably in Egypt in 2013 and in Tunisia in 2016. A further finding is that, in both countries, the protestors and claims that had dominated socioeconomic protests prior to the Arab uprisings have continued to shape protest dynamics in the years that have followed the revolutions (2011–2016).

Part II on labor starts with a focused discussion of the state of comparative research on organized labor and political change in Latin America. As Jonas Wolff shows, organized labor across Latin America played a significant role in the destabilization of authoritarian regimes and the (re)turn to democracy during "the long 1980s." At the same time, political democratization—and the turn from a state-centered to a market-oriented ("neoliberal") development model that accompanied it—dramatically changed the politico-institutional and socioeconomic context in which Latin America's labor movements operated. The overall result has been a marked weakening of organized labor throughout the region. The corresponding reduction in the level of contentious labor action in the course of the 1980s and 1990s had ambivalent effects on Latin American democracy: In facilitating a kind of democratization that combined the establishment of democratic institutions with persisting mass poverty and high socioeconomic inequalities, the weakness of organized labor, on the one hand, contributed to democratic stability by reducing the threat perception on the part of the elites. On the other hand, as labor movements did not push democratization further toward less low-intensity, more inclusive, or more social versions of democracy, this had clearly negative effects on the quality of the democratic regimes that emerged.

In Chap. 5, Bassem Karray analyzes the involvement of the Tunisian General Labor Union (UGTT) in the process of constitutional reform which followed the revolution and constituted a key element in the country's transition to democracy. A key question this chapter addresses is whether the UGTT used its political weight to enshrine socioeconomic goals in the constitution. As Karray shows, the UGTT did significantly contribute to the establishment of Tunisia's first democratic constitution, yet mainly in its indispensable role in facilitating a successful constitutional reform process. Based on a comparison of UGTT's own constitutional draft of 2011 and the Tunisian constitution of 2014, he finds that its specific contributions in terms of the contents of the new constitution were rather limited. The latter, however, also implies that the UGTT's role as a political mediator in the post-revolutionary transformation process has—to a certain extent—reduced its function as the national representation of organized labor.

The chapter argues that, while the mediating role of the UGTT constitutes its best-known contribution to Tunisia's transition to democracy, a focus on this "political" dimension misses important parts of the picture. In fact, the UGTT has contributed to the constitutional reform process by adopting three roles that are intertwined but can be distinguished analytically: as a force of proposal; as a force of equilibrium; and as a force of political pressure. The chapter analyzes these three roles empirically, by means of a qualitative case study based on interviews as well as on an analysis of primary documents and media reports.

While the UGTT is an example of an established and unusually powerful trade union federation, Chap. 6 analyzes the trajectory of a new and relatively weak actor: Egypt's independent trade union movement. Focusing on developments since the 2011 revolution, Nadine Abdalla explains why the movement proved unable to establish itself as a significant player in the post-uprising context and make its demands heard in the political arena. In particular, the chapter discusses structural and institutional features, namely the movement's socioeconomic base and its organizational structure, as well as its collective action frame.

The main argument put forward in this chapter is that workers' protests, even if they have remained surprisingly common even after the increase in repression since Morsi's ouster in July 2013, are scattered and largely take place at the local or factory level. This is the case because the rise of new forms of labor mobilization in Egypt has led to an institutionally fragmented, organizationally weak, and only partially representative movement which, at the national level, lacks the capacity to mobilize workers and/or exert significant political influence. In addition, the new trade union movement's predominant collective action frame is characterized by narrow and issue-specific economic claims—a frame that reflects and reinforces both the movement's internal structural weakness and its external lack of reliable sociopolitical allies.

Part III studies socioeconomic protests by marginalized people and, as in Parts I and II, begins with a review of literature on the relationship between protests by marginalized groups and political change in Latin America since the late 1970s. In Chap. 7, Jonas Wolff identifies key features that have characterized (socioeconomic) contention by marginalized groups in Latin American since the late 1970s: First, in some countries the contentious collective action by grassroots organizations representing marginalized sectors as well as their participation in broader, multi-class protests contributed to the destabilization, opening up and/or toppling of authoritarian regimes, even if in a secondary role (behind organized labor, middle-class protests, and/or the activities of opposition parties). Second, with the turn away from resistance to an authoritarian regime to the (contested) negotiation of regime change, marginalized groups generally played no significant role, neither as protestors continuing to push for change nor as participants at the negotiation table. Third, the dual transformation (political democratization and neoliberal restructuring) dramatically changed the structure of collective action among the popular sectors. These changes combined increasing diversity and less emphasis on common—class-based—popular sector claims; less hierarchical and centralized forms of organization and decreasing coordination; more emphasis on the local, territorial community level as well as on autonomy, self-help and self-organization, and less direct challenges to, and interaction with, the central state. Fourth, with a significant time lag, the combination of democracy and neoliberal reforms has enabled the emergence of broad anti-neoliberal protest alliances in which organizations and movements involving marginalized groups play an important role. These protest alliances, which emerged from local associational structures and societal networks and were able to move contentious collective action up to the national scale, put the social question back on the political agenda and facilitated the election of left-of-center governments that, at least partially, addressed a series of key socioeconomic concerns articulated by popular sector movements.

Chapter 8 looks at Tunisia, where unemployed activism has been the most important form of socioeconomic contention since the ouster of Ben Ali. Samiha Hamdi and Irene Weipert-Fenner analyze and compare the two most important types of unemployed mobilization in contemporary Tunisia: first, spontaneous, mostly disruptive contentious actions by unemployed people who operate outside formal organizations at the local level, using the example of the Gafsa mining basin; and second, formally organized activism within the framework of the Union of Unemployed Graduates (*Union des Diplômés Chômeurs*—UDC), the only unemployed organization at the national level.

The initial observation of the chapter is that unemployed mobilization in post-revolutionary Tunisia has been quite significant and has included massive outbursts of discontent, but has lacked political leverage. In fact, despite the greater political freedom that theoretically would allow unemployed groups to join forces and rally together, unemployed protests are characterized by growing fragmentation. The chapter offers an explanation for the general lack of cooperation of unemployed activists with each other, as well as with other societal and political actors, by systematically comparing the two different types of unemployed mobilization along three dimensions derived from social movement theory. First, in connection with collective action frames, the analysis finds substantial overlaps between the two cases and only minor discrepancies, which cannot explain the lack of cooperation. Second, the mobilizing structures are characterized by a general lack of trust among societal actors, on the one hand, and a predominance of the local level, even within the national UDC organization, on the other hand. This decentralized structure partly explains the weakness of the UDC at the national level. The lack of power, in turn, reduces the incentives on the part of other groups to join their ranks. Third, when it comes to political opportunities, the UDC has used the opening up of the political space to ally itself with leftist parties, but has remained wary of compromising its own autonomy. At the grassroots level, on the other hand, being "political" or "politicized" remains a negative attribute, which expresses a deeply felt mistrust of political institutions and parties as well as social organizations such as the UGTT trade union federation and the UDC. This difference in the perceived political opportunity structure has constituted a major obstacle to cooperation between autonomous unemployed groups and the UDC.

Chapter 9 focuses on one specific marginalized group in Egypt's informal economy: the tuktuk drivers. The overall aim is to understand how poor people in Egypt deal with the socioeconomic conditions they are living in and why they only very rarely engage in contentious action that voices socioeconomic demands. Nayera Abdelrahman Soliman argues that the few instances of protest can be explained as a conflict over the margins themselves. Empirically, the chapter analyzes and compares the experiences of tuktuk drivers in two different neighborhoods: one urban area (Ard El Lewa/Imbaba) in which no protest by tuktuk drivers was monitored and a rural area (Belqas) in which a protest was observed.

The chapter starts by discussing the process of marginalization and informalization of tuktuk drivers by presenting their socioeconomic conditions: their level of education, access to work, and work setting as well as work conditions. The second part then analyzes the impact of this positionality on the tuktuk drivers' interaction with the "center," mainly with governmental authorities such as either street police and/or traffic administrations. This analysis focuses on their tactics—contentious or not—for facing their degrading socioeconomic conditions within the margins they are pushed into, and for challenging the borders between margins and center. The analysis shows, first, that tuktuk drivers are in a continuous process of marginalization, which starts from the date and the place of birth. Second, the main conflict between tuktuk drivers and authorities is over space: contentious interactions emerge at the borders separating the margins from the center, whether formal or informal. Third, the tuktuk drivers' main claim is to have access to the "center" by being legal, by being able to move freely in places other than "poor" areas. The ways in which authorities deal with them in the streets, however, place them in a constantly vulnerable position and, thus, pushes them back to the margins.

As the studies compiled in this volume document, the overall dynamic of politico-economic development in post-revolutionary Egypt and Tunisia has had complex consequences for those actors who have continued to articulate socioeconomic grievances. Still, taking the different case studies together, one general observation stands out: key agents of socioeconomic contention, including movements involving organized labor and the unemployed, that were important in the run-up to the uprisings and that saw their political opportunities open up in the immediate aftermath of the revolutions, have since been effectively marginalized as political actors. The concluding chapter reflects on the causes of this weakness of socioeconomic contention by identifying comparative insights from the contributions to this volume and by situating them in the context of broader comparative and theoretical debates on the relationship between social movements and political change. More specifically, the conclusion first discusses Egypt's and Tunisia's post-revolutionary trajectories from a comparative perspective. Second, it discusses these comparative findings in the light of experiences in Latin America.

Drawing again on comparative scholarship on Latin America, the key argument presented in the volume's final chapter is that Egypt and Tunisia—and plausibly broader parts of the MENA region as well—are currently confronting a crisis of popular-sector incorporation that is fairly similar to the one Latin America has been facing since the 1980s. Large parts of the population—namely, those representing the lower strata of society—do not have access to effective mechanisms for linking them with the political arena, giving them an institutional voice in the political process and/or making policymakers responsive to their interests and values. With the popular uprisings of 2010–2011, this lack of incorporation, which reflects the breakdown of the previous scheme of incorporation (the "authoritarian social contract"), turned into a full-fledged crisis. In both post-revolutionary contexts studied in this volume, governments have been unwilling and/or incapable of establishing new mechanisms for incorporating organizations representing the popular sectors, while the latter have mostly been unable to apply pressure from below for their incorporation. This dynamic is remarkably similar in Egypt and Tunisia, despite the different political regimes that have taken shape in the two countries. The notion of a crisis of popular-sector incorporation helps to understand these surprising similarities, as it draws attention to the underlying social (sociopolitical and politico-economic) dynamics that shape contentious politics and are relatively independent of changes at the level of the political system.

References

Ababneh, S. (2018). Do you know who governs us? The damned monetary fund. *Middle East Report Online*, June 30. Retrieved December 21, 2018, from https://merip.org/mero/mero063018.

Abdelrahman, M. (2014). *Egypt's long revolution: Protest movements and uprisings*. Abingdon and Oxon: Routledge.

Achcar, G. (2013). *The people want: A radical exploration of the Arab uprisings.* London: Saqi Books.

Albrecht, H., & Bishara, D. (2011). Back on horseback: The military and political transformation in Egypt. *Middle East Law and Governance, 3,* 13–23.

Albrecht, H., & Ohl, D. (2016). Exit, resistance, loyalty: Military behavior during unrest in authoritarian regimes. *Perspectives on Politics, 14*(1), 38–52. https://doi.org/10.1017/S1537592715003217.

Allal, A. (2010). Réformes néolibérales, clientélismes et protestations en situation autoritaire. *Politique africaine, 117*(1), 107–125.

Allal, A. (2013). Becoming revolutionary in Tunisia, 2007–2011. In J. Beinin & F. Vairel (Eds.), *Social movements, mobilization, and contestation in the Middle East and North Africa* (pp. 185–204). Stanford, CA: Stanford University Press.

Allinson, J. (2015). Class forces, transition and the Arab uprisings: A comparison of Tunisia, Egypt and Syria. *Democratization, 22*(2), 294–314. https://doi.org/10.1080/13510347.2015.1010812.

Alvarez, S. E., Dagnino, E., & Escobar, A. (1998). *Cultures of politics: Politics of cultures: re-visioning Latin American social movements.* Boulder, CO and Oxford: Westview Press.

al-Anani, K. (2012). Islamist parties post-Arab spring. *Mediterranean Politics, 17*(3), 466–472. https://doi.org/10.1080/13629395.2012.725309.

Angrist, M. P. (2011). Understanding the success of mass civic protest in Tunisia. *Annual Meeting of the Middle East Studies Association,* Washington, DC.

Asadzade, P. (2018). New data shed light on the dramatic protests in Iran. Retrieved January 7, 2019, from https://www.washingtonpost.com/news/monkey-cage/wp/2018/01/12/what-data-show-us-about-irans-protests.

Asseburg, M., & Wimmen, H. (Eds.). (2017). *Dynamics of transformation, elite change and new social mobilization: Egypt, Libya, Tunisia and Yemen.* Abingdon and Oxon: Routledge.

Auyero, J. (2000). *Poor people's politics: Peronist survival network and the legacy of Evita.* Durham, NC: Duke University Press.

Bank, A. (2018). Comparative area studies and the study of Middle East politics after the Arab uprisings. In A. I. Ahram, P. Köllner, & R. Sil (Eds.), *Comparative area studies: Methodological rationales and cross-regional applications* (pp. 119–129). New York, NY: Oxford University Press.

Bayat, A. (2005). Islamism and social movement theory. *Third World Quarterly, 26*(6), 891–908.

Bayat, A. (2013). The Arab Spring and its surprises. *Development and Change, 44*(3), 587–601.

Bayat, A. (2017). *Revolution without revolutionaries: Making sense of the Arab Spring.* Stanford, CA: Stanford University Press.

Bayat, A. (2018). The fire that fueled the Iran protests. Retrieved January 7, 2019, from https://www.theatlantic.com/international/archive/2018/01/iran-protest-mashaad-green-class-labor-economy/551690/.

Beinin, J. (2012). The rise of Egypt's workers. *The Carnegie Papers*. Washington, DC: Carnegie Endowment for International Peace. Retrieved February 7, 2019, from https://carnegieendowment.org/files/egypt_labor.pdf.

Beinin, J. (2016). *Workers and thieves: Labor movements and popular uprisings in Tunisia and Egypt*. Stanford, CA: Stanford University Press.

Beinin, J., & Vairel, F. (Eds.). (2013a). *Social movements, mobilization, and contestation in the Middle East and North Africa*. Stanford, CA: Stanford University Press.

Beinin, J., & Vairel, F. (2013b). Introduction. The Middle East and North Africa beyond classical social movement theory. In J. Beinin & F. Vairel (Eds.), *Social movements, mobilization, and contestation in the Middle East and North Africa* (pp. 1–29). Stanford, CA: Stanford University Press.

Belakhdar, N. (2015). "L'Éveil du Sud" ou quand la contestation vient de la marge. Une analyse du mouvement des chômeurs algériens. *Politique africaine, 137*, 27–48.

Benford, R., & Snow, D. (2000). Framing processes and social movements: An overview and assessment. *Annual Review of Sociology, 26*(1), 611–639.

Bennani-Chraïbi, M., & Fillieule, O. (2003). Appel d'air(e). In M. Bennani-Chraïbi & O. Fillieule (Eds.), *Résistances et protestations dans les sociétés musulmanes* (pp. 17–42). Paris: Presses de Sciences Po.

Bishara, D. (2015). The politics of ignoring: Protest dynamics in late Mubarak Egypt. *Perspectives on Politics, 13*(4), 958–975. https://doi.org/10.1017/S153759271500225X.

Bishara, D. (2018). *Contesting authoritarianism. Labor challenges to the state in Egypt*. Cambridge: Cambridge University Press.

Boubekeur, A. (2016). Islamists, secularists and old regime elites in Tunisia: Bargained competition. *Mediterranean Politics, 21*(1), 107–127.

Brandes, N., & Engels, B. (2011). Social movements in Africa. *Stichproben. Wiener Zeitschrift für kritische Afrikastudien, 11*(20), 1–15.

Brownlee, J., Masoud, T., & Reynolds, A. (2013). Tracking the "Arab Spring": Why the modest harvest. *Journal of Democracy, 24*(4), 29–44.

Brumberg, D. (2013). Transforming the Arab world's protection-racket politics. *Journal of Democracy, 24*(3), 88–103.

Burnell, P. (2013). Democratisation in the Middle East and North Africa: Perspectives from democracy support. *Third World Quarterly, 34*(5), 838–855. https://doi.org/10.1080/01436597.2013.800742.

Cammett, M., & Salti, N. (2018). Popular grievances in the Arab region: Evaluating explanations for discontent in the lead-up to the uprisings. *Middle East Development Journal, 10*(1), 64–96. https://doi.org/10.1080/17938120.2018.1443606.

Chalcraft, J. (2016). *Popular politics in the making of the modern Middle East.* Cambridge: Cambridge University Press.

Chikhi, L. (2018). Protests by teachers, health workers spread in Algeria. Retrieved January 7, 2019, from https://www.reuters.com/article/algeria-protests/protests-by-teachers-health-workers-spread-in-algeria-idUSL8N1Q80XR.

Chomiak, L. (2014). Architecture of resistance in Tunisia. In L. Khatib & E. Lust (Eds.), *Taking to the streets. The transformation of Arab Activism* (pp. 22–51). Baltimore: John Hopkins University Press.

Clark, J. (2004). Social movement theory and patron-clientelism. *Comparative Political Studies, 37*(8), 941–968. https://doi.org/10.1177/0010414004267982.

Costello, M., Craig Jenkins, J., & Aly, H. (2015). Bread, justice, or opportunity? The determinants of the Arab awakening protests. *World Development, 67,* 90–100.

van Cott, D. L. (2005). *From movements to parties in Latin America: The evolution of ethnic politics.* Cambridge: Cambridge University Press.

Della Porta, D. (2014). *Mobilizing for democracy: Comparing 1989 and 2011.* Oxford: Oxford University Press.

Della Porta, D., & Diani, M. (2015). *The Oxford handbook of social movements.* Oxford: Oxford University Press.

Desai, R., Olofsgard, A., & Yousef, T. (2009). The logic of the authoritarian bargains. *Economics & Politics, 21*(1), 93–125.

Dihstelhoff, J. (2018). Tunisian politics between crisis and normalization. *Sada Middle East Analysis.* Retrieved December 21, 2018, from https://carnegieendowment.org/sada/77582.

Duboc, M. (2015). Reluctant revolutionaries? The dynamics of labor protests in Egypt, 2006–2013. In R. Abou-El-Fadl (Ed.), *Revolutionary Egypt: Connecting domestic and international struggles* (Routledge Studies in Middle Eastern Democratization and Government 9) (pp. 27–42). London and New York, NY: Routledge.

Dupont, C., & Passy, F. (2012). One year later, whither the Arab Spring? Domestic and regional challenges. *Swiss Political Science Review, 18*(1), 101–104. https://doi.org/10.1111/j.1662-6370.2012.02062.x.

Eckstein, S. (Ed.). (2001). *Power and popular protest: Latin American social movements.* Berkeley, CA: University of California Press.

Eckstein, S., & Wickham-Crowley, T. P. (Eds.). (2003). *Struggles for social rights in Latin America.* New York, NY: Routledge.

Eisenstadt, S. N. (1973). *Traditional patrimonialism and modern neopatrimonialism.* Sage research papers in the social sciences: Studies in comparative modernization series, 1 (90-003). Beverly Hills, CA: Sage.

El-Mahdi, R. (2009). Enough! Egypt's Quest for Democracy. *Comparative Political Studies, 42*(8), 1011–1039.

El-Mahdi, R. (2011). Labour protests in Egypt. Causes and meanings. *Review of African Political Economy, 38*(129), 387–402.

Emperador Badimon, M. (2013). Does unemployment spark collective contentious action? Evidence from a Moroccan social movement. *Journal of Contemporary African Studies, 31*(2), 194–212.

Francis, E. (2018). Jordan protesters press on, some unions strike after new PM appointed. Retrieved January 7, 2019, from https://www.reuters.com/article/us-jordan-protests/jordan-protesters-press-on-some-unions-strike-after-new-pm-appointed-idUSKCN1J118U.

Franklin, J. C. (2009). Contentious challenges and government responses in Latin America. *Political Research Quarterly, 62*(4), 700–714.

Giugni, M., McAdam, D., & Tilly, C. (Eds.). (1999). *How social movements matter*. Minneapolis, MN: University of Minnesota Press.

Gobe, E. (2010). The Gafsa mining basin between riots and a social movement: Meaning and significance of a protest movement in Ben Ali's Tunisia. Retrieved February 11, 2019, from https://halshs.archives-ouvertes.fr/halshs-00557826.

Goodwin, J., & Jasper, J. M. (1999). Caught in a winding, snarling vine: The structural bias of political process theory. *Sociological Forum, 14*(1), 27–54. https://doi.org/10.1023/A:1021684610881.

Goodwin, J., & Jasper, J. M. (Eds.). (2004). *Rethinking social movements: Structure, meaning, and emotion. People, passions, and power*. Lanham, MD: Rowman & Littlefield.

Grand, S. R. (2014). *Understanding Tahrir Square. What transitions elsewhere can teach us about the prospects for Arab democracy*. Washington, DC: Brookings Institution Press.

Grimm, J. (2015). Eine Schwalbe macht noch keinen Frühling: Die arabischen Umbrüche in der politikwissenschaftlichen Literatur. *Zeitschrift für Vergleichende Politikwissenschaft, 9*(1–2), 97–118.

Grimm, J., & Harders, C. (2017). Unpacking the effects of repression: The evolution of Islamist repertoires of contention in Egypt after the fall of President Morsi. *Social Movement Studies, 17*(1), 1–18. https://doi.org/10.1080/14742837.2017.1344547.

Guazzone, L., & Pioppi, D. (Eds.). (2009). *The Arab state and neo-liberal globalization: The restructuring of state power in the Middle East*. Reading: Ithaca Press.

Gurr, T. R. (1970). *Why men rebel*. Princeton, NJ: Princeton University Press.

Hagopian, F., & Mainwaring, S. P. (Eds.). (2005). *The third wave of democratization in Latin America. Advances and setbacks*. Cambridge: Cambridge University Press.

Harders, C. (2003). The informal social pact: The state and the urban poor in Cairo. In E. Kienle (Ed.), *Politics from above, politics from below: The Middle East in the age of economic reform* (pp. 191–213). London: Saqi.

Hinnebusch, R. (2015). Introduction: Understanding the consequences of the Arab uprisings—Starting points and divergent trajectories. *Democratization*, *22*(2), 205–217. https://doi.org/10.1080/13510347.2015.1010807.

Hoffmann, A., Bouziane, M., & Harders, C. (2013). Analyzing politics beyond the center in an age of transformation. In M. Bouziane, C. Harders, & A. Hoffmann (Eds.), *Local politics and contemporary transformations in the Arab world: Governance beyond the center* (pp. 1–21). Basingstoke: Palgrave Macmillan.

International Crisis Group. (2018). How to cope with Iraq's summer brushfire. Crisis Group Middle East Briefing No. 61. Retrieved February 11, 2019, from https://www.crisisgroup.org/middle-east-north-africa/gulf-and-arabian-peninsula/iraq/b61-how-cope-iraqs-summer-brushfire.

Johnston, H., & Almeida, P. (Eds.). (2006). *Latin American social movements: Globalization, democratization, and transnational networks*. Lanham, MD: Rowman & Littlefield.

Kamal, O. (2015). *Half-baked, the other side of Egypt's baladi bread subsidy. A study of the market intermediaries and middlemen in the system*. Barcelona: Barcelona Centre for International Affairs (CIDOB).

Karshenas, M., Moghadam, V. M., & Alami, R. (2014). Social policy after the Arab Spring: States and social rights in the MENA region. *World Development*, *64*, 726–739. https://doi.org/10.1016/j.worlddev.2014.07.002.

Kellogg Institute for International Studies and Kroc Institute for International Peace Studies. (2012). *The tipping point: Transitions to democracy in Latin America and the Middle East*. Notre Dame: University of Notre Dame.

Ketchley, N. (2017). *Egypt in a time of revolution: Contentious politics and the Arab Spring*. Cambridge Studies in Contentious Politics. Cambridge: Cambridge University Press.

Langohr, V. (2014). Labor movements and organizations. In M. Lynch (Ed.), *The Arab uprisings explained: New contentious politics in the Middle East* (pp. 180–200). New York, NY: Columbia University Press.

Lapegna, P. (2013). Social movements and patronage politics: Processes of demobilization and dual pressure. *Sociological Forum*, *28*(4), 842–863. https://doi.org/10.1111/socf.12059.

Lazar, S. (Ed.). (2017). *Where are the unions? Workers and social movements in Latin America, the Middle East and Europe*. London: Zed Books.

Levitsky, S., & Roberts, K. M. (Eds.). (2011). *The Resurgence of the Latin American Left*. Baltimore, MD: The Johns Hopkins University Press.

Marwane, A. (2018). Protests in southern Algeria: Causes and repercussions. Retrieved December 21, 2018, from https://www.washingtoninstitute.org/fikraforum/view/protests-in-southern-algeria-causes-and-repercussions.

Marzouki, N., & Meddeb, H. (2016). The struggle for meanings and power in Tunisia after the revolution. *Middle East Law and Governance, 8*(2–3), 119–130. https://doi.org/10.1163/18763375-00802001.

Masbah, M. (2017). A new generation of protests in Morocco? How Hirak al-Rif endures. Policy alternatives. Retrieved February 11, 2019, from https://www.arab-reform.net/en/node/1102.

McAdam, D., McCarthy, J. D., & Zald, M. N. (Eds.). (1996). *Comparative perspectives on social movements: Political opportunities, mobilizing structures, and cultural framings*. Cambridge: University Press.

McAdam, D., Tarrow, S., & Tilly, C. (2001). *Dynamics of Contention*. Cambridge: Cambridge University Press.

McCarthy, J. D., & Zald, M. N. (1977). Resource mobilization and social movements: A partial theory. *American Journal of Sociology, 82*(6), 1212–1241. https://doi.org/10.1086/226464.

Meijer, R. (2005). Taking the Islamist movement seriously: Social movement theory and the Islamist movement. *International Review of Social History, 50*, 279–291.

Mohammed, A., & Jalabi, R. (2018). Rockets fired at Basra airport as violent protests grip Iraq. Retrieved January 7, 2019, from https://www.reuters.com/article/us-iraq-protests/rockets-fired-at-basra-airport-as-violent-protests-grip-iraq-idUSKCN1LO0DV.

Morris, A. D., & McClurg Mueller, C. (Eds.). (1992). *Frontiers in social movement theory*. New Haven, CT: Yale University Press.

Netterstrøm, K. L. (2016). The Tunisian general labor union and the advent of democracy. *The Middle East Journal, 70*(3), 383–398.

O'Donnell, G., Schmitter, P. C., & Whitehead, L. (Eds.). (1986). *Transitions from Authoritarian Rule*. Baltimore, MD: Johns Hopkins University Press.

Omri, M.-S. (2016). *Confluency (tarafud) between trade unionism, culture and revolution in Tunisia*. Tunis: The Tunisian General Union of Labour.

Perletta, G. (2018). Street protests and socio-economic challenges in Iran: The Case of Khuzestan Province. IAI Commentaries. Retrieved February 11, 2109, from https://www.iai.it/it/pubblicazioni/street-protests-and-socio-economic-challenges-iran-case-khuzestan-province.

Phenix Center for Economics and Informatics Studies. (2017). *Labor Protests in Jordan 2016*.

Phenix Center for Economics and Informatics Studies. (2018). *Al-ihtijajat al-'ummaliyya fi-l-Urdun 2017* [Labor protests in Jordan 2017].

Pioppi, D. (2013). Playing with fire. The Muslim Brotherhood and the Egyptian Leviathan. *The International Spectator, 48*(4), 51–68. https://doi.org/10.1080/03932729.2013.847680.

Roberts, K. (1997). Beyond romanticism: Social movements and the study of political change in Latin America. *Latin American Research Review, 32*(2), 137–151.

Roll, S. (2016). Managing change: How Egypt's military leadership shaped the transformation. *Mediterranean Politics, 21*(1), 23–43. https://doi.org/10.10 80/13629395.2015.1081452.

Rossi, F. M. & von Bülow, M. (Eds.) (2015). *Social movement dynamics. New perspectives on theory and research from Latin America.* Farnham: Ashgate.

Rucht, D., Koopmans, R., Neidhardt, F., et al. (1999). *Acts of dissent: New developments in the study of protest.* Lanham, MD: Rowman & Littlefield.

Ruiz de Elvira, L., Schwarz, C. H., & Weipert-Fenner, I. (Eds.). (2018). *Clientelism and patronage in the Middle East and North Africa: Networks of dependency* (Routledge Studies in Middle Eastern Democratization and Government). London and New York, NY: Routledge.

Sadiki, L. (2009). *Rethinking Arab democratization: Elections without democracy.* Oxford and New York, NY: Oxford University Press.

Schlumberger, O., & Matzke, T. (2012). Path toward democracy? The Role of economic development. *Swiss Political Science Review, 18*(1), 105–109. https://doi.org/10.1111/j.1662-6370.2012.02058.x.

Schock, K. (1996). A conjunctural model of political conflict. The impact of political opportunities on the relationship between economic inequality and violent political conflict. *Journal of Conflict Resolution, 40*(1), 98–133.

Shigetomi, S. (2009). Rethinking theories on social movements and developments. In S. Shigetomi & K. Makino (Eds.), *Protest and social movements in the developing world* (pp. 1–18). Cheltenham and Northampton, MA: Edward Elgar.

Sika, N. (2017). *Youth activism and contentious politics in Egypt.* Cambridge: Cambridge University Press.

Silva, E. (2009). *Challenging neoliberalism in Latin America.* Cambridge and New York, NY: Cambridge University Press.

Simmons, E. (2014). Grievances do matter in mobilization. *Theory and Society, 43*(5), 513–546.

Singerman, D. (2004). The networked world of Islamic social movements. In Q. Wiktorowicz (Ed.), *Islamic activism: A social movement theory approach* (pp. 143–163). Bloomington, IN: Indiana University Press.

Tarrow, S. (1998). *Power in movement: Social movements, collective action and politics.* Cambridge: Cambridge University Press.

Tarrow, S. (2008). Charles Tilly and the practice of contentious politics. *Social Movement Studies, 7*(3), 225–246.

Teti, A., Abbott, P., & Cavatorta, F. (2018). *The Arab uprisings in Egypt, Jordan and Tunisia: Social, political and economic transformations.* Basingstoke: Palgrave Macmillan.

Tilly, C. (1979). *From mobilization to revolution.* Reading: Assison-Wesley.

Tilly, C., & Tarrow, S. (2007). *Contentious politics*. Boulder, CO and London: Paradigm Publishers.

Valbjørn, M. (2015). Reflections on self-reflections—On framing the analytical implications of the Arab uprisings for the study of Arab politics. *Democratization*, *22*(2), 218–238. https://doi.org/10.1080/13510347.2015.1010808.

Vatthauer, J.-P. & Weipert-Fenner, I. (2017). The quest for social justice in Tunisia. Socioeconomic protest and political democratization post 2011. *PRIF Report 143*. Frankfurt: Peace Research Institute Frankfurt.

Volpi, F. (2017). *Revolution and authoritarianism in North Africa*. London: Hurst & Company.

Volpi, F., & Clark, J. A. (2019). Activism in the Middle East and North Africa in times of upheaval: Social networks' actions and interactions. *Social Movement Studies*, *18*(1), 1–16. https://doi.org/10.1080/14742837.2018.1538876.

Walton, J. (1989). Debt, protest, and the state in Latin America. In S. Eckstein (Ed.), *Power and popular protest. Latin American social movements* (pp. 299–328). Berkeley, CA: University of California Press.

Weipert-Fenner, I. (2013). Wegbereiter oder treibende Kraft? Die Rolle der Arbeiter in der ägyptischen Revolution. In H. Albrecht & T. Demmelhuber (Eds.), *Revolution und Regimewandel in Ägypten* (pp. 209–231). Baden-Baden: Nomos.

Weipert-Fenner, I. (2014). Neue Akteure, neue Prozesse—alles beim Alten? Über den schwierigen Umgang mit der Ambivalenz der arabischen Transformationsprozesse. *Politische Vierteljahresschrift*, *55*(1), 145–167.

Weipert-Fenner, I. (2018). Unemployed mobilisation in times of democratisation: The Union of Unemployed Graduates in post-Ben Ali Tunisia. *The Journal of North African Studies*. https://doi.org/10.1080/13629387.2018.1535317.

Weipert-Fenner, I., & Wolff, J. (2015). Socioeconomic contention and post-revolutionary political change in Egypt and Tunisia: A research agenda. *PRIF Working Paper 24*. Frankfurt: Peace Research Institute Frankfurt.

Wickham, C. R. (2002). *Mobilizing Islam: Religion, activism, and political change in Egypt*. New York, NY: Columbia University Press.

Wiktorowicz, Q. (Ed.). (2004). *Islamic activism: A social movement theory approach*. Indiana series in Middle East Studies. Bloomington, IN: Indiana University Press.

Wolf, A. (2018). Morocco's Hirak movement and legacies of contention in the Rif. *The Journal of North African Studies*, *24*(1), 1–6.

Wolff, J. (2007). (De-)mobilising the marginalised: A comparison of the Argentine piqueteros and Ecuador's indigenous movement. *Journal of Latin American Studies*, *39*(1), 1–29. https://doi.org/10.1017/S0022216X0600201X.

Wolff, J. (2008). *Turbulente Stabilität: Die Demokratie in Südamerika diesseits ferner Ideale*. Baden-Baden: Nomos.

Wolff, J. (2009). De-idealizing the democratic civil peace: On the political economy of democratic stabilization and pacification in Argentina and Ecuador. *Democratization, 16*(5), 998–1026. https://doi.org/10.1080/13510340903162143.

Yashar, D. J. (2005). *Contesting citizenship in Latin America: The rise of indigenous movements and the postliberal challenge.* Cambridge: Cambridge University Press.

Zeghal, M. (2013). Competing ways of life: Islamism, secularism, and public order in the Tunisian transition. *Constellations, 20*(2), 254–274.

Zemni, S. (2013). From socio-economic protest to national revolt: The labor origins of the Tunisian revolution. In N. Gana (Ed.), *The making of the Tunisian revolution: Contexts, architects, prospects* (pp. 127–146). Edinburgh: Edinburgh University Press.

Zorob, A. (2013). Der Zusammenbruch des autoritären Gesellschaftsvertrags: Sozio-ökonomische Hintergründe der arabischen Proteste. In A. Jünemann & A. Zorob (Eds.), *Arabellions: Zur Vielfalt von Protest und Revolte im Nahen Osten und Nordafrika* (pp. 229–256). Wiesbaden: Springer VS.

PART I

General Trends

CHAPTER 2

Beyond Regime Change: The State and the Crisis of Governance in Post-2011 Egypt and Tunisia

Amr Adly and Hamza Meddeb

2.1 Introduction

Despite the diverging trajectories that the two countries have followed since the 2011 revolutions, Egypt and Tunisia have witnessed relative political stabilization since 2014. Despite the persistence of terrorist threats and the occasional outburst of social and political protests at the time of writing (in late 2018), neither country is facing the risk of a total and abrupt change in the structure or personnel of political authority. This stabilization has, however, taken place on diverging terms in the two countries. Whereas in Egypt a military-backed authoritarian regime took charge in mid-July 2013, in Tunisia a political regime with democratic and pluralist features resulted from a major political pact in 2014.

A. Adly (✉)
American University in Cairo (AUC), New Cairo City, Egypt

H. Meddeb
Mediterranean School of Business,
South Mediterranean University, Tunis, Tunisia
e-mail: Hamza.meddeb@smu.tn

© The Author(s) 2020
I. Weipert-Fenner, J. Wolff (eds.), *Socioeconomic Protests in MENA and Latin America*, Middle East Today,
https://doi.org/10.1007/978-3-030-19621-9_2

Both political regimes are far from being consolidated in the sense of following well-observed rules—formal, informal, or a mix of the two—that regulate the practice of political authority within the state apparatus as well as between state and society. In fact, as different as they are, Egypt's authoritarian regime and Tunisia's fragile democracy are facing similar economic restraints and, interestingly, have reacted quite similarly to them, despite their different regime dynamics. Economically, there has been an inability to re-launch the economy after six bad years of low growth, high unemployment and low investment, large fiscal imbalances in the form of deficits and public debts, and worsening external financial positions as tourism has collapsed, capital flight has intensified, and foreign reserves have all but evaporated, exposing national currencies to tremendous pressure and posing the threat of higher inflation combined with economic recession. This critical combination has translated into lower standards of living for a majority of Egyptians and Tunisians, and it has exacerbated many of the structural socio-economic issues that were behind the earlier revolutionary upheavals in the first place.

These economic crises have also taken their toll on the attempts of the two regimes to stabilize and consolidate power in democratic or authoritarian terms. The lack of resources and the continuous need to introduce unpopular measures that promise further hardship such as currency depreciation, fuel and food subsidy cuts, and higher consumption of taxes have further weakened the prospects of consolidation of both kinds of power arrangement, as divergent and different as they are. Against this background, this chapter aims at explaining why the two diverging regime paths taken by Egypt and Tunisia have led to a basically similar policy impasse.

We argue that Egyptian and Tunisian incumbents have demonstrated limited political capacity to tackle the structural roots of the economic and fiscal problems the two countries are facing. This incapacity has transcended regime type and involves the dynamics governing socio-political coalitions on which social and political stabilization has depended. What explains the limited political capacity in both cases, we argue, is the ruling incumbents' vulnerability to representatives of old distributional coalitions (including state-dependent constituencies of labor and private business) whose support, or at least acquiescence, has been essential for post-revolution stabilization, either on a pluralist or an authoritarian basis.

This persisting vulnerability has undermined the autonomy and capacity of ruling incumbents to move against old interests and patterns of distribution of public resources, even if this meant protracted economic crises and a decline in general welfare, especially of less organized constituencies. Since the beginning of serious attempts at political re-stabilization in Egypt and Tunisia in 2013 and 2014, respectively, incumbents have largely refrained from taking measures that would have negatively impacted old beneficiaries of state distributional policies in a direct and politically traceable fashion. Facing mounting deficits in their budgets, balances of payments, and foreign currency shortages, their preference has gone to less politically costly options such as external aid (both cash and in-kind, as well as cheap credit and central bank deposits), indirect taxation such as value-added tax (VAT) or customs duties, accumulating foreign debt, and tolerating higher inflation and currency depreciation.

2.2 Egypt and Tunisia After the 2011 Revolutions: So Different, yet So Similar!

It is fair to say that Egypt and Tunisia started from similar points back in early 2011, only to diverge in their paths toward post-revolution stabilization and consolidation of power. In both countries, popular revolutions managed to bring down long-standing dictators. In neither country did central state authority fully collapse and lead to chaos, territorial disintegration, or civil strife. Both nations initially underwent some post-revolution transformation toward more pluralistic and competitive political orders. However, both processes of transformation were plagued by deep divisions and polarization among the elites—Islamist versus non-Islamist—but also within the populace, over the importance of religion vis-à-vis state authority and religion vis-à-vis public life (Achcar 2013).

Whereas, in Tunisia, elite pacting was successful in drafting and adopting the constitution of 2014, Egyptian elites failed to agree on a basic minimum for the functioning of the then new political regime. The stakes were high in Egypt, and the constitution passed by the Muslim Brotherhood in 2012 only deepened the Islamist-secularist divide. With the lack of consensus and the perceived mutual threats of power transfer between the two camps, the post-revolution political system collapsed in the wake of massive demonstrations and a subsequent military coup in mid-2013. These developments put an end to Egypt's brief and tumultuous experiment with political pluralism. It ushered the country into a period of intense political repression and violence that ended by mid-2014 with an authoritarian military-backed regime seeking the consolidation of its power after Sisi's ascent to the presidency.

By contrast, Tunisia took the opposite direction. Possibly learning the lesson from what had just happened in Egypt but also given the inability of any single actor to completely dominate the political arena, Islamist, secularist, and corporatist elites (namely the leadership of the Tunisian General Labor Union—Union Générale Tunisienne du Travail—UGTT and the Tunisian Confederation of Industry, Trade and Handicrafts—UTICA) managed to form a transition pact (see Chap. 5 in this book). The country's largest trade union, the Tunisian General Labor Union (UGTT), claims a total membership of around 750,000 mostly public-sector employees and workers in a country with a working population of 4.125 million. Since its founding in 1946, the UGTT has played a crucial role in the anti-colonial struggle for independence. Following independence in 1956, it assumed the role of a major institutional channel for expressing dissent and economic grievances, thanks to its role as a junior partner of Bourguiba's and Ben Ali's regimes. The UGTT has always benefited from its bargaining power in Tunisian political and economic life (Khiari 2003; Camau and Geisser 2003; Yousfi 2015). Along with the Tunisian Confederation of Industry, Trade, and Handicrafts (UTICA), which represents the employers and economic elites connected to the old regime, the Tunisian League for Human Rights, and the Tunisian Order of Lawyers, the UGTT formed the so-called Quartet which in 2013 and 2014 led the mediation between secularists and Islamist elites in order to forge a political compromise. Consensus was reached in the 2014 constitution over the foundations of the post-revolution regime, especially over religion in politics and public life (Marzouki 2015). To a certain extent, this lowered the stakes involved in the power transfer. In the same year, free and fair presidential and parliamentary elections shifted power to a new alliance of old interests (Nidaa Tounes). However, the consensus-founding myth was an important factor in the new regime failing to function properly (Marzouki and Meddeb 2015). A national unity government was formed. Tunisia started its long, bumpy, and still inconclusive path toward democratic consolidation.

The political turmoil since 2011 has exacerbated many of the structural problems the two economies have traditionally suffered. Egypt and Tunisia faced declining gross domestic product (GDP) growth rates, high unemployment, and low levels of investment. In Tunisia, the average GDP growth rate from 2011 to 2015 was a mere 1.8 percent, compared with a much higher rate (4.6 percent) for the period between 2006 and 2010. In Egypt, the average growth rate was 2.5 percent between 2011 and 2015, down from 6.2 percent between 2006 and 2010 (World Bank 2017a).

Unemployment increased in both countries, from approximately 9 percent in 2010 to 12.6 percent in 2016 in Egypt (Trading economics 2017a) and from approximately 13.0 percent in 2010 to 15.5 percent in 2016 in Tunisia (Trading economics 2017b). Net foreign direct investment as a percentage of GDP shrank in both countries after the uprisings. In Egypt, it dropped from 2.9 percent in 2010 to 2.1 percent in 2015, whereas in Tunisia it went down from 3.0 percent to 2.2 percent during the same period (World Bank 2017b).

These macroeconomic trends had a negative impact on public finances in both countries. In Egypt, the budget deficit jumped from an already high rate of 8.1 percent of GDP in 2010 to an even higher one (11.6 percent) in 2015 (Trading economics 2017c). Despite sizable subsidy cuts in 2017, the deficit still hovered around 10 percent of GDP by the end of the fiscal year 2017–2018. Egypt's public debt as a percentage of GDP rose sharply from 73.7 percent in 2010 to 85.0 percent in 2015, then to 92 percent of GDP, primarily because of the unprecedented expansion in foreign borrowing after the adoption of the International Monetary Fund (IMF) deal in November 2016 (Trading economics 2017d).

In Tunisia, the budget deficit increased from 2.6 percent of the GDP in 2010 to 3.7 percent in 2015. Tunisia's public debt, in turn, increased from 44.5 percent of GDP in 2013 to 54.6 percent in 2016. According to the World Bank (2016), the country's total external debt stock denominated in dollars, which includes both public and private debt, increased substantially from 53.5 percent of gross national income (GNI) in 2010 to 65.6 percent in 2015.

The two countries' balance of payment outlooks deteriorated as their capacity to generate foreign currency earnings declined rapidly after the 2010–2011 uprisings. Tourism collapsed because of mounting terrorist attacks, capital flight increased, and foreign currency reserves decreased sharply. According to the Central Bank of Egypt, foreign reserves fell by more than half after the uprising, declining from US$37.0 billion in 2010 to US$15.9 billion in 2015. This trend could only be reversed in 2017 through the massive expansion in foreign borrowing coupled with the flotation of the Egyptian pound. However, the rebuilding of foreign reserves has hitherto been a mere reflection of an inflated foreign debt stock. In Tunisia, the decline was less dramatic, but still remarkable, falling from US$9.8 billion in 2010 to US$5 billion in 2018 (Reuters 2018b). This put downward pressure on the national currencies, leading to higher inflation rates combined with an economic slowdown.

The two countries received massive inflows from abroad in the form of cheap loans and financial assistance that enabled competing or cooperating elites in each context to avoid unpopular austerity measures for some time and hence to protect fragile political arrangements from the pressure of economic decay and worsening standards of living. Egypt was one dramatic case. Between 2013 and 2015, Egypt received around US$23 billion in cheap credit and in-kind (oil and natural gas) and cash aid from the United Arab Emirates (UAE), Saudi Arabia, and Kuwait (Reuters 2015). The figure does not include other aid streams, estimated to exceed US$10 billion by 2015 (Colonna 2018). These funds were used to finance arms purchases from France and Russia following an American halt to military aid to Egypt in the wake of the military takeover of July 2013. In the meantime, workers' remittances kept flowing to Egypt despite plunging international oil prices since the summer of 2014. Egypt received US$19.2 billion in remittances in 2015, predominantly from the Gulf Cooperation Council (GCC) countries. The figure was US$16.7 billion in 2016, US$18.3 billion in 2017, and is projected to US$23.4 billion in 2018, making remittances almost four times as large as Suez Canal revenues (Abu basha 2018, p. 17).

Between 2011 and 2015, Tunisia was the recipient of generous capital inflows from all the major international financial institutions, development banks, and international partners, amounting to almost US$7 billion in various forms (Muasher et al. 2016). Capital inflows received by 2015 came to constitute almost 15 percent of GDP. In 2016, international partners continued their support: the World Bank established a new country partnership framework that would provide Tunisia with up to US$5 billion in loans to help restore economic growth, create jobs for young people, and reduce the disparities between the coastal centers and the underdeveloped regions (World Bank 2016). Also, in 2016, the IMF approved an extended fund facility of US$2.8 billion over four years to support economic reform in Tunisia (IMF 2016). Finally, during an international conference organized in Tunis in November 2016 to support the five-year development plan (2016–2020), Tunisia signed US$4.3 billion in project finance deals. The total financial support pledged to Tunisia by participating countries and financial institutions which took part in the conference thus totals US$14 billion, equivalent to 35 percent of GDP (Meddeb 2017a).

Nonetheless, these inflows have failed to offer a way out of the structural ordeals the two economies have been facing. The situation has worsened further as the global economy suffered yet another downturn in 2015, followed by President Trump's launching of trade wars with China, mounting more pressure on already troubled economies.

Overall, post-revolution Tunisia and Egypt provide an excellent example of a most-different-systems case (Przeworski and Teune 1970). Similar policy outcomes resulted in both countries despite different regime dynamics and almost contradictory political choices. This suggests that the inability of the ruling elites to tackle tough economic issues goes beyond regime type (democratizing vs. authoritarian).

In Egypt, the overwhelming force through which the regime suppressed dissent did not translate into a heightened capacity to effect economic restructuring measures. It was not until the Persian Gulf allies stopped pumping money (for political as well as economic reasons, including tensions over the stance on Syria and plummeting international oil prices) into state coffers that the IMF became the lender of last resort.

In Tunisia, the new elites could not use their consensus and formation of pacts to redefine the (re)distributional role[1] of the state and to adopt the measures for the re-launch of the economy and the repair of financial imbalances as prescribed by the International Financial Institutions (IFI). To make this possible, the government sought to freeze hiring in the public sector and suspend a salary increase that had already been agreed upon with the UGTT. However, corporatist representatives of labor, business, and professional groups pushed back. Lawyers and primary and secondary school teachers took to the streets, and the UGTT threatened to hold a general strike on December 8, 2016. The government eventually had to back down from implementing its fiscal and economic reform programs. When the IMF halted disbursement of the second tranche of the loan in response to this, the prime minister, desperate to show his commitment to reform, removed the minister in charge of public-sector reform, who was close to the UGTT. This created a political crisis, with the UGTT threatening to end its support for the government (Soudani 2017).

---

[1] Distributional acts are distinctive from redistributional ones depending on the source of money that is collected or dispensed by the state. The former refers to resources that are allocated by the state to social groups or constituencies directly from state non-tax revenues. The latter refers to state action through which income and/or wealth is passed from one group to another through authoritative acts by the state, such as actively through progressive taxation or passively through tax exemptions.

2.3 The Argument: Beyond Regime and into Distributional Alliances

This chapter aims at analyzing the broader political context in Egypt and Tunisia in which socio-economic protests have been unfolding. The specific focus of this comparative analysis is on state and regime dynamics during the period starting in 2013–2014. The rationale for focusing on this period is the beginning of a stabilization of political authority in both countries, although on a different basis, after almost three years of revolutionary turmoil and chaos since 2011. The aim is to analytically reconstruct the economic policies pursued by the ruling incumbents which had distributional implications. In doing so, this chapter aims at explaining the puzzling observation that incumbents in both countries, despite the different regime trajectories, have revealed limited capacity to adopt economic reforms with distributional implications through authoritative state action.

Conceptually, political capacity refers to the extent to which states can authoritatively and effectively decide on the distribution and redistribution of economic resources vis-à-vis different social constituencies without undermining the basis of their power (control over public order and the reproduction of the regime). It is labeled "political" in the sense of David Easton's (1965) classical definition of politics as the authoritative allocation of values.

The notion of political capacity here differs markedly from the overly Weberian approach to state capacities put forward by Skocpol (1985), Amsden (1992), and Evans (1995). Developmental state literature since the attempt at "bringing the state back in" in the mid-1980s was based on Weber's definition of state capacity in bureaucratic terms, where the capacity of the state to formulate and pursue cohesive action is a function of having a meritocratic, autonomous, and coherent bureaucracy. Whereas Weberian concepts of state capacity can be regarded as absolute, based on the characteristics of the state bureaucracy, political capacity is relative and relational. It is closer to the Gramscian understanding of state authority as a reflection of hegemony (or the lack thereof) over and within civil society. The focus here is hence not on the absolute bureaucratic capacity of the state apparatus but rather on its relative (in)capacity, which refers to the ability of ruling incumbents to mobilize societal allies with the aim of transforming social and economic relations (Shafer 1994).

It is already well established in the literature on the Middle East and North Africa (MENA) that Arab states may be authoritarian, or even "fierce," to use Nazih Ayubi's term (1996), but they are, nevertheless, weak. Since independence in the middle of the previous century, Arab states have followed a paradoxical path of evolution that has combined large bureaucracies, extensive mandates over the allocation of resources, and authoritarian modes of governance within their societies together with limited capacity to transform social relations and fulfill the long-claimed mission of transforming society and modernizing economies (Ayubi 1996; Skocpol 1985; Evans 1995). The late Samer Soliman (2006, 2011) paraphrased and reiterated this argument elegantly in the title of the Arabic edition of his book about Egypt's fiscal crisis under Mubarak, "Weak state and strong regime." We will follow this scholarly tradition, but critically. Our analysis tends to be more conscious of agency factors through which structural restraints, economic as well as sociological and institutional, manifest themselves. The focus here is on political actors who represent relevant societal groups and constituencies and their capacity to collectively act given their organizational ability, collective identity, and historical patterns of interaction with their bases and with other socio-political actors within state and civil society.

We hence argue that the limited political capacity demonstrated by Egyptian and Tunisian incumbents transcends regime type and is based in the socio-political dynamics within the ruling coalitions on which these regimes depend in order to govern. What explains the limited political capacity in both cases is the vulnerability to representatives of old state-dependent distributional alliances (labor as well as private business) necessary for the consolidation of power, whether on a pluralist or an authoritarian basis. This vulnerability has undermined the relative autonomy and capacity of ruling incumbents to take action even if this means a prolonged economic crisis. Such vulnerability to the old distributional alliances springs from two factors related to post-revolutionary trajectories in Egypt and Tunisia:

The first is that, in 2014, power passed in both cases into the hands of old elites who were overtly committed to the restoration of public order and security and economic and political stability rather than bringing about change. This made the new rulers eager to avoid socio-economic protest in urban centers and in critical sectors, primarily among civil servants and public-sector workers. It also made them less inclined to estrange old business interests by levying more taxes, cutting subsidies, or pursuing corruption charges against them, as they had come to rely on these very people for any viable economic recovery in the immediate term.

Tactics accommodating old interests within the public sector and the private business community apply to Egypt's military-backed regime as much as to Nidaa Tounes, despite the very different contexts. The accession of these old elites to power depended partly on defending the old distributional alliances against the Islamists, who had plans for reconfiguring business-state relations in favor of new cronies and inserting their own beneficiaries and adherents into patronage networks within the bureaucracy.

The military coup of 2013 in Egypt happened partly with the stated objective of pushing back against the Brotherhood infiltration of the state bureaucracy (Adly 2015). Similarly, in Tunisia, there was rising tension within the national unity government over the exclusion of Ennahda adherents from the networks of patronage and clientelism rejuvenated under Caid Essebsi. In fact, as shown by the results of the 2011 and 2014 elections, Ennahda has been perceived as representing Tunisia's South and large parts of the interior regions that had historically been marginalized (Gana et al. 2012). The political incorporation of Ennahda was expected to open the door for the emergence of affiliated business elites and bureaucrats who would compete with the established interests in the economy and the state apparatus. It was possibly to combat this probable outcome by President Caid Essebsi proposing an Economic Reconciliation Bill through which economic crimes, including corruption, committed by civil servants and businessmen under Ben Ali, would be officially granted amnesty in exchange for confessions and financial restitution negotiated behind closed doors (Adly and Meddeb 2017). However, apart from formalities, the bill clearly aims at consolidating financial backing and support for the president's party: Nidaa Tounes.

The second factor contributing to the incumbents' vulnerability to existing interests is the latter's continued ability to collectively resist any measures explicitly and directly attacking their access to state resources (Waterbury 1992). Collective action may be institutionalized through organizations that aggregate and represent the interests of labor or business like the UGTT and the UTICA in Tunisia, which have become powerful veto groups in the past three years. However, it may also take less institutionalized forms such as localized protest, including strikes, demonstrations, and sit-ins that occur at factory or agency levels in Egypt, especially among civil servants and workers in state-owned enterprises (Abdalla 2018; Beinin and El-Hamalawy 2007; Beinin and Vairel 2013).

Not surprisingly, both before and after the 2011 uprisings in Egypt and Tunisia, it was public-sector workers, which is a category that includes civil servant and state-owned enterprise (SOE) worker, who were the most active in opposing neoliberal reforms and attempts to privatize state-owned enterprises and downsize the civil service. In 2013 and 2014, for instance, almost two-thirds of strikes, sit-ins, and demonstrations in Egypt were concentrated in the public sector and were carried out either by blue-collar workers in state-owned enterprises or by civil servants (Ramadan and Adly 2015). Historically, the public sector has been the most unionized sector in the two countries, and in Egypt, it used its functional importance as leverage to extract economic concessions from the state during the presidency of Hosni Mubarak. In Tunisia, the UGTT's local and regional branches similarly played a major role in calling for strikes and other forms of protest before and during the uprising.

Ruling incumbents in Egypt and Tunisia have sought to appease and neutralize these state-dependent constituencies through higher wages, increased public employment, and subsidies. In Egypt, because, unlike blue-collar workers in state-owned enterprises, civil servants were historically not unionized, such an approach took a less institutionalized form than in Tunisia where the UGTT acted as a systematic interlocutor with the government on all matters related to employees. After 2011, more and more young people were recruited into the civil services of both countries, increasing their public-sector wage bills and adding to their budget deficits.

Democratic pact making in Tunisia took place with the heavy presence and effective mediation of the UGTT (see Chap. 5, in this volume). Islamists were brought into the national consensus-building process, first hesitantly but ultimately successfully. Conversely, in Egypt, there was no UGTT to directly and collectively claim to represent state-dependent classes, primarily made up of public-sector workers. Neither state-dominated nor newborn independent unions had the autonomy or resources to assume such a role (Ramadan and Adly 2015; see also Chap. 6, in this volume). Instead, the military was a powerful actor that had enough resources, historical legitimacy, and strong penetration of the state bureaucracy after independence. Moreover, the military would potentially represent the state-led coalition, primarily made up of civil servants (Adly 2015). With contingent factors such as the kind of choices made by the leaders of the Brotherhood in 2012, such structural factors translated into a bigger role for the military and paved the way for the 2013 takeover. The military's attempt to return to state authoritarianism depended again on appealing to the same state-dependent constituencies (Adly and Meddeb 2017).

Stabilization and the restitution of state authority in both countries, whether on pluralist or authoritarian terms, depended on the very same social coalitions that had ruled before the revolution. This had to do with a long legacy of the domination and legitimation of the modernizing post-independence state. It also had to do with critical junctures that had shaped the paths toward a market-led capitalist model since the 1970s. The crisis of the reproduction of state domination, under whichever regime, was reincarnated in both countries despite diverging political choices made by the incumbent elites after the revolutions of 2010–2011.

2.4 The "Eternal Return" of Weak States in Egypt and Tunisia

Old elites back in power dependent on potent old distributional alliances is the explanation we put forward for the perpetual lack of political capacity to effect measures that could pull the economies of Egypt and Tunisia out of their immediate quagmire. This situation is, however, hardly new. Post-independence states in the MENA region have continually lacked the legitimacy and political capacity to use their authority for the distribution or redistribution of income and wealth. The situation in Egypt and Tunisia demonstrates that the dominance of old interests in post-revolution contexts constitutes yet another episode of weak political capacity.

A state's political capacity is a result of the socio-historical process through which the state was formed as a centralized authority. The political capacity to undertake and effect decisions with (re)distributional consequence is formed through episodes of historical interaction with various societal groups that resist the state or ally themselves with it (Migdal 1988). The institutional features that persist can be regarded as historical junctures that set the state-society relations on a certain course (Steinmo et al. 1992; Karl 1997). Weak political capacity of a state is a result of past choices made by ruling elites in given social contexts. There is nothing inevitable, natural, or essentialist in it. Weak capacity persists if state-society relations that once created it become perpetuated. Breaking away from historical trajectories usually comes at a cost, and hinges on many contingencies that define the broader context within which the state functions, both in its national territory and also in the international arena.

Following independence and throughout most of the MENA region, the state was the motor behind nation building and socio-economic modernization via industrialization, urbanization, and universal education. At that historical juncture, a social coalition was formed of state-dependent urban middle and labor classes together with the middle peasantry in the countryside (Kandil 2012; Posusney 1997; King 2009). Nation building and modernization required the suppression of class and subnational ethnic and regional differences in the name of national unity and independence (Abdel-Malek 1962; Bono et al. 2015; Beinin and Lockman 1988). In Egypt and Tunisia, this coalition assumed a state corporatist form of unionized labor primarily in the public sector, a huge bureaucracy staffed by newly graduated youth from free universities that came to constitute the then new middle classes and some collective representation of peasants. The only acts of (re)distribution were carried out in the context of decolonization, targeting specific and often very small groups who were either foreigners, residents of foreign origin, or members of religious and ethnic minorities through nationalization, or a thin layer of the landed aristocracy through land reform. In both instances, (re)distributional acts were limited in frequency and were far from radical, and they were definitely carried on a national rather than a class basis.

Weak political capacity was reinforced when post-independence state elites replaced earlier policies of state-led development with more market-oriented reforms in the 1970s and 1980s under Bourguiba and Sadat. The ability of the state to undertake (re)distributional acts by slashing subsidies and downsizing its bloated bureaucracy proved extremely limited, given the January 1977 and January 1978 riots in Egypt and Tunisia, respectively. The violent popular reaction was another critical juncture that perpetuated the weak political capacity of the state, emphasizing it as an historic trait of states in the region that have little legitimacy to take from one social group and give to another in any direct and politically traceable manner (Bayat 1993; Posusney 1997).

Neither the Mubarak nor the Ben Ali regime was spared this dilemma. Their choice was to pursue liberalization, privatization, or divestiture of state-owned enterprises and the support of private-sector development, but within the limits of reproducing state authority by maintaining the old coalition of beneficiaries to the greatest extent possible. This led to an incoherent strategy where a huge bureaucracy was retained and even more jobs offered to newly educated graduates in the public sector while pushing for gradual trade liberalization, deregulation, and attraction of foreign investments (Waterbury 1983). The outcome of this was huge fiscal imbalances, on the one hand, as expenditure on subsidies, wages, and debt service (incurred in the first place to finance the first two items) was constant, while revenue dwindled as a percentage of the GDP. On the other hand, the state could only support the transformation to a market-led development model by allowing the expansion of the private sector. It could, however, contribute very little to its competitiveness and robustness through public investment in infrastructure and human capital. These limitations and the choices made by the incumbent elites in the 1980s and 1990s and through the 2000s faced the Egyptian and Tunisian states with the task of cushioning the impact of market-making reforms in order to sustain public order and hence state authority instead of redefining state structures and functions to service the burgeoning capitalist order.

The Egyptian and Tunisian civil service continued to expand throughout the 1990s and 2000s, and so did the wage bill. Egypt had a bureaucracy of around six million employees, with roughly 56 percent of the workforce in low-paying and often redundant jobs in local government (El-Merghani 2010, p. 162). The Central Authority for Public Mobilization and Statistics (CAPMAS) estimated the share of state employment in total active workers in 2012 as a massive 36.9 percent. For Tunisia, the World Bank estimated the rise in public-sector staff to have been from 350,000 in 2000 to 400,000 in 2005 and to have continued to more than 500,000 in 2011. This would make the share of public-sector staff in the total active population as high as 11.5, 12, and 13.5 percent in 2000, 2005, and 2011, respectively (Brockmeyer et al. 2015, p. 5).

Not only did the number of public-sector workers increase, but the wage bill also kept growing as a percentage of total expenditure. In Egypt, the share of wages increased from 23.4 percent in 1990–1991 to a massive 30.57 percent in 1997–1998, and it hovered around 29 percent in 2006–2007 (Central Bank of Egypt). In Tunisia, the increase was even more pronounced. According to the Ministry of Finance, the share of the wage bill in total government expenditure was as high as 40 percent in 1990 and continued to increase from the mid-1990s, rising from 41.3 percent in 1996 to a peak of 50.3 percent in 2003, and was as high as 47.56 percent in 2010 (Tunisian Ministry of Finance 2018). If wages and subsidies are added to other forms of recurrent expenses, nearly two-thirds of public expenditure in Tunisia and Egypt are recurrent. Direct investment averaged a meager 11.15 percent in the interval between 1986 and 2010. The share was around 10 percent in Egypt. This may help explain why the two states had very little input into investing in infrastructure and human development.

State revenue continuously declined as a percentage of GDP through the 1990s and 2000s. The Tunisian and Egyptian states suffered from generally weak capacity, political as well as administrative, to collect taxes from the property- and capital-holding classes due to a plethora of factors (Soliman 2011; Hibou 2006). The global context may be relevant here, as increasing capital mobility limited the already restricted capacity of many developing (as well as developed) states to tax capital (Rodrik 1998). A combination of all of these factors resulted in the overall stagnation of revenues, primarily tax-based, as a percentage of national incomes.

In the case of Egypt, average state revenue as a percentage of GDP was 30.8 percent in 1990. It declined to 26.4 percent in the interval between 2005 and 2010. By 2010, the ratio of tax revenue to GDP was barely equal to that of 1990 (Central Bank of Egypt). In Tunisia, a similar yet less dramatic decline could be observed. The ratio of total revenue to GDP averaged 28 percent in the interval 1990–2004 and declined slightly to 27.7 percent for the period 2005–2010. The ratio stagnated at around 19 percent of the total GDP, which is a low percentage, although higher than that of Egypt (16 percent). The increase in the share of taxes to total state revenue in Tunisia resulted primarily from the sheer decline in non-tax revenue, mainly external grants and direct sales of oil and phosphates (Soliman 2006, p. 205). However, the percentage of tax revenue to total GDP hardly changed throughout the same period.

Whereas successive waves of privatization and liberalization managed to transfer the bulk of output and added value to the private sector, the two states hardly augmented their capacity to collect taxes. Corporate taxes constituted only a humble share of total tax revenue in both countries. In Tunisia, they averaged 12 percent between 1986 and 2010. This compared with a share of 11.67 percent for payroll taxes, largely collected from public-sector employees (Tunisian Ministry of Finance 2018). Most expansion in tax collection happened in the domain of indirect taxation, which constituted a massive average of 72 percent of total tax revenue during the same period (1986–2010). The story is all too similar in Egypt, where capital and industrial and commercial profits taxes averaged around 5 percent of total tax revenue between 1990 and 2010 (Central Bank of Egypt). Indirect taxes, namely sales and customs taxes, accounted for around two-thirds of tax revenue. The share of property taxes averaged less than 3 percent during the same period.

Weberian-inspired explanations that focus on the limited administrative capacity of state bodies to collect information about the economy and to process it in a meaningful way in order to obtain resources via taxation cannot explain the situation fully in the two countries being studied. Doubtless, administrative capacities have been weak in both countries, but they could have been built up. In fact, tax policy and tax administration systems have been targets of reform since the 1990s in both countries, often with a considerable presence of international financial institutions and Western donors and trade partners. The fact that such reform initiatives aiming at capacity building did not lead anywhere itself requires explanation. This explanation is likely to be found in the relational aspects of state capacity that have to do with the capacity to redistribute from one group to another, which has been consistently limited in both nations.

In summary, neither the Egyptian nor the Tunisian state has had the political capacity to undertake authoritative acts of redistribution, whether along neoliberal lines or any other alternative program or ideology. In Egypt, as repressive as the regime could be, it failed to pursue the strategy adopted by authoritarian regimes in Asia such as in China or Vietnam which could use their power to suppress imports and consumption and raise domestic savings. It equally failed to use repression dynamics to dismantle old distributional coalitions *a la* Chile under Pinochet, despite the harsh crackdown on political opposition. In Tunisia, a democratically elected national unity government lacked the legitimacy—and, fortunately, the context of escalating debt and hyperinflation crisis—that some democratic governments in Latin America such as Argentina under Menem were able to use in the 1980s and 1990s to pass severe austerity and privatization measures. It also lacked the power to pursue alternatives to austerity altogether or to change the foundations of the country's political economy after the revolution.

The revolutions of 2010 and 2011 ironically formed another critical juncture at which state political incapacity to undertake (re)distribution was reinforced. Egypt and Tunisia witnessed waves of labor strikes and protest throughout the 2000s. In Egypt, two-thirds of these strikes, sit-ins, and demonstrations were concentrated in the public sector, either the state bureaucracy or state-owned enterprises (Ramadan and Adly 2015). In Tunisia, non-labor protests such as the 2008 protests in the Gafsa region played a similar role (see Chap. 8, in this volume). When these local revolts merged with the broader political protest movement against the Ben Ali and Mubarak regimes in 2010 and 2011, the closest definition possible of "social justice" among laborers and middle-class protestors was some ambiguous invocation of Nasserism and Bourguibism: a strong developmental role for the state, a large public sector (against privatization), and social security policies toward workers, students, and employees. This old Nasserist and Bourguibist imaginaire of social justice was no coincidence, for labor protests, as mentioned before, were concentrated among state workers, including civil servants. However, such a stance was conservative in many senses, as it was primarily fighting against further neoliberalization and for the conservation of the remnants of state-led development. This impacted upon the choices taken by elites seeking stabilization of their rule in both countries, as none could afford to offend these constituencies, at least as long as resources could be made available by means of external aid or borrowing.

2.5 Sisi's Egypt: Don't Look for a Pinochet

Under Egypt's struggling authoritarianism, until late 2016, there seemed to be little need to use repression to impose (re)distributional measures (Abrams 2015). Observing state policies after 2013, especially before the adoption of the IMF package in November 2016, suggests a rather limited capacity to enforce austerity measures with the aim of bringing down the budget deficit. Indeed, some partial austerity measures were put into effect in 2014, following the election of Sisi as president. However, they have been far from radical or consistent. Their implementation has also been governed by short-term and immediate security concerns to avoid potential popular protest against higher prices or a decline in real wages. In July 2014, for instance, Sisi issued a decree raising local oil prices and slashing the fuel subsidy. The original plan set by the Ministry of Finance had the objective of phasing out all fuel subsidies in five years. Despite this, a second phase of fuel subsidy cuts was halted in the fiscal year 2015–2016. The government preferred to keep things as they were, taking advantage of low world oil prices to avoid the unpopular raising of local energy prices.

The inability to carry out actions with distributional consequences translated into a rapid deterioration in state finances. In 2013 and 2014, the deficits were 12.2 percent and 11.5 percent, respectively. However, these figures are quite conservative as they include the massive inflows of GCC budget support. According to former Minister of Finance, the deficit in 2014 without the inclusion of foreign aid was a staggering 14 percent of GDP. The increase in the deficit was translated into an exponential rise in domestic debt, which jumped from 73.6 percent in 2010 to 87.1 percent in 2014, the highest in ten years. Such an increase in domestic debt made the government the biggest borrower from domestic banks, crowding out the private sector, raising interest rates, and hence further stifling the chances of economic recovery.

Given the general inability to levy taxes and hence raise government revenue or to cut expenses in any meaningful way, it is no surprise that the government resorted to negotiating loans with the IMF as a means of countering the widening financial gap and a worsening foreign currency shortage. In November 2016, the Egyptian government took steps to secure a US$12 billion IMF loan. These measures included floating the Egyptian pound, slashing fuel subsidies, and introducing a value-added tax (VAT). Consequently, the value of the dollar almost doubled overnight from 8.88 pounds to around 18. The introduction of the VAT in 2017 raised taxes on consumption to 13 percent—before the rate increased again to 14 percent in 2018 (Aljazeera 2016).

As painful as these measures may have been, they deliberately refrained from injuring the distributional coalition of state-dependent labor and private business. They also reflect an attempt to accommodate the IMF conditions for badly needed funding, rather than a clear strategy of economic liberalization. With the exception of the flotation of the Egyptian pound, the government continues to be reluctant to completely and finally phase out fuel subsidies, which is deemed crucial for bringing down the budget deficit. As a result of this disagreement with the IMF, the second tranche of the loan was unofficially suspended and the IMF delegation visit in April 2017 postponed (it took place in July). The government complied a short time later, and the flow of loans resumed. However, Egypt's budget deficit in 2017 was still 9.5 percent (Trading economics 2017c), up from a projection of 9 percent (Reuters 2018a). The government's public debt meanwhile jumped from 92 percent of GDP in 2016 to 101 percent in 2017 (Trading economics 2018).

It is safe to note that the Sisi regime has consciously avoided angering public-sector workers and civil servants, at least so far. In the face of mounting fiscal and economic problems, together with international conditionality, until now, the focus has been on indirect measures such as currency devaluation (and later on flotation) and the imposition of indirect taxes on consumption. Of course, such measures impose a burden on final consumers and often have an inflationary impact. However, they affect everyone and hence are politically more affordable than targeting specific business or state workers' constituencies with direct tax hikes or wage cuts, respectively.

Civil servants remain a potent force. In 2015, they mobilized against a civil service law (No. 18/2015) that Sisi had issued by decree and successfully blocked it in parliament (see Chap. 6, in this volume). This has actually been the one single piece of legislation from among more than 300 laws that was fully rejected by the newly elected parliament. The law would have allowed the downsizing of the civil service and encouraged early retirement. It also had the objective of restructuring state administration in a way that would have made it more investment-friendly and less costly for doing business. A new watered-down version of the law was passed in 2016. It was designed to achieve the same goals but in a less radical manner and without mass layoffs. Nonetheless, it commits the government to ensuring that the annual increase in public-sector salaries remains lower than the annual inflation rate.

Similarly, the regime showed no political capacity to solve its financial crisis at the expense of private business. The Sisi regime recognized, very much like the Supreme Council of the Armed Forces (SCAF) and the Muslim Brotherhood before them, that a positive investment climate was a necessity for economic recovery, job creation, and, above all, attracting foreign investment. Egypt had to prove its continuing commitment to the neoliberal measures undertaken during Mubarak's time (Adly 2017). That was one reason why the state did not expropriate any of the assets of businessmen indicted on corruption charges.

Whereas Sisi's regime raised indirect taxes on consumption, it cut tax rates on capital, reversing even earlier measures that were taken in the name of social justice after the 2011 revolution. For example, the real estate law, prepared in 2014, has not come into effect. Another example is the capital gains tax levied in 2014, which was suspended for two years and is almost forgotten now. Moreover, tax rates were reduced from 25 percent to 22.5 percent, and a temporary high-income tax was rescinded before even going into effect.

The overall picture in Egypt supports our argument. The state, as authoritarian and repressive as it has been since mid-2013, has largely shied away from implementing measures with direct (re)distributional repercussions on the two most significant beneficiaries of state policies under Mubarak: state workers and big business. Relying on a tight core of coercive state apparatuses, the military-backed regime lacked formal or informal institutional channels for the representation of interest groups. Consolidation of its rule, in this context, depended on winning the support or at least muting the dissent of civil servants and public-sector workers. Otherwise, the regime would be risking going against its base.

It would also risk the return of socio-economic protest that might lead to a renewal of political protest. The same logic applies to big businesses, on which the regime has to depend for re-launching the economy after five long years of recession.

2.6 Tunisia: Too Much Elite Pacting

Tunisia's contemporary socio-economic landscape looks grim. Without tackling the structural roots of the socio-economic crisis, most gains in the form of political and civil rights and freedoms of the January revolution remain precarious. Like Egypt and despite very different regime dynamics, the current economic predicament is the outcome of the state's incapacity to implement much needed fiscal reforms and (re)distributional measures.

Facing an ever-worsening economic crisis, the coalition of Nidaa Tounes and Ennahda has focused on short-term stability rather than on long-term development or economic restructuring (Hibou and Meddeb 2018). Since 2015, the new coalition has adopted the same economic policies and tactics of incorporation that once existed under the Ben Ali regime. The alliance that the new regime is trying to build is more likely to include the strata that profited from the growing globalization of the Tunisian economy. The securitization and the discourse emphasizing *haybat addawla*—state prestige—illustrate the attempted return of the police state, in the hope of applying selective repression to protect the new arrangements. Such arrangements would ineluctably imply the taming of labor and threaten to exacerbate the socio-political crisis.

The current ruling coalition of political and corporatist actors seems bent on preserving the status quo in the name of national consensus (Fabiani 2018). Transformative policy ideas that might offer solutions to Tunisia's long-standing political and economic problems are generally rejected from the political and, to a certain extent, the public sphere. Such measures might include higher taxes on corporations and private wealth, tariff protections for the development of domestic industry, investment in agriculture, land reform that could entail redistribution and collective ownership, as well as the nationalization of confiscated private firms that benefited from corrupt deals made during the Ben Ali era or even during the *Infitah* years of wealth transfer in the 1980s through the 2000s. Instead, the dominant institutional and policy prescriptions for economic reform are based on a "race to the bottom" logic by calling for a wage freeze or increasing taxation of salaries in order to attract capital that merely reinforces distorted patterns of accumulation and distribution.

The increasingly dominant narrative shared by the international financial institutions and governing parties alike is that reform has been blocked due to the rule of *hizb Al Idara*, or the party of the bureaucracy. As one member of Ennahda's leadership put it in early 2016:

> "Nowadays Tunisia is governed by a four-party coalition and a party formed by the bureaucracy. The bureaucracy is slow and conservative. Reforms will place undoubtedly the government in opposition with business interests or with the interests of the working class. It's because there is no long term political vision that the bureaucracy can take charge of."[2]

Such absence of alternative visions for organizing the state and the economy have paved the way for a strategy that justifies keeping the status quo in the name of national consensus, embodied by both the governments of Habib Essid (2015–2016) and Youssef Chahed (since 2016). Ironically, this situation has been one of the causes of the call for a return to a presidential system, as parliamentary politics have proven too unruly to push through the kinds of reforms deemed necessary. In placing the blame on the bureaucracy or on specific parties, such framing downplays structural factors, the absence of a robust social coalition supportive of change, and the entrenched interests that actually support maintaining the status quo at all cost. For instance, the predominance of importers in the UTICA has blocked every attempt to reduce or limit imports as a means of countering the widening trade deficit, leading to the continued depreciation of the Tunisian dinar. Similarly, the UGTT has kept calling for increasing public-sector salaries, which have fed the rising inflation rate, given that productivity has not improved much.

In general terms, the victory of Nidaa Tounes in the 2014 legislative elections has led to the reaffirmation of the power of the old business elites. Anxious to preserve their interests in a climate of uncertainty and keen to carry weight on economic strategies, businessmen have done more than support political parties financially. They have actually entered politics: 10 percent of members of parliament are businessmen, of which 60 percent are elected representatives of Nidaa Tounes.

---

[2] Interview with Ennahda's leader, Tunis, January 2016.

Despite its positive role in pushing for a redistribution of power and the protection of workers' rights in the post-revolutionary period, the UGTT has at times neglected some of the deeper socio-economic divides in the country. Under Ben Ali, the UGTT was part and parcel of the authoritarian governance, and often worked together with the state to manage labor in a way that suited the interests of capital, and reinforced geographical and class divides (Hibou 2011). It has taken a more activist position in the aftermath of the uprising, often backing more radical actions by groups like the Union of Unemployed Graduates (UDC). In addition, the UGTT has condemned the implication of businessmen in tax evasion and has been calling for fiscal reform to overcome the budget deficit. Despite this, its position vis-à-vis the kinds of structural transformation required to expand and protect the interests of Tunisians in all domains remains vague and inconsistent.

Generally represented as a driving force behind the uprising, regional disparities account for much of the social and political unrest in Tunisia today. The development of these regions is a major challenge. More than underdevelopment, a general feeling of dispossession feeds perceptions of social injustice in these regions (Hibou 2015). There is a historical imbalance between the inland regions and the coastal areas, with important resource transfers (gas, oil, phosphate, water) from the former to the latter that are still ongoing. And yet these transfers have been mostly taken for granted at the national level. The regions producing the natural resources that have largely contributed to the macroeconomic balance of the whole country and to the prosperity of the coastal areas have never been fairly compensated with national budget redistributions. Instead, the weak level of public investments has further aggravated these regional imbalances. For decades, 80 percent of public spending has benefited the coast, with only 20 percent remaining for the inland regions. This also holds true for tax policies that have favored coastal activities: in the 2000s, 72 percent of the tax reductions went to exporting companies against just 12 percent for regional and agricultural development (the remaining 8 percent covered common incentives). Patterns of foreign direct investment have reinforced this historic imbalance.

The social instability in southern Tunisia not only indicates the post-2011 government's inability to contain the protests; it mainly expresses the inability of the political system to include all societal forces and its limited capacity to channel and mediate the social claims of the disenfranchised populations, who feel excluded from political representation and from enjoying the benefits of the revolution. It points also to the limits of consensus between Islamists and secularists that frame formal politics. For large swathes of the population, this consensus has turned into a power-sharing pact that has disregarded long-standing and deeply rooted structural socio-economic grievances. In the absence of a strong and representative political opposition, this has opened the door to informal political contention (see Chap. 8, in this volume). The worsening of the situation in Libya and the failure of the Tunisian political elites to kick-start development in the periphery will only further foster the conditions in which radical politics could thrive (Meddeb 2017b).

2.7 Conclusion

This chapter has sought to explain similar policy outcomes under different political regime dynamics in Egypt and Tunisia after the 2011 revolutions. In developing an answer to this puzzling observation, we have proposed looking into the social coalitions under which incumbent regimes have depended to win and retain office. We have argued that similar policy outcomes in both countries had to do with similar state incapacities perpetuated by the vulnerability of incumbents to old distributional alliances, rather than to particular post-revolutionary regime dynamics, whether democratic or authoritarian. In both countries, the state as a pact of domination has been the hostage of an historical deal that dates back to independence, and that continues to weaken the political capacity of the state to decide authoritatively over the (re)distribution of resources from one social group to another. This has been a persistent feature that has been reinforced at many historical junctures through the past six decades.

These institutional restraints have shaped the paths and dynamics of the post-revolutionary regimes in both countries. In Tunisia, the interplay between various structural and contingent factors made it possible for a pluralist regime to emerge against a background of successful elite pacting and consensus building. Egypt took the opposite direction with the abrupt abandonment of a brief political opening and returning to authoritarianism. Nonetheless, both regimes have been dependent on appeasing the same old state-dependent coalitions of social actors. This helps explain the two countries' similar inability to tackle fiscal and economic crises through the last several years.

Does this mean that regime type does not matter? Of course not. Regime type does matter, but its impact on policy-making is mediated and restrained by state structures and by the broader features of the political economy in which political regimes are embedded, at least in the short- and medium terms. In the long term, regimes can be decisive in their own right in determining the chances of changing state institutions and the socio-economic coalitions on which state domination rests. Authoritarianism may provide the institutional framework for dismantling or reconfiguration of earlier coalitions and for the redefinition of state functions in the realm of economic regulation or (re)distribution of resources from one group to another. Conversely, a democratic regime may allow the elites more room to maneuver and to play off one group against another. An exact answer to this question lies beyond the scope of this chapter. The two cases studied here do suggest, however, that a better understanding of the complex relationship between political regimes and state structures is crucial when it comes to explaining economic policy-making.

References

Abdalla, N. (2018). Al-haraka al-niqabiyya al-mostaqila fi Misr bayn guhud al-tanzeem wa tahadiyyat al-taetheer (The independent union movement in Egypt between effort at organization and limited impact). In A. Adly & F. Ramadan (Eds.), *Su'ud wa Uful Al-haraza Al-omaliyya fi Misr (2006–2016): Al-omaal, Wal-siyasa wal-dawla (The rise and fall of Egypt's labor movement [2006–2016]: Workers, politics and the state)* (pp. 39–79). Cairo: Dar Al-maraya.

Abdel-Malek, A. (1962). *Égypte, société militaire*. Paris: Éditions du Seuil.

Abrams, E. (2015, April 24). Sisi is no Pinochet. *The Washington Post*. Retrieved November 26, 2018, from https://www.washingtonpost.com/opinions/hes-no-pinochet/2015/04/24/8c8d642e-e212-11e4-905f-cc896d379a32_story.html.

Abu Basha, M. (2018, April 23). 4Q17 BOP Chartbook: CAD stable at three-year low as remittances keep breaking record high. *EFG Hermes*. Retrieved November 28, 2018, from https://www.efghermesone.com/News/Index/egypt-economics-4q17-bop-chartbook.

Achcar, G. (2013). *The people want: A radical exploration of the Arab uprising*. Berkeley, CA and Los Angeles, CA/London: University of California Press.

Adly, A. (2015, January 31). Triumph of the bureaucracy: A decade of aborted social and political change in Egypt, *Jadaliyya*. Retrieved November 26, 2018, from http://www.jadaliyya.com/pages/index/20708/triumph-of-the-bureaucracy_a-decade-of-aborted-soc.

Adly, A., & Meddeb, H. (2017). *Why painful economic reforms are less risky in Tunisia than Egypt?* Beirut: Carnegie Middle East Center.

Amsden, A. (1992). *Asia's next giant, South Korea and late industrialization.* New York, NY: Oxford University Press.

Ayubi, N. N. (1996). *Over-stating the Arab state: Politics and society in the Middle East.* London and New York, NY: IB Tauris.

Bayat, A. (1993). Populism, liberalization and popular participation: Industrial democracy in Egypt. *Economic and Industrial Democracy, 14,* 65–87.

Beinin, J., & El-Hamalawy, H. (2007). Strikes in Egypt spread from center of gravity. *Middle East Report Online,* May 9. Retrieved November, 28, 2018, from http://www.merip.org/mero/mero050907.

Beinin, J., & Lockman, Z. (1988). *Workers on the Nile: Nationalism, communism, Islam and the Egyptian working class, 1882–1954.* Princeton, NJ: Princeton University Press.

Beinin, J., & Vairel, F. (Eds.). (2013). *Social movements, mobilization, and contestation in the Middle East and North Africa.* Stanford, CA: Stanford University Press.

Bono, I., Hibou, B., Meddeb, H., & Tozy, M. (2015). *L'État d'injustice au Maghreb: Maroc et Tunisie.* Paris: Karthala.

Brockmeyer, A., Khatrouch, M., & Raballand, G. (2015). Public sector size and performance management: A case-study of post-revolution Tunisia. World Bank Group, Governance Global Practice Group: Policy Research Working Paper 7159. Retrieved November, 27, 2018, from http://documents.worldbank.org/curated/en/574821468166165145/pdf/WPS7159.pdf.

Camau, M., & Geisser, V. (2003). *Le syndrome autoritaire. Politique en Tunisie de Bourguiba à Ben Ali.* Paris: Presses de Sciences Po.

Central Bank of Egypt. (2001–2014). *Annual Report.* Cairo: Central Bank of Egypt.

Colonna, J. (2018, March 12). SIPRI: Egypt's arms imports skyrocket amidst greater security threats. *Egypt Today.* Retrieved November, 26, 2018, from http://www.egypttoday.com/Article/1/45059/SIPRI-Egypt's-arms-imports-skyrocket-amidst-greater-security-threats.

Easton, D. (1965). *A systems analysis of political life.* New York, NY: Wiley.

El-Merghani, I. (2010). Awda' Ilaqat Al-amal (Labor Relations). In Al-Hiali Foundation (Ed.), *Al-omal Al-misriyoon Fi Alam Motaghayer: Tareekh, Nidhal (Egyptian Workers in a Changing World: History and Struggle)* (pp. 131–165). Cairo: Al-Hilali Foundation. (in Arabic).

Evans, P. (1995). *Embedded autonomy: States and industrial transformation.* Princeton, NJ: Princeton University Press.

Fabiani, R. (2018). Tunisia and the international economy since 2011: Rentierism, patronage and moral hazard. *Jadaliyya.* Retrieved November, 26, 2018, from http://www.jadaliyya.com/Details/35142.

Gana, A., Van Hamme, G., & Ben Rebah, M. (2012). Géographie électorale et disparités socio-territoriales: les enseignements des élections pour l'assemblée constituante en Tunisie. *L'Espace Politique, 18.* Retrieved November, 28, 2018, from http://journals.openedition.org/espacepolitique/2486.

Hibou, B. (2006). Domination & control in Tunisia: Economic levers for the exercise of authoritarian power. *Review of African political economy*, *33*(108), 185–206.

Hibou, B. (2011). *The force of obedience. The political economy of repression in Tunisia*. Cambridge: Polity Press.

Hibou, B. (2015). La formation asymétrique de l'Etat en Tunisie. Les territoires de l'injustice. In I. Bono, B. Hibou, H. Meddeb, & M. Tozy (Eds.), *L'État d'injustice au Maghreb: Maroc et Tunisie* (pp. 99–149). Paris: Karthala.

Hibou, B., & Meddeb, H. (2018). Tunisie: la démocratisation ou l'oubli organisé de la question sociale, *AOC media*, January 29.

IMF (International Monetary Fund). (2016). *IMF reaches staff-level agreement with Tunisia on a four-year US$2.8 billion extended fund facility* (press release, April 15). Retrieved November, 26, 2018, from https://www.imf.org/en/News/Articles/2015/09/14/01/49/pr16168.

Kandil, H. (2012). Why did the Egyptian Middle Class March to Tahrir Square? *Mediterranean Politics*, *17*(2), 197–215.

Karl, T. L. (1997). *The paradox of plenty: Oil booms and petro-states*. Studies in International Political Economy, 26. Berkeley, CA; Los Angeles, CA; London: University of California Press.

Khiari, S. (2003). *Tunisie, le délitement de la cité*. Paris: Karthala.

King, S. J. (2009). *The new authoritarianism in the Middle East and North Africa*. Bloomington, IN: Indiana University Press.

Marzouki, N. (2015, July 10). Tunisia's rotten compromise. *Middle East Report Online*. Retrieved November, 28, 2018, from http://www.merip.org/mero/mero071015.

Marzouki, N., & Meddeb, H. (2015). Tunisia: Democratic miracle or mirage? Jadaliyya. Retrieved November, 26, 2018, from http://www.jadaliyya.com/Details/32181.

Meddeb, H. (2017a). *Peripheral vision. How Europe can help preserve Tunisia's fragile democracy*. London: European Council on Foreign Relations.

Meddeb, H. (2017b, April 5). Precarious resilience. Tunisia's Libyan predicament. *MENARA Future Notes*. Retrieved November, 27, 2018, from http://www.iai.it/sites/default/files/menara_fn_5.pdf.

Migdal, J. S. (1988). *Strong societies and weak states. State-society relations and state capabilities in the Third World*. Princeton, NJ: Princeton University Press.

Muasher, M., Pierini, M., Djerassi, A. (2016). *Between peril and promise: A new framework for partnership with Tunisia*. Washington, DC: Carnegie Endowment for International Peace. Retrieved November, 26, 2018, from https://carnegieendowment.org/files/CP_269_Tunisia.pdf.

Posusney, M. (1997). *Labor and the state in Egypt: Workers, unions and economic restructuring*. New York, NY: Columbia University Press.

Przeworski, A., & Teune, H. (1970). *The logic of comparative social inquiry*. New York, NY: Wiley.
Ramadan, F., & Adly, A. (2015). Low-cost authoritarianism. The Egyptian regime and labor movement since 2013. Carnegie Middle East Center. Retrieved November, 26, 2018, from https://carnegie-mec.org/2015/09/17/low-cost-authoritarianism-egyptian-regime-and-labor-movement-since-2013-pub-61321.
Reuters. (2015). Egypt got $23 billion in aid from Gulf in 18 months-minister. Retrieved November, 28, 2018, from http://uk.reuters.com/article/uk-egypt-investment-gulf/egypt-got-23-billion-in-aid-from-gulf-in-18-months-minister-idUKKBN0LY0UT20150302.
Reuters. (2018a, January 30). Egypt sees budget deficit at 9.4 pct/GDP in 2017-18-deputy finmin. Retrieved November, 28, 2018, from http://www.reuters.com/article/egypt-economy-deficit/egypt-sees-budget-deficit-at-9-4-pct-gdp-in-2017-18-deputy-finmin-idUSL8N1PP2CW.
Reuters. (2018b). Tunisia's foreign reserves fall to level equal to 84 days of imports. Retrieved November, 28, 2018, from http://www.reuters.com/article/tunisia-economy-currency/tunisias-foreign-reserves-fall-to-levels-equal-to-84-days-of-imports-idUSL8N1PW2YN.
Rodrik, D. (1998). Capital mobility and labor. Draft paper prepared for the NBER workshop on trade, technology, education, and the U.S. labor market, April 30–May 1, 1998. Harvard University. Retrieved November, 26, 2018, from https://sites.hks.harvard.edu/m-rcbg/research/d.rodrik_ksg_capital.mobility.and.labor.pdf.
Shafer, D. M. (1994). *Winners and losers: How sectors shape the developmental prospects of states*. Ithaca, NY: Cornell University Press.
Skocpol, T. (1985). Bringing the state back in: Strategies of analysis in current research. In P. B. Evans, D. Rueschemeyer, & T. Skocpol (Eds.), *Bringing the state back in* (pp. 3–37). Cambridge University Press.
Soliman, S. (2006). *Aldawla al daeefa wal nizam al-qawi, Idarat al azma al maleya fi misr*. Cairo: el-Dar Press.
Soliman, S. (2011). *The autumn of dictatorship: Fiscal crisis and political change in Egypt*. Stanford, CA: Stanford University Press.
Soudani, S. (2017, February 27). Tunisie. Le limogeage surprise d'Abid Briki annonce une grave crise gouvernementale. *Le Courier de l'Atlas*. Retrieved November, 27, 2018, from https://www.lecourrierdelatlas.com/tunisie-le-limogeage-surprise-d-abid-briki-annonce-une-grave-crise-gouvernementale-7548.
Steinmo, S., Thelen, K. A., & Longstreth, F. (Eds.). (1992). *Structuring politics: Historical institutionalism in comparative analysis*. Cambridge and New York, NY: Cambridge University Press.

Trading Economics. (2017a). Egypt unemployment rate 1993–2018. Retrieved November, 27, 2018, from https://tradingeconomics.com/egypt/unemployment-rate.
Trading Economics. (2017b). Tunisia unemployment rate 2005–2018. Retrieved November, 27, 2018, from https://tradingeconomics.com/tunisia/unemployment-rate.
Trading Economics. (2017c). Egypt government budget 2002–2018. Retrieved November, 27, 2018, from https://tradingeconomics.com/egypt/government-budget.
Trading Economics. (2017d). Tunisia government budget 2007–2018. Retrieved November, 27, 2018, from https://tradingeconomics.com/tunisia/government-budget.
Trading Economics. (2018). Egypt public debt rate 2002–2018. Retrieved November, 27, 2018, from https://tradingeconomics.com/egypt/government-debt-to-gdp.
Tunisian Ministry of Finance. (2018). Les Indicateurs: Dépenses. Retrieved November, 28, 2018, from http://www.finances.gov.tn/index.php?option=com_content&view=article&id=127&Itemid=303&lang=fr.
Waterbury, J. (1983). *The Egypt of Nasser and Sadat. The political economy of two regimes*. Princeton, NJ: Princeton University Press.
Waterbury, J. (1992). The heart of the matter? Public enterprise and the adjustment process. In S. Haggard & R. R. Kaufman (Eds.), *The politics of economic adjustment: International constraints, distributive conflicts and the state* (pp. 182–220). Princeton, NJ: Princeton University Press.
World Bank. (2016). New program of support for Tunisia focused on supporting youth and employment, equal opportunities for regions (press release, May 17). Retrieved November, 27, 2018, from http://www.worldbank.org/en/news/press-release/2016/05/17/new-program-of-support-for-tunisia-focused-on-supporting-youth-employment-equal-opportunities-for-regions.
World Bank. (2017a). GDP Growth (annual %) 1961–2017, Egypt and Tunisia. Retrieved November 27, 2018, from https://data.worldbank.org/indicator/NY.GDP.MKTP.KD.ZG?locations=EG-TN.
World Bank. (2017b). Foreign direct investment, net inflows (% of GDP) 1976–2017. Retrieved November 27, 2018, from https://data.worldbank.org/indicator/BX.KLT.DINV.WD.GD.ZS?locations=TN-EG&name_desc=true&view=chart.
Yousfi, H. (2015). *L'UGTT, une passion tunisienne, enquête sur les syndicalistes en revolution (2011–2014)*. Paris: IRMC-Karthala.

CHAPTER 3

Socioeconomic Contention in Post-2011 Egypt and Tunisia: A Comparison

Prisca Jöst and Jan-Philipp Vatthauer

3.1 Introduction

Since the uprisings that provoked the toppling of presidents Ben Ali and Mubarak in early 2011, Tunisia and Egypt have continued to experience serious socioeconomic problems: Both North African countries faced high rates of unemployment of young adults in less-developed regions as well as social instability and a slowdown of economic growth (ILO 2014, pp. 62–64; Schulz 2012). This is also reflected in popular perceptions. In a survey conducted during the 2014 parliamentary elections in Tunisia, Chantal Berman and Elizabeth Nugent asked about citizens' main concerns in 2011 and at the time the survey was carried out. The survey reveals that unlike 2011, when people found democracy, civic freedoms,

---

P. Jöst (✉)
University of Gothenburg, Gothenburg, Sweden
e-mail: prisca.jost@gu.se

J.-P. Vatthauer
Die Linke, Berlin, Germany

Peace Research Institute Frankfurt (PRIF), Frankfurt am Main, Germany

© The Author(s) 2020
I. Weipert-Fenner, J. Wolff (eds.), *Socioeconomic Protests in MENA and Latin America*, Middle East Today,
https://doi.org/10.1007/978-3-030-19621-9_3

and transitional justice to be most important, Tunisians identified economic growth, employment, and living costs as the most pressing issues in 2014 (Berman and Nugent 2015, p. 7). These findings are in line with results from the Arab Barometer (2011, 2013, 2015), which reveal that Tunisians have become increasingly concerned about economic development since 2011. In the 2015 survey, respondents identified "the economic situation" as Tunisia's most important challenge. Egyptians also named "the economic situation" as one of the two most urgent challenges that their country faces, even though they found that the country's economy had improved since 2013 (Arab Barometer 2015).

At the same time, however, this chapter shows that—while socioeconomic concerns undoubtedly played a very prominent role in the uprisings in both cases (see El-Meehy 2014; Beissinger et al. 2012)—the two countries differ markedly when it comes to the evolution of socioeconomically motivated protests since 2011. When looking at protests in which at least one socioeconomic claim was raised, Tunisia experienced a comparably higher number of such socioeconomic protests between 2011 and 2016 than Egypt. In terms of both absolute numbers and a share of all types of protests, socioeconomic protests in Tunisia have been at a very high level. By contrast, Egypt was marked by massive protests, in which mainly political issues were raised, whereas socioeconomic demands seem to have been less relevant.

At first glance, these differences seem to be easy to explain: In line with the established argument that political opportunities are fundamental in shaping contentious action (see McAdam 1999; Tilly 1977), one could argue that different political developments in those countries led to different outcomes. Since the long-standing dictators were overthrown in early 2011, Tunisia and Egypt have undergone very different trajectories of political transformation. Whereas in Tunisia conflicts and political turbulences generally followed a path of democratic transition, a process of democratization in Egypt was reversed by a military coup in 2013. Since then, Egypt's political regime has experienced an increasingly authoritarian development. Thus, as outlined by Adly and Meddeb (in this volume), both countries developed different regime types in the aftermath of the uprisings. In this sense, the higher number of socioeconomic protests in post-revolutionary Tunisia would simply reflect the much more facilitating political context, as compared to much more repressive Egypt.

However, there is more to the dynamics of socioeconomic protests than such a macro-perspective suggests. As we show in this chapter, a closer look at the actual protest actors, their claims and tactics, as well as at the geographical patterns of socioeconomic protests reveals micro-dynamics that are much more complex in both cases—and suggest both interesting similarities between the countries and important temporal continuities within the two cases.

The following chapter seeks to map and analyze the evolution of socioeconomically motivated protests in Tunisia and Egypt over a period of six years (between 2011 and 2016). In a first step, the methodological approach is presented in more detail. The analysis is based on the *Armed Conflict Location & Event Data Project* (ACLED), which provides a detailed data set that entails information on protest events in both Arab countries between 2011 and 2016. In a second step, we present the main findings from our data analysis on socioeconomic protests in Tunisia and Egypt in the aftermath of the Arab uprisings. The chapter describes the dynamics of socioeconomic contestation in both countries—starting with Tunisia. After looking at the protest numbers in both countries and their evolution over time, we discuss the protest actors and how they changed between 2011 and 2016. We also study the claims of the protesters and how they differ between actors and between countries. We then give an overview of the different tactics used by protest actors to express their demands. Furthermore, we analyze the extent to which geographical patterns of socioeconomic protest can be identified. We compare the numbers of socioeconomically motivated protests in the wealthier regions with those in the impoverished governorates of both countries. In a final step, we discuss the results of the data analysis from a comparative perspective.

3.2 Data and Methodology

The comparative analysis of socioeconomic protest in Egypt and Tunisia draws on the ACLED data set, which currently represents the only ongoing comprehensive, qualitative data collection covering protests in both Arab states going back to 2010. It focuses on acts of political violence by state and non-state actors alike, but it also includes non-violent protests. ACLED is a manually coded data set which is based on daily local, regional, and national media in English and French as well as reports by non-governmental organizations (NGOs) and humanitarian agencies.

Because of the limited available information about the individual protest events provided by ACLED, the database was further refined by means of original research. Using newspapers in English, French, and Arabic, additional data on the actors, demands, and types of the protests mentioned in the ACLED database were collected and manually coded. The coding of socioeconomic protests was based on the definition provided in the introduction to this volume: Protests were coded as "socioeconomic" when the claims made during the event touched on at least one of the following issues: productive activities (access to land, subsidies, credits, taxes), social services (public services, health, education, water, transportation, price/tariff subsidies), income (wages, collective contracts, pensions, work), and worker rights (such as the right to organize and employment standards). Protests in which none of these demands were raised were coded as "other."

Even though protests obviously differ in terms of number of participants, duration, and so on, every protest in the data set is coded as a single protest. A protest with many participants in the capital city counts as much as a small protest, such as a hunger strike. Instead of considering the specifics mentioned previously as a measure of the significance of a protest, ACLED provides a different possibility. By definition, ACLED only considers protests that have certain political significance for the country at hand. As a result, ACLED's protest numbers are much lower than other country-specific protest databases covering Egypt and Tunisia. As previously mentioned, an advantage of this definition is that all protests in ACLED meet a "significance threshold." In this way, we do not compare significant protest events with very insignificant protests as other databases tend to do.

Because it draws on media articles and reports, a number of possible biases and limitations have to be considered when making use of ACLED. *First*, the reliance on English- and French-speaking media may imply a regional bias within a country. Foreign language sources tend to cover densely populated areas rather than peripheral areas. As a consequence, protests in peripheral areas might be underrepresented in the database (Vatthauer and Weipert-Fenner 2017, p. 9). *Second*, country-specific censorship by the regime and the degree of press freedom in a country are also a possible source of bias. Given the reliance on local media coverage, the database is prone to these effects. A *third* possible bias is that media reporting of protests usually follows public attention, which means that the database portrays only those events that received the most attention—such as violent protests—and not the full range of protests. These biases are certainly important, but they arguably do not significantly distort the analysis presented later.[1] As most biases are stable over time, they do not distort our findings, which are based on temporal comparisons.

---

[1] To test our findings from the ACLED database we compared them with findings from other sets of data on protest events in both North African countries provided by different national NGOs. In all data sets we found similar dynamics. For further details see footnotes 2 and 6 in this chapter.

3.3 The Evolution of Protest in Egypt and Tunisia

Over the period of six years (2011–2016), 1755 protests (total numbers) were counted in Tunisia compared to 4285 in Egypt (see Table 3.1). In Tunisia, after a small decrease in the number of socioeconomic protests in the years 2013 and 2014, in 2015 and even more strongly in 2016, the numbers rose enormously. The numbers of other protests in Tunisia remained relatively stable over time. In Egypt, we find a more similar trend for socioeconomic and other protests. Both types of protests increased massively in the year 2013, while the numbers remained relatively low in other years. Estimating the significance of socioeconomic contestation in both countries, we find that socioeconomic protests play a bigger role in the Tunisian protest landscape than they do in Egypt. While in Tunisia there are between 3.56 and 35.3 socioeconomic protests per year per million inhabitants, the range in Egypt is between 0.16 and 1.82. In comparison to other protests, our findings suggest that in Tunisia almost every second protest is a socioeconomic protest, whereas in Egypt less than every ninth protest is a socioeconomic one.

If we compare these numbers with the overall population in both countries, we find that Tunisia experienced remarkably higher numbers of protests per million inhabitants than Egypt. The ratio varies from 2.92 (protests per million inhabitants) in 2016 to 21.49 in 2013 in Egypt and from 17.14 in 2011 to 50.51 in 2016 in Tunisia. Moreover, Tunisia experienced remarkably higher numbers of socioeconomic protests than Egypt, whereas non-socioeconomic protests in Egypt outnumbered those in Tunisia by far. However, as will be seen in the following sections, dynamics become much more complex with regard to the protest actors, their claims, and the types of protest.

3.4 Socioeconomic Protests in Tunisia

From 2011 to 2014, numbers of "other" protests were always significantly higher in Tunisia than those of socioeconomic protests, with an average of 169 "other" protests each year. This pattern changed in 2015, when 176 socioeconomic protests were counted (but only 145 "other" protests). In 2016, the number of socioeconomic protests (399) in one year more than doubled "other" protests (172). Socioeconomic protests thus increased in absolute numbers as well as relative to non-socioeconomic protests, which marked a new trend in the country's recent protest history (see Fig. 3.1). In January 2016, 124 socioeconomic protests were counted in one month

Table 3.1 Protest numbers in Tunisia and Egypt (in brackets: per million inhabitants)

Year	Socioeconomic protests		Other protests		Total	
	Tunisia	Egypt	Tunisia	Egypt	Tunisia	Egypt
2011	38 (3.56)	88 (1.09)	145 (13.58)	561 (6.97)	183 (17.14)	649 (8.06)
2012	71 (6.58)	13 (0.16)	189 (17.53)	293 (3.55)	260 (24.11)	306 (3.71)
2013	42 (3.85)	154 (1.82)	180 (16.52)	1665 (19.67)	222 (20.38)	1819 (21.49)
2014	34 (3.09)	39 (0.45)	164 (14.89)	898 (10.34)	198 (17.98)	937 (10.79)
2015	176 (15.77)	44 (0.49)	145 (12.99)	267 (3.00)	321 (28.76)	311 (3.50)
2016	399 (35.30)	75 (0.83)	172 (15.22)	188 (2.09)	571 (50.51)	263 (2.92)
Total	760	413	995	3872	1755	4285

Source: Authors' data collection based on the ACLED data set

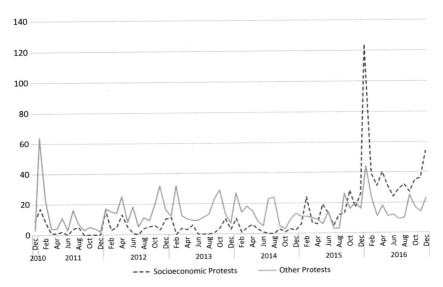

Fig. 3.1 Protests in Tunisia. Source: Authors' data collection based on the ACLED data set

alone, which surpassed former record numbers, including those during the month of the revolution in January 2011.[2]

In December 2010, protests occurred in Sidi Bouzid and soon after spread to the other regions in the marginalized south and interior. They marked the beginning of the Arab uprisings and pointed to socioeconomic marginalization of those regions. January 2011 was marked by mass protests in the capital city Tunis, where people demonstrated for the removal of President Ben Ali and demanded political change. The protests continued

---

[2] Since May 2014 the Tunisian Forum for Economic and Social Rights (*Forum Tunisien pour les Droits Economiques et Sociaux, FTDES*) has published monthly reports on protest events all over the country. The so-called OST (*Rapports de l'Observatoire Social Tunisien*) reports contain information on the protest actors and their demands as well as on the types of action. The protest numbers are considerably higher than in ACLED, which might be due to their inclusion of Arabic-speaking media articles, in which small-scale protest actions are also mentioned. Furthermore, FTDES owns local offices in the marginalized regions, in which information and data on protest actions in those regions are collected. However, since both databases ACLED and OST showed very similar trends, ACLED represents a valid set of data for further analysis. For further information, see https://ftdes.net/ (accessed 26 June 2017).

after Ben Ali resigned on 14 January 2011, demanding that the old cadres—including Mohamed Ghannouchi who became the president of the new interim government—give up their power (see Willsher 2011). Until Ghannouchi's removal on 27 February 2011, politically motivated protests dominated the scene, and socioeconomic protests became less common.

The same developments continued throughout the years from 2011 to 2014, when large protests accompanied the constitution-making process (see Boubekeur 2016). Following the election of the National Constituent Assembly (*Assemblée nationale constituante*, ANC) in October 2011, the Islamist Ennahda party governed the country as part of a troika government with the secular Congress for the Republic (*Congrès pour la république*) and Democratic Forum for Labor and Liberties (*Forum démocratique pour le travail et les libertés*, Ettakatol) (Antonakis-Nashif 2016, p. 131; Boubekeur 2016, p. 113f.). During this period, the government had to deal with deep internal conflicts between the Islamist Ennahda party and the two secular troika members (Boubekeur 2016, p. 115). At the same time, it did not show any evidence of efforts to really alter the country's economic and social policies, but it remained dependent on financial support from the International Monetary Fund (IMF) and other external actors (Paciello 2013, p. 19). Socioeconomic protests demanding improvement of the economic situation of the country in Tunis in April and in Siliana in November 2012 were heavily suppressed by police forces (Boubekeur 2016, p. 115). After the two opposition leaders Chokri Belaid and Mohamed Brahmi were assassinated in February and July 2013, respectively (Antonakis-Nashif 2016, p. 131; Boubekeur 2016, pp. 115–117), people were mostly concerned about the unstable political situation and the future of the country under the leading Islamist Ennahda Party. During the so-called Bardo protests in July and August 2013, oppositional, secular political groups—including the *Union Générale Tunisienne du Travail* (UGTT)—demonstrated outside the parliament against the current government led by the Ennahda Party (Antonakis-Nashif 2016, p. 131).

In December 2013, the National Dialogue Quartet came together to support the democratic transition in Tunisia in times of political crisis (see Antonakis-Nashif 2016, p. 131). It was organized by four key players in the Tunisian civil society: The Tunisian General Labor Union (UGTT, *Union Générale Tunisienne du Travail*), the Tunisian Confederation of Industry, Trade and Handicrafts (UTICA, *Union Tunisienne de l'Industrie, du Commerce et de l'Artisanat*), the Tunisian Human Rights League (LTDH, *La Ligue Tunisienne pour la Défense des Droits de l'Homme*), and the

Tunisian Order of Lawyers (*Ordre National des Avocats de Tunisie*) (see Chap. 5, in this volume).³ Thus, until the new constitution was finally adopted and Ennahda gave up its power to a new cabinet of technocrats in January 2014 (Boubekeur 2016, p. 119; Schäfer 2015, p. 23), protests concerned mostly political issues such as demands for the removal of Ennahda (Ocampos 2016). During this period, socioeconomic protests played only a minor role. In October and November 2014, the parliamentary and presidential elections were held and a new government was finally installed in February 2015, with Habib Essid from the secular Nidaa Tounes Party as Prime Minister.

The year 2015 was marked by crucial changes: Socioeconomic protests increased, whereas "other" protests decreased slightly in the first quarter of the year. The new government under Essid announced its commitment to reducing unemployment and regional inequalities as well as to undertaking new tax reforms and minimizing public spending (European Commission 2015, p. 43). Nonetheless, its inauguration was accompanied by large socioeconomic contestation in early 2015. Among the most important protest events was a wave of protests in different cities of the governorate of Gafsa in May, when protesters criticized the lack of industrial policies in the neglected hinterland. During this period of time, phosphate production in the Gafsa mining basin came to a complete standstill due to strikes and sit-ins of unemployed workers in front of the factory site, blocking, for example, the railway, which is needed to carry the phosphate (see Chap. 8, in this volume). Unemployed young people, demanding the creation of jobs, became important protest actors. Moreover, workers from the informal sector called for their activities to be regularized and legalized. The introduction of a new tax on transborder trade and the closing of the Ris Jedir border further triggered protests among the informal workers and smugglers in the marginalized south (see Meddeb 2017).

In January 2016, the number of socioeconomic protests grew dramatically and outnumbered those of "other" protests. The first protest broke out in the city center of Kasserine in the marginalized interior of the country after a young unemployed person died in an accident while denouncing corruption in recruitment procedures in the public sector. In slightly more than one week, large protests spread across the marginalized southern and interior regions and finally led to solidarity protests in the capital city and the northern parts of the country. Protesters demanded economic reforms, the

---

³The National Dialogue Quartet received the Nobel Peace Prize in 2015 for its outstanding contributions to the political development of post-revolutionary Tunisia.

creation of new jobs, and an end to the marginalization of the southern and interior regions (see Jöst 2017). Even though socioeconomic protests had already started to decrease at the end of January, the wave of protests had a lasting effect in the following months. Thus, the year 2016 was marked by high numbers of socioeconomic protests—in absolute numbers as well as compared to "other" protests. Non-socioeconomic protests remained only slightly above the level of previous years.

Regarding the types of actors engaged in socioeconomic protests in Tunisia, we observe major changes after December 2010 (see Fig. 3.2). Socioeconomic protests in 2011 and 2012 were almost exclusively organized by "unspecified societal actors," meaning mass protests characterized by unorganized people, as well as by "unions, political parties and protest alliances."[4] Together, these two types of protest actors account for 90 percent (33 protests in total) of all socioeconomic protests in 2011 and 92 percent (65 protests in total) in 2012.

In terms of the demands raised, we observe changes within the category of "unspecified societal actors" during the first two years after the revolution. In 2011, mass protests almost exclusively raised demands for fundamental change and economic reforms. Moreover, protest alliances between different trade unions and civil society organizations presented crucial protest actors. In 2012, however, mass protests were making very different claims, focusing on living standards—including improved health care—the right to employment and individual demands for jobs as well as economic reform. At the same time, protest alliances uniting several trade unions and civil society organizations became marginal. Within the category "unions, political parties, and protest alliances," the UGTT represented the most prominent protest actor in 2012 and 2013.

In 2011 and 2012, government employees and workers in the industrial sector and agricultural and fishing sectors organized barely 5 percent of the socioeconomic protests.[5] Service-sector employees did not play any active

---

[4] The category "unions, political parties, and protest alliances" includes mostly protest actions organized by one specific trade union or political party. However, few protest alliances between different trade unions and civil society organizations were counted—most of them in 2011. Those protest alliances also fall under this category.

[5] Different groups of workers from the service, industrial, or fishing and agricultural sectors have been placed in a different category from trade unions such as the UGTT. First, those groups of protest actors have been named "employees" in media reporting, mostly without any reference to external support by the trade unions. Second, as Beissinger et al. (2012, p. 15) point out, in most of the cases, people who described their occupation as "workers"

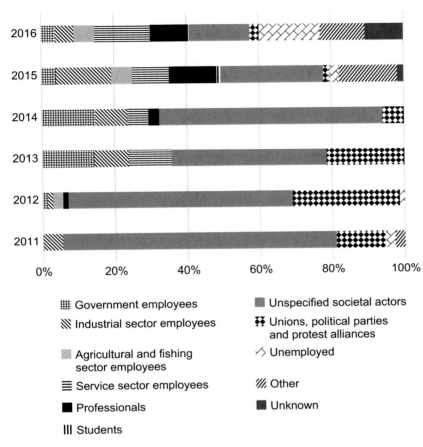

Fig. 3.2 Socioeconomic protesters in Tunisia. Source: Authors' data collection based on the ACLED data set

role as protest actors during that time. This changed at the beginning of the year 2013. In 2014, workers in the public, industrial, and service sectors became crucial protest actors, organizing 36 percent (15 protests in total) of the socioeconomic protests. By contrast, the role of mass protests and unions, political parties and protest alliances started to decrease slightly.

in the Arab Barometer (2011) were not members of a trade union. By contrast, trade union members were mostly government employees or professionals and people in "other occupations" (Beissinger et al. 2012, p. 15).

Nonetheless, these groups of actors still organized more than 60 percent (on average 25 protests per year) of all socioeconomic protests in 2013 and 2014, raising issues like living standards, the right to employment, or economic reforms. In 2015, almost half of all socioeconomic protests (48 percent) were organized by workers from the public, service, and agricultural and fishing sectors or by professionals (e.g., journalists and lawyers), who had previously played only a marginal role. At the same time, unions, political parties, and protest alliances accounted for barely 2 percent of the socioeconomic protests. Now, even mass protests which had previously raised very different issues mostly called for better working conditions for their participants. Furthermore, in 2015, unemployed people became crucial protest actors. In 2016, this trend became even stronger: Unemployed people, who had not previously played a crucial role as a group of actors, now accounted for 17 percent (85 protests in total) of the socioeconomic protests. In general, mass protests demanding employment increased, so that it can be assumed that a share of those protest actors were also unemployed.

In sum, over the years, protest alliances between trade unions, civil society organizations, and political parties, which organized mass protests in 2011 and 2012, were replaced as the dominant protest actors by individual protest groups representing specific economic sectors (and unemployed people) who were demonstrating in their own right.

Similar developments can be observed in the demands of the protesters which also became much more specific between 2011 and 2016 (see Fig. 3.3). In 2011, slightly more than 60 percent (32 protests in total) of the protests demanded fundamental changes, economic reforms, and the creation of new jobs. In the following years, demands for improved living standards and working conditions became more important issues. In 2012, the number of protests demanding better living standards increased significantly from 8 percent (in 2011) to 28 percent. At the same time, the numbers of protests demanding fundamental changes and economic reform dropped from 60 percent (19 protests in total) to 27 percent. Still, demands for the creation of new jobs continued to be raised in 34 percent of the protests (24 protests). In 2013, demands for better working conditions became most important—accounting for more than 30 percent of the socioeconomic protests. Since 2013, claims for fundamental change have declined steadily, and they finally disappeared from the protest scene in 2016. By contrast, protest actors started to raise more specific demands for jobs, better working conditions, and improved living

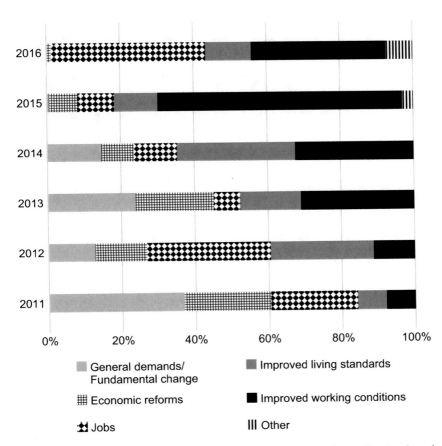

Fig. 3.3 Protesters' demands in Tunisia. Source: Authors' data collection based on the ACLED data set

standards. In 2015, working conditions peaked, with a share of 67 percent of all socioeconomic protests (113 protests). This category covers issues like higher pay, as well as legalizing work in the informal sector. Demands for jobs—including the creation of new jobs as well as individual demands for employment—were raised most importantly in 2011 and 2012 (29 percent on average). From 2013 to 2015, these demands lost importance before they dominated socioeconomic protests in 2016, holding a 42 percent share (166 protests) of all socioeconomic protests.

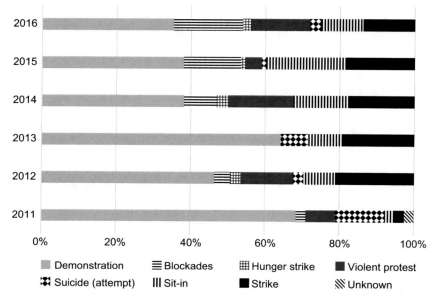

Fig. 3.4 The types of protest in Tunisia. Source: Authors' data collection based on the ACLED data set

In sum, the demands of the protesters became more specific over the period of six years. This development mirrors the differentiation of the protest actors presented earlier. In 2011, when mass protests organized by various actors dominated the protest scene, very general demands for fundamental change and economic reform were raised. In the following years, when specific groups of actors dominated the protests, their demands became more specific as well.

The years from 2011 to 2016 are further marked by an increase in disruptive protests and a shifting away from non-violent forms of protests to more confrontational tactics (see Fig. 3.4). Until 2013, demonstrations represented the most frequent form of protest, with an average share of 59 percent (between 26 and 33 demonstrations per year) of all socioeconomic protests. From 2014 onward, the protesters started to use more unconventional and confrontational forms of protest to express their demands: Blockages, sit-ins, violent protests, and suicide attempts became much more important—accounting for an average of 45 percent of all socioeconomic protests. In 2014, 42 percent of all protests were disruptive protests, whereas in 2015, 43 percent, and in 2016, 49 percent were in this category. Nonetheless, on average, 37 percent of all socioeconomic protests were demonstrations, which represent a rather conventional type of protest. Over the years, strikes became a crucial tactic for demanding better working conditions. In 2011, they accounted for barely 3 percent of all socioeconomic protests. However, in 2012, already more than 20 percent (15 protests) of the socioeconomic protests were strikes. In the following years, they had an average share of 17 percent of all socioeconomic protests.

In sum, demonstrations as a more conventional form of protest have decreased steadily since 2014. Nonetheless, they have remained the most frequent form of action. At the same time, however, the use of disruptive forms of protest steadily increased between 2014 and 2016.

It is important to say that Tunisia faces huge regional disparities that are reflected in the geographical pattern of protest. The overall development of the coastal regions is considerably higher than in the interior regions of the country. Data from the study on regional development in Tunisia, published in 2012 by the Ministry of Regional Development and Planning, dramatically confirms these findings. According to the research group from the Tunisian Institute for Competitiveness and Qualitative Studies, the interior areas are a third less developed than their coastal counterparts (ITCEQ 2012, pp. 9–10). The study uses development indicators from the fields of education and training, technology, unemployment, income, health, justice, and equality to measure differences in regional development. Whereas Tunisia's northeastern regions achieved an average score of 0.61 (with a maximum score of 1), the southern and western regions reached only 0.40. The three least developed governorates showed an average value of 0.23 (0.16 Kasserine, 0.25 Kairouan and 0.28 Sidi Bouzid), whereas the most developed governorates achieved an average score of 0.70 (0.76 Tunis, 0.69 Ariana, 0.66 Ben Arous).

Comparing the numbers of socioeconomic protests that have been organized in the marginalized interior and southern regions with those of the wealthier coastal regions shows very interesting results (see Table 3.2): Over the period of six years, almost twice (1.79) as many protests took place in the neglected south and interior than in the wealthier coastal regions. Whereas in the Tunisian hinterland up to 333 (in 2016) protests were organized in a single year, the highest yearly number of protests in the wealthier coastal regions was only 169. If Tunis, as the capital where most protests usually take place, is omitted, only 102 protests are counted in the wealthier governorates.

Table 3.2 Socioeconomic protests by region in Tunisia

	Protests in marginalized regions[a]	Protests Per million inhabitants	Protests in wealthier regions (w/o Tunis)[b]	Protests Per million inhabitants	Protests in Tunis	Protests Per million inhabitants
2011	21	4.83	9	1.70	7	6.75
2012	49	11.22	4	0.74	18	17.24
2013	20	4.56	4	0.73	18	17.12
2014	22	5.00	4	0.72	8	7.56
2015	108	24.30	33	5.84	35	32.91
2016	333	74.27	102	17.73	67	62.79
Total	553	–	156	–	153	–

Source: Authors' data collection based on the ACLED. Numbers of inhabitants are taken from Tunisia's National Statistical Institute (Institut National de la Statistique Tunisie—INS). See INS (2017).

Notes: [a]Marginalized regions include Béja, Gabès, Gafsa, Jendouba, Kairouan, Kasserine, Kebili, Kef, Medenine, Sidi Bouzid, Siliana, Tataouine, Tozeur, and Zaghouan. [b]Wealthier regions include Ariana, Ben Arous, Bizerte, Mahdia, Manouba, Monastir, Nabeul, Sfax, Sousse (excluding Tunis)

If we take the population numbers into account, we see that up to 74.27 protests per million inhabitants took place in the marginalized regions in 2016. By contrast, the ratio in the coastal regions only reached a maximum of 17.73 in the same year, if Tunis is omitted. The governorate of Tunis shows a ratio of 62.79 protests per million inhabitants in 2016, which is also extremely high. Thus, most protests took place in the marginalized regions (4.4 million people) and in the capital city (1.05 million people). The coastal regions, however, where more than 5.5 million people live, organized considerably fewer protests. Despite the regional differences described earlier, we clearly observe some national dynamics as well: Numbers of socioeconomic protests have been increasing steadily all over the country since 2014.

3.5 Socioeconomic Protests in Egypt

Compared to Tunisia, socioeconomic protests in Egypt have played only a minor role in the country's post-revolutionary protest history—at least in the English- and French-speaking media coverage, on which the ACLED data set is based. From 2011 through 2016, as seen earlier (Table 3.1), only 413 socioeconomic protests were counted compared to 3872 non-socioeconomic

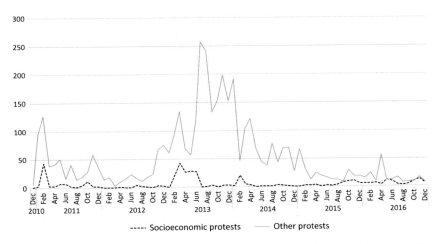

Fig. 3.5 Protests in Egypt. Source: Authors' data collection based on the ACLED data set

protests. The number of socioeconomic protests increased from 13 in 2012 to 154 in 2013. At the same time, a minimum of 306 "other" protests (in 2012) and a maximum of 1819 (in 2013) were counted. During the six-year period, only two major peaks were observed, in February 2011 and March 2013, with the number of socioeconomic protests per month only peaking to around 40 one time (see Fig. 3.5). By contrast, non-socioeconomic protests remained at a significantly higher level until February 2015, with five major peaks between February 2011 and March 2014. Since then, protest numbers have been on the decline, with only one more minor peak in April 2016.[6] Thus, socioeconomic contestation did exist in post-2011 Egypt, but, compared to "other" protests, socioeconomic protests did not achieve much importance—neither in terms of absolute protest numbers nor in relation to other protests between 2011 and 2016.

[6] A few other databases on labor protests in Egypt since 2011 are provided by Egyptian NGOs. In their reports on workers' protests, the Economic Center for Economic and Social Rights (ECESR) analyzed labor protests in post-revolutionary Egypt. ECESR counted significantly more labor protests than ACLED. These differences in protest numbers, again, might stem from the fact that they coded Arab-speaking media coverage, in which even small-scale strikes and protest events have been reported on. Yet, we observe very similar trends in both databases. Consequently, we decided to work with ACLED, which represents the most comprehensive of all three databases.

In January 2011, massive protests marked Egypt's revolution, in which the independent trade unions as well as workers from different economic sectors acted as important protest actors (see Beinin 2011, p. 194; Bishara 2014, p. 3).[7] During the Egyptian uprisings, youth activists also played a key role as Nadine Abdalla (2016) and others have shown. The January protests were inspired by the wave of protests that started in Tunisia in December 2010. Furthermore, those protests built upon what Dianiela Pioppi (2013, p. 54) calls a newly formed "culture of protest," which partly emerged out of the period of youth and workers' movements prior to the uprisings.[8] The first major peak in socioeconomically motivated protests in Egypt falls exactly into this revolutionary period, when tensions were high and people raised political as well as socioeconomic demands in mass protests at Tahrir Square in Cairo. During the last three days of the Mubarak regime, groups of workers who organized nationwide strikes played a key role as protest actors, acting independently from the state-controlled Egyptian Trade Union Federation (ETUF) (Bishara 2014).

Until December 2012, we find only minor peaks in June, July, and October 2011 and very small ones in July and November 2012. Whereas socioeconomic protests were of little importance, "other" protests continued throughout the years between 2011 and 2012. Violent protest actions were reported from the city center of Cairo, where various actors protested in favor of a speeding up of political changes and against the military's attempt to retain its influence after the overthrow of the regime in February 2011 (El-Mahdi 2014). In January and June 2012, the first parliamentary and presidential elections since the fall of the Mubarak regime were held (Paciello 2013, p. 9). Neither the Muslim Brotherhood's (MB) Freedom and Justice Party (FJP), which became the majority party in the legislative elections (Pioppi 2013, p. 57),[9] nor the newly elected President Mohammed

---

[7] For the role of workers' strikes and the independent trade unions in Egypt during the 2011 uprisings and beyond, see Chap. 6 (in this volume).

[8] Egypt's 2000s were marked by workers' movements demanding higher wages and the payment of bonuses and "other wage supplements critical to bringing income to a level that can sustain survival" (Beinin 2011, p. 191). Those protests, as Beinin (2011, p. 192) argues, lacked "a national or regional trade union or political organizational framework." In the same vein, workers' protests that accompanied the ouster of Mubarak in 2011 were held by workers who demonstrated as individuals without any organizational support (Beinin 2011, p. 194).

[9] After the first round of parliamentary elections and only four months after its first session had taken place, the parliament was dissolved by the Supreme Council of the Armed Forces (SCAF), which thus gained legislative power before Mursi became president (Pioppi 2013, p. 58).

Morsi tackled the economic challenges Egypt was facing during this period (Paciello 2013, p. 9). Pioppi (2013, p. 60) argues that this was partly because the MB-FJP was mostly concerned with its attempt to consolidate its power, while struggling with the former elites and the state institutions as well as with internal problems. In addition, as Stephan Roll (2016, p. 28) argues, the MB-FJP had to deal with the Supreme Council of the Armed Forces (SCAF), which continued to control the constitutional process. Instead of implementing alternative programs to strengthen the Egyptian economy, the government took unpopular decisions to reduce subsidies for energy resources and to ration gasoline, in an attempt to guarantee further IMF loans (see Elhelwa 2013; Pioppi 2013; Paciello 2013, p. 11).

Between February and March 2013, the number of socioeconomic protests steadily increased. In contrast, president Morsi's attempt to weaken the power of the judiciary in November 2012 through a new constitutional declaration provoked non-socioeconomic protests (Kirkpatrick and El Sheikh 2012). The announcement of the declaration was followed by massive protests and the formation of the National Salvation Front, representing an "anti-Brotherhood platform" for secular forces (Pioppi 2013, p. 61). Moreover, in spring 2013, the *tamarrod* (Rebel) movement was founded which united businessmen as well as youth activists and security forces (Pioppi 2013, p. 65), who called for the removal of the president (Brown 2016, p. 25). The movement obtained the financial support of Naguib Sawiris, founder of the "Free Egyptians Party" and majority shareholder of one of the leading newspapers "Al-Masry al-Youm" (Richter 2013). Roll (2013, p. 6) makes the point that different established interest groups such as the Egyptian business elite had planned the failure of the Morsi regime long beforehand. Knowing about the crossholdings between media companies and business elites, Carola Richter (2013) further argues that different private media channels and newspapers owned by those who had reaped benefits from former President Mubarak, stirred up public opinion against President Morsi in the month previous to the military coup.

In June 2013, Morsi's appointment of new governors—ten were MB members (Pioppi 2013, p. 63)—caused violent anti-Brotherhood protests in different governorates (ACLED). On 30 June 2013, the first anniversary of Morsi's inauguration as president, mass protests were initiated by the *tamarrod* movement, which enabled the overthrow of the Morsi regime by military forces (Brown 2016, p. 25). Immediately after the coup on 3 July 2013, Saudi Arabia, United Arab Emirates, and Kuwait provided financial assistance to Egypt. According to Roll (2016, p. 33), this lends additional support to the idea that SCAF was already preparing to take power prior to this.

The military coup in July and insecurity concerning the future of the political system accounted for a constant wave of politically motivated protests in the second half of the year. Massive protests in support of Morsi and against the military coup were held for several months (see Grimm and Harders 2017). As a reaction, Interim President Adly Mansour signed a new Protest Law (No. 107/2013) in November 2013, which put every type of protest—including non-violent protests as well as any other kind of public meeting—under the control of the government. With the new law the security services have the power to "cancel or postpone the demonstration, change the location, and modify the activity path" on the basis of a "potential threat" to the security situation in Egypt (Hamzawy 2016). The new Protest Law triggered further protests in November. At the same time, continuing demonstrations supporting the Muslim Brotherhood were brutally dispersed by police forces. The summer of 2014 saw a peak in non-socioeconomic protests which occurred in the period when al-Sisi became president. Until mid-2015, Egypt experienced a steady decline in total protest numbers. Whereas socioeconomically motivated protests remained at the same—even though low—level, non-socioeconomic protests dropped down to the lowest level since 2012, with only one minor peak in April 2016. In August 2015, the new Anti-Terrorism Law (No. 94/2015) was signed by President al-Sisi. The law "contains many draconian articles, including ones that criminalize news reporting that contradicts the government's official accounts" (Mandour 2015). Furthermore, it criminalizes individuals participating in politically motivated protests as well as "anyone who privately urges another to participate in such actions" (HRW 2015). By 2013, violent repression had already been used by the al-Sisi regime in addition to legal repression as a strategy for controlling the people and to avoid any form of public resistance: "The authorities have killed unarmed civilians; used sexual violence against women, men, and children with greater impunity; and conducted forced disappearances at unprecedented levels" (Mandour 2015).

In the second half of 2015, socioeconomic protests began to increase slightly. In August and September, government employees demonstrated against the proposed Civil Service Law (No. 18/2015). Throughout the whole year, protests were organized by public service employees, unions, and NGOs. Yet, as in 2011, when ETUF put pressure on the workers not to protest (Bishara 2014, p. 3), ETUF did not support the protests (Charbel 2015; also see Chap. 6, in this volume). After massive protests in January 2016, the parliament rejected a law which contained the possibility of extensive job cuts in the public service and restricted basic labor rights (Kasseb 2016; El Din 2016). After amendments had been made, the new law was finally approved in October 2016, despite ongoing opposition by labor unions (Youssef 2016).

In Egypt, socioeconomic opposition since 2011 has been dominated by labor-related protests. Whereas in Tunisia "unspecified societal actors" and "unions, political parties, and protest alliances" accounted for most of the socioeconomic protests in the immediate aftermath of the Arab uprisings, in Egypt government employees as well as workers in the industrial and service sectors organized more than half (58 percent) of the socioeconomic protests in 2011 (see Fig. 3.6). Between 2012 and 2016, this share of protests driven by public-, industrial-, and service-sector employees has fluctuated between 38 percent and 61 percent. Professionals make up an additional 10–24 percent (between 3 and 18 protests per year) of the socioeconomic protests between 2011 and 2016. In the years 2011 and 2013, unspecified societal actors accounted for 16 percent of socioeconomic protests (14 and 24 protests per year). In 2014, they had a significantly smaller share (3 percent/1 protest per year), which increased once again in 2016 (21 percent/16 protests per year). By contrast, protests by unemployed workers have been marginal over the whole period, accounting for only 1–4 protests per year and completely disappearing from the scene in 2014.

In sum, since the share of "unspecified societal actors" has been significantly smaller in Egypt than in Tunisia, protests have been more homogenous. Already, in 2011, different groups of actors acted on the protest scene with different worker groups as central protest actors. Mass protests with unspecified societal groups as their main actor did not play a decisive role in Egypt.

Thus, despite some minor changes in the share of the different protest actors, no major changes could be identified in the Egyptian case. The same holds true for the demands of the protesters, which clearly reflect the predominance of labor-related protest (see Fig. 3.7). Other than in Tunisia, where protesters expressed general demands for fundamental changes in 2011, demands for improved working conditions dominated the socioeconomic protests in Egypt (60 percent/53 protests in 2011). Over the following six years, protesters continued to primarily demand improved working conditions—including demands for higher pay as well

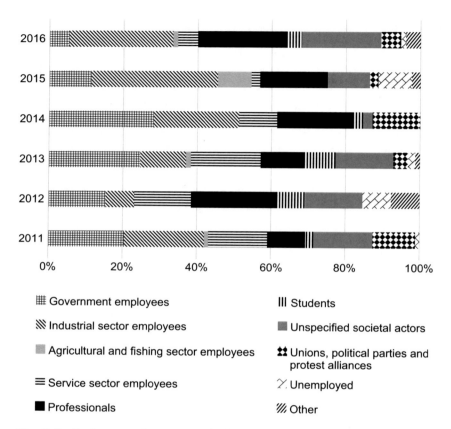

Fig. 3.6 Socioeconomic protesters in Egypt. Source: Authors' data collection based on the ACLED data set

as safety measures at the workplace. Such demands finally peaked in 2015, with 66 percent (29 protests) of the socioeconomic protests demanding improved working conditions. Second, and most importantly, protesters demanded improved living standards, with numbers varying from 4 protests in 2012 to 33 in 2013. This category includes various demands such as for better quality of education as well as for the construction of social housing and a decrease in food prices.

Unlike in Tunisia, demands for economic reform and fundamental change did not play a decisive role in post-revolutionary Egypt. Only, in 2012, did demands for economic reforms and fundamental change temporarily become

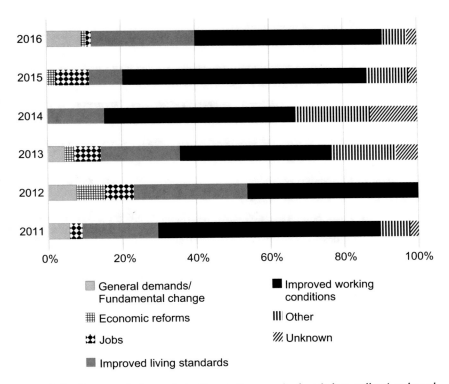

Fig. 3.7 Protesters' demands in Egypt. Source: Authors' data collection based on the ACLED data set

prominent in the protests: In 16 percent (8 percent each) of the protests, demands were made for economic reform and fundamental change. In 2014, however, these demands were not mentioned at all. Demands for fundamental change only came back on the scene in 2016, when 9 percent (7 protests) of the socioeconomic protests raised such demands. In addition, in 2015 and 2016, in only two protests did demonstrators demand economic reform. Unlike Tunisia, demands for jobs—including demands for individual employment as well as the claim of a right to employment—never reached high relevance after the Egyptian revolution in 2011. Only in 2012 were they raised in 8 percent of all socioeconomic protests. Thereafter, they disappeared almost entirely from the protest scene, with only four protests demanding employment in 2015 and one protest in 2016.

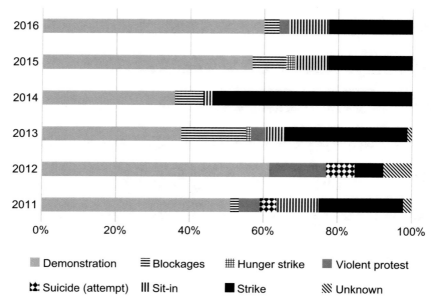

Fig. 3.8 Types of protests in Egypt. Source: Authors' data collection based on the ACLED data set

To put it briefly, demands for better working conditions were most frequently raised in post-2011 Egypt. Furthermore, protesters also demanded improved living standards. By contrast, more general demands for development and economic reform have not played a decisive role in socioeconomic protests since 2011.

Whereas in Tunisia we have observed increasing numbers of disruptive protests since 2011, Egypt, again, faced no major changes when it comes to the types of protests (see Fig. 3.8). Over the past six years, the forms of protest have remained almost unchanged in Egypt: Demonstrations have been the most common form of protest, followed by strikes. Only, in 2014, did the number of strikes (21) exceed the number of demonstrations (14). Disruptive forms of protest such as sit-ins, blockades, violent protest, suicides, and hunger strikes never made up more than 30 percent (between 3 and 41 protests per year) of the socioeconomic protests between 2011 and 2016. Thus, more organized forms of protest such as demonstrations (including protest marches) exceed unconventional and disruptive forms of protest.

In Egypt, regional disparities go along with the division into Upper (southern) and Lower (northern) Egypt and a strong urban/rural divide (EHDR 2010, p. 22). According to the United Nations Development Programme (UNDP), 923 of the 1000 poorest villages are all located in governorates in Upper Egypt (EHDR 2010, p. 22). By contrast, the five highest ranked governorates are located in Lower Egypt.[10] In addition, the UNDP Report on Poverty in Egypt (2011) shows that all governorates in Lower Egypt show remarkably lower levels of poverty than their counterparts in Upper Egypt, except for Luxor (El Laithy 2011, p. 7).[11]

In the marginalized regions where some 33 million people lived between 2011 and 2016, only 90 socioeconomic protests were counted (see Table 3.3). By contrast, in the non-marginalized regions (without Cairo), where more than 42 million people live, 143 socioeconomically motivated

Table 3.3 Socioeconomic protests by region in Egypt

	Protests in marginalized regions[a]	Protests Per million inhabitants	Protests in wealthier regions (w/o Cairo)[b]	Protests Per million inhabitants	Protests in Cairo	Protests Per million inhabitants
2011	22	0.71	23	0.57	43	4.97
2012	1	0.03	1	0.02	11	1.25
2013	44	1.34	49	1.16	61	6.78
2014	6	0.18	20	0.46	13	1.42
2015	0	0.00	23	0.52	21	2.25
2016	17	0.48	27	0.60	31	3.28
Total	90	–	143	–	180	–

Source: Authors' data collection based on the ACLED data set. Numbers of inhabitants are taken from CAPMAS (2016).

Notes: [a]The category "marginalized regions" covers marginalized Upper Egypt governorates (including Luxor). [b]The category "wealthier regions" covers wealthier Lower Egypt (excluding Cairo)

[10] The highest ranked governorates are Port Said, Suez, Cairo, Alexandria, and Damietta. Only in 2010 was Cairo replaced by Ismailia in the group of the top five ranks for the first time since 1995. This is partly explained by Ismailia's remarkable increase in the education index as a sub-index of the Human Development Index (EHDR 2010, p. 21).
[11] Among the 13 best-performing governorates, only Luxor, which is a very small governorate located in Upper Egypt, is listed at rank number 12. It performs slightly better than the Lower Egypt governorate Beheira (rank number 13) in the UNDP Report on Poverty in Egypt. However, this does not crucially influence our findings on the gap between Lower and Upper Egypt. Consequently, Luxor has been placed in the category of the lower performing Upper Egypt regions in following discussions.

protests took place plus another 180 protests in the government of Cairo, where another 9 million people live. Thus, a considerably higher number of protests was counted in the governorates of the non-marginalized Lower Egypt—even when Cairo is omitted. This is also mirrored in the protest actors themselves, who have most prominently been employees from the different economic sectors, who most frequently live in the urban centers of Lower Egypt. By contrast, Egyptians who live in the most impoverished areas of Upper Egypt suffer from lack of job opportunities due to a poor industrial infrastructure. According to our findings, they have not constituted relevant groups of protest actors since 2011.

However, when we relate the numbers of socioeconomic protests per governorate to regional population numbers, we see a different picture: A maximum of 1.34 protests annually per million inhabitants was counted in the marginalized governorates, but only up to 1.16 in the non-marginalized governorates, and only if Cairo is left out. Yet, the most protests per inhabitant were measured in Cairo as one of the urban and well-developed centers of the country (see Table 3.3).[12] If we compare the numbers of protests per year since 2011, we find that until 2014, protest numbers were on a similar level in the marginalized and wealthier regions (such as Cairo). Since 2014, protest numbers (absolute and relative to the number of inhabitants) in Lower Egypt have remained at a significantly higher level than in marginalized Upper Egypt, even though they have decreased compared to 2013.

3.6 Conclusion

Even though socioeconomic problems are still striking in both post-revolutionary contexts, we find that socioeconomic protest activities—in terms of actors, demands, tactics, and regional distribution—took different paths in Egypt and Tunisia. Generally speaking, socioeconomic protests have been much more relevant in Tunisia than in Egypt. First, Tunisia has faced significantly higher numbers of socioeconomic protests relative to its population. Second, socioeconomic protests in Tunisia have been shown to be more relevant when compared to the overall number of protests. In particular, since 2014, the number of socioeconomically motivated protests has steadily increased and finally even outnumbered those of "other" protests in 2016. In Egypt, in contrast, there have consistently

[12] Official population numbers are taken from the Statistical Yearbook (2016) of the Central Agency for Public Mobilization and Statistics (CAPMAS) in Egypt. For further information, see CAPMAS (2016).

been much more non-socioeconomic protests than socioeconomic protests. After overall protests had peaked in 2013, the number of socioeconomic protests in Egypt has decreased even more since 2014. This decline arguably reflects the changing political environment after the military coup in 2013 and the rise in violent repression by the al-Sisi government.

However, it is important to note that even in Egypt socioeconomic protests *did occur* during the years after the 2011 uprisings, even if they did not reach a high level of political and societal relevance compared to non-socioeconomic contention. Whereas non-socioeconomic protests such as the anti-regime protests in summer 2013 led to the overthrow of the Morsi regime by military forces (Brown 2016, p. 25), socioeconomic protests did not result in observable changes in social and economic policies. Neither, as further outlined in the chapter by Nadine Abdalla (see Chap. 6, in this volume), were the independent trade unions able to reach political influence and organize systematic labor protests.

Since the differences in the role of socioeconomic protests in Egypt and Tunisia are puzzling—especially against the background of continuing economic stagnation, rising food prices, and persisting unemployment in both North African countries—this chapter looked in greater detail at the socioeconomic protests that have been organized since 2011.

Regarding the actors and their demands, we find that socioeconomic contention in Egypt was mainly driven by sector-specific labor protests asking for improvement of their working conditions. An exemption from this can be seen in the protests around the 2011 revolution, in which workers took to the streets as politicized individuals and not as part of an organized entity (see Beinin 2011, p. 194; Bishara 2014, p. 3). In Tunisia, the picture is different. Until 2014, most socioeconomic protests were staged by unspecified societal actors demanding fundamental changes and reforms to end the marginalization of certain regions. These protests mostly had the form of mass protests. Yet, since 2014, protest actors in Tunisia have become more diverse, and protests were increasingly composed of groups of employees from different economic sectors making sector-specific claims such as raising salaries or improving working conditions.

It is only in Tunisia that we find a shift toward combative tactics. Since 2014, when protest actors in Tunisia started to differentiate, disruptive forms of protest have become more frequent. At the same time, more conventional forms of protest such as (mass) demonstrations decreased. In Egypt, in contrast, demonstrations remained the most common type of action. This finding might be surprising in view of the changing political environment in Egypt: Increasing repression by the al-Sisi government since 2013 led to neither more violent forms of protest nor to the contrary response among socioeconomic protesters. At the same time, it is remarkable that demonstrations were still held despite a higher degree of repression—particularly after a new anti-protest law had been issued in November 2013.

Significant differences also concern the geographical patterns of socioeconomic protest. In Tunisia, the marginalized south and interior regions have proven to be the most prominent protest scene since 2011. Thus, also in the aftermath of the Arab uprisings, when protests first occurred in Sidi Bouzid in the Tunisian hinterland, socioeconomic protests primarily involved the marginalized governorates of the country. In Egypt, by contrast, socioeconomic protests were mostly organized in the comparatively "wealthier" governorates of "Lower Egypt." In both countries, however, a large number of protests were organized in the capital cities Tunis and Cairo.

This regional pattern matches our findings on protest actors and claims in the two countries: In Tunisia, where in 2011 groups of "unspecified societal actors" and "unions, political parties and protest alliances" in the marginalized regions made demands for fundamental change and economic reform, post-revolutionary protests were primarily staged in these marginalized regions of interior and southern Tunisia. Interestingly, the difference in protest numbers in the marginalized versus those in the wealthier regions became even more pronounced in the following years, when protesters started to cluster along group-specific issues. In this context, unemployed people became key protagonists driving protest waves in May 2015 and in January 2016 (see Chap. 8, in this volume).

In Egypt, where protest actors were already more heterogeneous in 2011, most socioeconomic protests—in absolute numbers as well as relative to the number of inhabitants—took part in Cairo and the governorates of Lower Egypt. Until 2014, protest numbers in the wealthier regions (without Cairo) were similar to those in the marginalized regions. Since 2014, protest numbers in the wealthier regions have outnumbered those in marginalized Upper Egypt. This does not seem much of a surprise, given our findings on protest actors and their claims. As shown, socioeconomic protests in Egypt were mostly staged by groups of employees from different economic sectors claiming higher wages and better working conditions.

In a study on the participants in the Arab uprisings, Beissinger et al. (2012) show that the revolution in Egypt has not been driven by a "cross-class coalition," as in the case of Tunisia, but mainly by people from the urban middle class. As our analysis demonstrates, these differences in the composition of protest groups have continued to shape socioeconomic protests in the years that followed the revolutions. This continuity becomes even more evident against the background of protest events prior to the Arab uprisings:

As, for example, Amin Allal (2013), Laryssa Chomiak (2014), and Eric Gobe (2010) have shown, Tunisia had already experienced waves of protests during the last years of the Ben Ali regime. Most prominent examples are protests by the unemployed in front of the Gafsa mining basin in January 2008 (Allal 2013; Gobe 2010) and the Ras Jdir border protests in August 2010 (Allal 2013). In both protest episodes, young and unemployed Tunisians of the impoverished regions as well as workers who felt deprived were the primary actors (Allal 2013, pp. 187, 189). As is further analyzed by Samiha Hamdi and Irene Weipert-Fenner (see Chap. 8, in this volume), such protests by unemployed people in the Tunisian hinterland have continued to play a crucial role in Tunisia since the 2011 uprisings.

By contrast, Egypt was hit by a massive wave of workers' protests in the years before the 2011 uprisings (see Beinin 2009, 2011; Beinin and Duboc 2013), in which the unemployed did not play an active role. In December 2006, the biggest workers' strike was held in the Misr Spinning and Weaving Company in Al-Mahalla Al-Kubra, which is located in the Nile delta in Lower Egypt (Beinin and Duboc 2013, p. 218). In 2007 and 2008, the number of labor protests reached a peak of 614 and 609, respectively, actions per year (Beinin 2009, p. 450). These protests were initially limited to the textile industry but soon after also embraced every industrial sector as well as public service workers and professionals (Beinin 2009, p. 450). The protests primarily arose in the regions of Lower Egypt where people demanded their rights as employees.

In both countries, thus, the protesters and claims that had dominated socioeconomic protests prior to the Arab uprisings continued to shape protest dynamics in the years that followed the revolutions (2011–2016). Thus, our analysis shows a high degree of continuity in both cases.

Finally, there are also remarkable similarities between Egypt and Tunisia. In the two countries, the years between 2011 and 2016 have been characterized not by more or less continuous socioeconomic protests but rather by passing outbursts of socioeconomic discontent, most notably in Egypt in 2013 and in Tunisia in 2016. Also, there seems to be a certain convergence when it comes to actors and claims. Whereas in Tunisia broader protest alliances that dominated the years 2011 and 2012 were later replaced by individual protest groups representing specific economic sectors who were demonstrating in their own right, Egypt throughout the years was characterized by a rather fragmented landscape of issue- and sector-specific socioeconomic protests.

References

Abdalla, N. (2016). Youth movements in the Egyptian transformation: Strategies and repertoires of political participation. *Mediterranean Politics, 21*(1), 44–63.

Allal, A. (2013). Becoming revolutionary in Tunisia 2007–2011. In J. Beinin & F. Frédéric (Eds.), *Social movements, mobilization and contestation in the Middle East and North Africa* (2nd ed., pp. 185–204). Stanford, CA: Stanford University Press.

Antonakis-Nashif, A. (2016). Contested transformation: Mobilized publics in Tunisia between compliance and protest. *Mediterranean Politics, 21*(1), 128–149.

Arab Barometer. (2011). Arab barometer survey wave ii. Retrieved October 23, 2018, from http://www.arabbarometer.org/waves/arab-barometer-wave-ii/.

Arab Barometer. (2013). Arab barometer survey wave iii. Retrieved October 23, 2018, from http://www.arabbarometer.org/content/arab-barometer-iii-0.

Arab Barometer. (2015). Arab Barometer Survey Wave IV. Retrieved May 22, 2019, from http://www.arabbarometer.org/waves/arab-barometer-wave-iv/.

Beinin, J. (2009). Workers' protest in Egypt: Neo-liberalism and class struggle in 21st century. *Social Movement Studies, 8*(4), 449–454.

Beinin, J. (2011). Workers and Egypt's January 25 revolution. *International Labor and Working-Class History, 80*(1), 189–196. https://doi.org/10.1017/S0147547911000123.

Beinin, J., & Duboc, M. (2013). A workers' social movement on the margin of the global neoliberal order, Egypt 2004–2012. In J. Beinin & F. Vairel (Eds.), *Social movements, mobilization, and contestation in the Middle East and North Africa* (2nd ed., pp. 205–227). Stanford, CA: Stanford University Press.

Beissinger, M.R., Jamal A., & Mazur K. (2012). Who participated in the Arab Spring? A comparison of Egyptian and Tunisian revolutions. Retrieved October 23, 2018, from https://pdfs.semanticscholar.org/bf96/ad6d9ce044ee0dd1865ded7dcaae-75f198eb.pdf.

Berman, C.E. & Nugent, E.R. (2015). Defining political choices: Tunisia's second election from the ground up. *Analysis Paper 38, 2015*. The Center for Middle East Policy at Brookings.

Bishara, D. (2014). Labor movements in Tunisia and Egypt: Drivers vs. objects of change in transition from authoritarian rule. *SWP Comments 1*.

Boubekeur, A. (2016). Islamists, secularists and old regime elites in Tunisia: Bargained competition. *Mediterranean Politics, 21*(1), 107–127.

Brown, N. J. (2016). The transition: From Mubarak's fall to the 2014 presidential election. In E. Hokayeme & T. Hebatalla (Eds.), *Egypt after the spring: Revolt and reaction* (The International Institute for Strategic Studies) (pp. 15–29). New York, NY: Routledge.

CAPMAS. (2016). Statistical yearbook 2016—Population, central agency for public mobilization and statistics. Retrieved June 20, 2018, from http://www.capmas.gov.eg/Pages/Publications.aspx?page_id=5104&Year=16539.

Charbel, J. (2015, August 10). Workers protest civil service law in one of biggest street actions since 2013. *Mada Masr*. Retrieved October 23, 2018, from https://www.madamasr.com/en/2015/08/10/feature/politics/workers-protest-civil-service-law-in-one-of-biggest-street-actions-since-2013/. Accessed 23 October 2018.

Chomiak, L. (2014). Architecture of resistance in Tunisia. In L. Khatib & E. Lust (Eds.), *Taking to the streets: The transformation of Arab activism* (pp. 22–50). Baltimore, MD: Johns Hopkins University Press.

EHDR Egypt Human Development Report. (2010). Youth in Egypt: Building our future, United Nations Development Programme and the Institute of National Planning, Egypt. Retrieved June 20, 2018, from http://hdr.undp.org/sites/default/files/reports/243/egypt_2010_en.pdf.

El Din, M.S. (2016, February 11). What happened after February 11, 2011? *Mada Masr*. Retrieved October 23, 2018, from https://www.madamasr.com/en/2016/02/11/feature/politics/what-happened-after-february-11-2011/.

El Laithy, H. (2011). The ADCR 2011: Poverty in Egypt (2009). Arab Development Challenges Background Paper, 2011 (11). United Nations Development Programme. Retrieved from http://www.undp.org/content/dam/rbas/doc/poverty/BG_11_Poverty%20in%20Egypt.pdf.

Elhelwa, S. (2013, March 25). Egypt's economic crisis growing. *Daily News Egypt*. Retrieved October 23, 2018, from. https://dailynewsegypt.com/2013/03/25/egypts-economic-crisis-growing/.

El-Mahdi, R. (2014). Egypt: A decade of Ruptures. In L. Khatib & E. Lust (Eds.), *Taking to the streets. The transformation of Arab activism* (pp. 52–75). Baltimore, MD: Johns Hopkins University Press.

El-Meehy, A. (2014). Relative deprivation and politics in the Arab uprisings, Research report on social justice and development policy in the Arab world. Issam Fares Institute for Public Policy and International Affairs, American University of Beirut. Retrieved October 23, 2018, from https://website.aub.edu.lb/ifi/programs/social_justice/Documents/papers/20140507ifi_SocialJustice_AsyaElMeehy.pdf.

European Commission. (2015). *Social dialogue in Morocco, Tunisia and Jordan. Regulations and realities of social dialogue*. Brussels: European Commission.

Gobe, E. (2010). The Gafsa mining basin between riots and a social movement: Meaning and significance of a social movement in Ben Ali's Tunisia. *Working Paper*. Retrieved October 21, 2018, from https://halshs.archives-ouvertes.fr/halshs-00557826.

Grimm, J., & Harders, C. (2017). Unpacking the effects of repression: The evolution of Islamist repertoires of contention in Egypt after the fall of President Morsi. *Social Movement Studies*. https://doi.org/10.1080/14742837.2017.1344547.

Hamzawy, A. (2016, November 24). Egypt's anti protest law: Legalising authoritarianism. Carnegie Middle East Center. Retrieved October 23, 2018, from

http://carnegieendowment.org/2016/11/24/egypt-s-anti-protest-law-legalising-authoritarianism-pub-66274.
HRW. (2015, August 19). Egypt: Counterterrorism law erodes basic rights. Human Rights Watch. Retrieved October 23, 2018, from https://www.hrw.org/news/2015/08/19/egypt-counterterrorism-law-erodes-basic-rights.
ILO. (2014). ILO—Global employment trends: Risk of a jobless recovery? International Labour Organization, Geneva. Retrieved October 23, 2018, from http://www.ilo.org/wcmsp5/groups/public/%2D%2D-dgreports/%2D%2D-dcomm/%2D%2D-publ/documents/publication/wcms_233953.pdf.
INS. (2017). Bulletin mensuel de statistique, Mars 2017. Institut National de la Statistique, Tunisie. Retrieved June 26, 2018, from http://www.ins.tn/fr/publication/bulletin-mensuel-de-la-statistique-mars-2017.
ITCEQ. (2012). Institut Tunisien de la Compétitivité et des Etudes Quantitatives. http://www.itceq.tn/fr/.
Jöst, P. (2017): *Work, freedom and dignity—Once more? Contentious politics, emotions and organizational constraints in Tunisia since 2011*. Master thesis (unpublished), University of Tübingen.
Kasseb, B. (2016, January 31). The saga with Egypt's civil service law continues. *Mada Masr*. Retrieved October 23, 2018, from https://www.madamasr.com/en/2016/01/31/feature/politics/the-saga-with-egypts-civil-service-law-continues/.
Kirkpatrick, D.D. & El Sheikh, M. (2012, November 22). Citing deadlock, Egypt's leader seizes new power and plans Mubarak retrial. *New York Times*. Retrieved October 23, 2018, from http://www.nytimes.com/2012/11/23/world/middleeast/egypts-president-morsi-gives-himself-new-powers.html.
Mandour, M. (2015). Repression in Egypt from Mubarak to Sisi. Carnegie Middle East Center. Retrieved October 23, 2018, from http://carnegie-mec.org/sada/60985.
McAdam, D. (1999). *Political process and the development of black insurgency, 1930–1970*. Chicago, IL: University of Chicago Press.
Meddeb, H. (2017). Peripheral vision: How Europe can help preserve Tunisia's fragile democracy. Policy Brief European Council on Foreign Affairs. Retrieved October 23, 2018, from http://www.ecfr.eu/publications/summary/peripheral_vision_how_europe_can_preserve_tunisias_democracy_7215.
Ocampos, T. I. (2016). Islamists and secularists in Tunisia: A democratic success in the making. *Middle East Eye*. Retrieved October 23, 2018, from http://www.middleeasteye.net/columns/islamists-and-secularists-tunisia-democraticsuccess-making-72380 3950.
Paciello, M. C. (2013). Delivering the revolution? Post-uprising socio-economics in Tunisia and Egypt. *The International Spectator, 48*(4), 7–29.

Pioppi, D. (2013). Playing with fire. The Muslim Brotherhood and the Egyptian Leviathan. *The International Spectator, 48*(4), 51–68.
Richter, C. (2013, September 16). Media in Egypt: Fall into line or switch off. Qantara. Retrieved October 23, 2018, from https://en.qantara.de/content/medien-in-agypten-gleichschalten-oder-abschalten.
Roll, S. (2013). Ägyptens Unternehmerelite nach Mubarak. Machtvoller Akteur zwischen Militär und Muslimbruderschaft. *SWP Studie S14.* Berlin: Stiftung Wissenschaft und Politik.
Roll, S. (2016). Managing change: How Egypt's military leadership shaped the transformation. *Mediterranean Politics, 21*(1), 23–43.
Schäfer, I. (2015). The Tunisian transition: Torn between democratic consolidation and neo-conservatism in an insecure regional context. European Institute of the Mediterranean. Retrieved October 23, 2018, from https://www.diegdi.de/uploads/media/Tunisian_Transition_EuroMeSCo_Paper_25_Isabel_Schaefer.pdf.
Schulz, S. (2012). After spring comes? Recent development investments into the MENA region. Heinrich-Böll-Stiftung. Retrieved October 23, 2018, from https://www.boell.de/en/2012/10/31/after-spring-comes-recent-development-investments-mena-region.
Tilly, C. (1977). From mobilization to revolution. *CRSO Working Paper 156.* Michigan, MI: University of Michigan.
Vatthauer, J.-P. & Weipert-Fenner, I. (2017). The quest for social justice in Tunisia. Socioeconomic protest and political democratization post 2011. *PRIF Report No. 143.* Frankfurt: Peace Research Institute Frankfurt.
Willsher, K. (2011, February 27). Tunisian prime minister Mohamed Ghannouchi resigns amid unrest. *The Guardian.* Retrieved October 23, 2018, from https://www.theguardian.com/world/2011/feb/27/tunisian-prime-minister-ghannouchi-resigns.
Youssef, A. (2016, October 4). After months of negotiations, parliament passes civil service law. *Daily News Egypt.* Retrieved October 23, 2018, from https://dailynewsegypt.com/2016/10/04/months-negotiations-parliament-passes-civil-service-law/.

PART II

Organized Labor

CHAPTER 4

Organized Labor and Political Change in Latin America: An Overview

Jonas Wolff

4.1 Introduction

In the twentieth century, throughout Latin America, labor unions had been "the most important organizations through which the urban lower classes framed and attempted to promote their interests." While certainly not the only popular-sector organizations, labor unions "were politically privileged both by their own resources and capacity to undertake collective action and typically by their affiliation to political parties" (Collier and Handlin 2009, p. 3; see also Valenzuela 1989, p. 447). It is, therefore, not surprising that organized labor played a significant role in the destabilization of authoritarian regimes and the (re-)turn to democracy between the late 1970s and the early 1990s. From a comparative perspective, this role has been assessed (and generally confirmed) most prominently by Arturo Valenzuela (1989), Ruth Collier (1999), and Steven Levitsky and Scott

---

J. Wolff (✉)
Peace Research Institute Frankfurt, Frankfurt am Main, Hessen, Germany
e-mail: wolff@hsfk.de

© The Author(s) 2020
I. Weipert-Fenner, J. Wolff (eds.), *Socioeconomic Protests in MENA and Latin America*, Middle East Today,
https://doi.org/10.1007/978-3-030-19621-9_4

Mainwaring (2006).[1] At the same time, political democratization—and the turn from a state-centered to a market-oriented ("neoliberal") development model that accompanied it—dramatically changed the politico-institutional and socioeconomic contexts in which Latin America's labor movements operated. The overall result has been a marked weakening of organized labor throughout the region (see Kurtz 2004; Oxhorn and Ducatenzeiler 1998; Roberts 1998), which essentially meant that labor unions lost their privileged status as *the* channel through which the working class, or, to use a broader term, the popular sectors, articulate their claims vis-à-vis the state (Collier and Handlin 2009).

Against this backdrop, this chapter offers a focused discussion of the state of comparative research on organized labor and political change in Latin America. In line with the overall questions guiding this volume, I try to identify general answers to two questions: First, to what extent, how, and determined by what factors has organized labor shaped political change in Latin America? Second, to what extent, how, and determined by what factors has organized labor, and labor-based contentious action in particular, been affected by political change in Latin America?[2] In both instances, I define political change narrowly and focus on the transitions to democracy in the 1970s and 1980s. At the end of the chapter, however, I also briefly look at more recent political changes, namely, the so-called leftist turn in the early 2000s.

4.2 Organized Labor's Role in Democratization

By the late 1980s, Arturo Valenzuela emphasized that "the labor movement is hardly ever a completely unitary actor" but rather "usually a complex and diverse one" and that periods of "transition out of authoritarian rule often lead to an increase in the internal differences and tensions between the various constituent elements of labor movements" (Valenzuela 1989, p. 446). This important observation notwithstanding, he and scholars who subsequently tried to assess organized labor's role in processes of democratization in Latin America and beyond have been able to identify general empirical patterns and overarching causal dynamics.

---

[1] With a focus on the Southern Cone, including Brazil, see also Drake (1996).

[2] This is precisely the twofold question addressed by Arturo Valenzuela in a 1989 piece in which he discussed "the special relationship between labor movements and processes of redemocratization, both in terms of labor's reactions to the overall change and the latter's effects on it" (Valenzuela 1989, p. 446).

Valenzuela, on his part, basically argued that labor movements occupy "a special place among the forces of civil society" when it comes to mobilizing against an authoritarian regime (Valenzuela 1989, p. 447). In trying to account for the variation in organized labor's role in democratization processes, Valenzuela suggested four reasons, or "sources": "the strength or weakness of the labor movement and the economic context of the transition," "the centralisation or decentralisation of the labor movement and its unity or division," "the authoritarian regime's treatment of labor and its political allies prior to redemocratisation," and "the modalities of the transition to democracy and the relationship between the labor movement and the elites guiding the transition" (Valenzuela 1989, p. 452). Organized labor, for instance, is able to play an important (and positive) role in democratization when the labor movement is strong and when union organization and collective bargaining are centralized (Valenzuela 1989, pp. 452–457); syndically harsh and/or politically closed authoritarian regimes as well as transitions that are abrupt and unplanned tend to produce labor movements that will push for democratization (and actively engage in labor conflict) on the streets, rather than acting with restraint and in a dialogue-oriented style (Valenzuela 1989, pp. 458, 463).[3]

In one of the most prominent contributions on the subject, Ruth Collier (1999) systematically analyzed and basically confirmed Valenzuela's argument that organized labor has played a significant role during the processes of democratization in Latin American (and Southern Europe) since the late 1970s. According to Collier, labor movements specifically contributed to democratization by mobilizing against and destabilizing authoritarian regimes; but, at later stages, labor protests also helped prevent an authoritarian backlash, and in some cases, organized labor also participated in the negotiation of political change (which was, however, by and large dominated by middle- and upper-class actors). In the cases of South American and Southern European democratization since the late 1970s analyzed by Collier, she observes that

> the union movement, or important parts of it, was typically one of the major actors in the political opposition, explicitly demanding a democratic regime. More than merely one component or 'layer' of a resurrected civil society

---

[3] In general, in his 1989 essay, Valenzuela only illustrated the overall relevance of these four sources of variation, which in the end are really four internally complex sets of factors, rather than showing how precisely differences in these four dimensions interact with and impact labor's varying political role.

that moved into the interstices of political space opened by incumbents and followed the lead of many other groups, the union movement was sometimes able to create political space for anti-authoritarian, pro-democratic protest. In some cases, union-led protest for democracy contributed to a climate of delegitimation that provoked the initiation of the transition; in others it helped derail the legitimation projects of authoritarian regimes. Protest continuing to the end of the transition rather than creating an authoritarian backlash, often kept the transition moving forward. Finally, while the protest of other groups also put the regime on the defensive, labor-based organizations went further in affecting democratic transitions in two ways: in many cases labor-based parties and sometimes unions won a place in the negotiations, and they derailed the transformative projects of the authoritarian rulers to exclude any future participation of left and labor-based parties, thereby expanding the scope of contestation in the successor regimes. (Collier 1999, p. 165)

At the same time, Collier emphasizes that democratization since the 1970s "did not single out the working class as a beneficiary" and, therefore, looked "less like a class-based process" (in contrast to democratization in the nineteenth and early twentieth centuries). This is, she argues, due to the fact that "the antecedent regimes were not restricted democracies but outright authoritarian regimes or autocracies" and that, with "virtually all the components of a democratic regime lacking, democratization and the recovery of political rights affected virtually all groups in civil society, including rival elites and opposition party leaders"; in addition, socioeconomically speaking, recent processes of democratization have occurred in a historical context in which "the working class was decidedly on the defensive" (Collier 1999, p. 13).

Collier's assessment is generally in line with Paul Drake's comparative analysis of South America's Southern Cone (including Brazil). In his *Labor Movements and Dictatorships,* Drake (1996) argues that labor movements played a crucial role in the first phase of mobilization that responded to tactical liberalization by the dictatorships and pressured for more significant change. With democratization approaching, however, organized labor ceded leadership of the broad opposition movements to political parties. At that time, labor movements mostly acted with restraint in order not to threaten the transition to democracy. According to Drake, this restraint was due to "legacies from the authoritarian experience: (1) its fear of a recurrence; (2) the economic constraints on its leverage; (3) the weakness of its institutions; (4) the moderation of its beliefs, programs, and comportment; and (5) its heightened appreciation for classic liberal democracy" (Drake 1996, p. 183).

Theoretically, Collier emphasizes three dimensions of democratization—class, prior inclusion, and arena of action—and, then, identifies different patterns characterized by "different constellations of the three dimensions" (Collier 1999, p. 21). With a view to democratization in the 1970s and 1980s, there are four such patterns (Collier 1999, chap. 4):

1. In the "destabilization/extrication" pattern in which the authoritarian regime exited from power in a defensive way (without an incumbent project of restricted reforms), organized labor combined mobilization/protest with participation in negotiation/deliberation and, more specifically, contributed to destabilizing the authoritarian regime, opening up space, triggering the transition, and expanding contestation. South American examples include Argentina and Peru.
2. In the "transition game," the authoritarian regimes' attempts to increase their legitimacy by allowing for restricted contestation were derailed by labor (and non-labor) protests. Here, organized labor contributed to promoting the transition and expanding contestation, but the negotiation of change was essentially limited to the middle and upper classes. Examples are Bolivia, Brazil, and Uruguay.
3. In the "parallel tracks" pattern, which characterizes the Chile transition, there is an explicit transitional project and timetable set by the authoritarian regime. The parallel tracks consist of the exclusive process of negotiation between middle- and upper-class insiders only and mobilization initiated by a cross-class alliance of outsiders at various points. Organized labor, specifically, contributed to opening up space, building a democratic opposition, enforcing the transition, and expanding contestation.
4. The "inter-elite game" is the only pattern in which organized labor did not play a significant role. The transition here is driven by opposition from middle- and upper-class outsiders and essentially negotiated without organized labor either participating or exerting pressure from below. A South American example of this pattern is Ecuador.

Levitsky and Mainwaring (2006, p. 21), in their analysis of the relationship between "Organized Labor and Democracy in Latin America," on the one hand, support Collier's and Drake's finding that "Latin American labor movements have often played a leading role in struggles against dictatorships" (see also Birle 1999, pp. 192–198). On the other hand, however, they emphasize that organized labor's overall "record with respect to democracy has been mixed" (Levitsky and Mainwaring 2006, p. 21). They take particular issue with the notion that labor movements are generally pro-democratic forces. In contrast to Rueschemeyer et al. (1992), they emphasize that (1) organized labor aims not only at "maximizing workers' material gains" but also at pursuing "organizational, political, ideological, and career benefits" that are, to a substantial degree, defined by the union leadership and that (2) "labor movements may pursue their interests successfully within various political regimes" because, for instance, "a variety of inclusionary authoritarian regimes have offered union leaders avenues for achieving their collective and individual goals" (Levitsky and Mainwaring 2006, p. 24).[4] In comparing nine Latin American countries, they suggest that labor movements' regime orientation depends on two factors: (1) the nature of their partisan alliances and, in particular, whether allied parties have an instrumental or a genuine orientation toward democracy; (2) the perceived regime alternative and, in particular, whether a non-democratic but pro-labor regime seems viable (Levitsky and Mainwaring 2006, pp. 25–27).[5]

---

[4] It should, however, be noted that Rueschemeyer et al. (1992, p. 8) cite the working class—rather than labor organizations—as "the most consistently pro-democratic force," while also noting exceptions to this general rule—which "occurred where the class was initially mobilized by a charismatic but authoritarian leader or a hegemonic party linked to the state apparatus." As concerns Latin America, they observe that the working class "generally, but not always, played a strong pro-democratic role in so far as it demanded an opening of the political system to achieve its own inclusion. Given the social construction of class interests, however, working-class organizations in some cases readily supported authoritarian regimes which accorded them material and status concessions [...]. This was particularly likely if the leaders of such regimes were the first to mobilize and organize labor on a large scale" (Rueschemeyer et al. 1992, p. 168). This argument is, in fact, quite similar to the one presented by Levitsky and Mainwaring.

[5] Based on a different set of cross-regional comparisons, Bellin (2000) also suggested that labor movements are "contingent democrats" only, and suggested two different variables in order to account for the observable variance: With a view to (1) "the degree to which organized labor depends on state support for its organizational viability, vitality, and clout," "organized, state-dependent labor believes its interests are better served by maintaining collaborative, not contestatory, relations with the state." In terms of (2) "the degree to which organized labor is economically privileged vis-à-vis the general population," organized labor that enjoys "a privileged stance" will "perceive its interests to be better served by maintaining a cozy relationship with the state (even if the institutional arrangements are authoritarian), rather than by championing institutions that make the state accountable to mass interests (that is, democracy)" (Bellin 2000, p. 183).

A different argument suggests that, while labor movements contributed to the destabilization of authoritarian regimes in Latin America, it was, in the end, not the strength but rather the weakness of organized labor that facilitated democratization: By eliminating "any serious working class 'threat,'" it enabled the acceptance of the democratic rules of the game on the part of the elites (Levitsky and Mainwaring 2006, p. 38; see also Drake 1996, p. 186; Huber et al. 1997; Kurtz 2004; Roberts 1998; Wolff 2009). This two-stage observation is in line with Valenzuela's suggestion that democratic transitions work best when high labor mobilization "at certain critical moments of breakdown of the authoritarian institutions" is followed by a "decline of that mobilization" and "restraint" on the part of organized labor in order to "demonstrate that democratization can lead to greater social and political order rather than to revolution, instability, and chaos" (Valenzuela 1989, p. 450).[6] But in contrast to Valenzuela's actor-centered approach (which emphasized different labor strategies), the argument here emphasizes rather the socio-structural weakening of organized labor and its capacity for collective action (see Oxhorn and Ducatenzeiler 1998; Kurtz 2004; Roberts 1998). At the same time, however, this weakness of organized labor arguably had "negative implications for the quality of democracy," in that it contributed to the emergence of elite-centered, fairly formal democracies undermined and distorted by persistent (if not increasing) socioeconomic inequalities (Levitsky and Mainwaring 2006, p. 38; see also Huber et al. 1997; Kurtz 2004; Oxhorn and Ducatenzeiler 1998; Roberts 1998; Wolff 2009). As Paul Drake has summarized the situation:

> With their restraint, unionists had more success at facilitating democratization than at pursuing fundamental reforms. None of the unbound labor movements obtained big changes in the balance of power or the socioeconomic order [...]. In most countries, the working class failed to transform basic macroeconomic policies. (Drake 1996, p. 188)

---

[6] Empirically, at least for the Southern Cone countries Argentina, Chile, and Uruguay as well as for Brazil, Paul Drake (1996, p. 49) has observed that labor movements did in fact act with "relative restraint during the delicate stages of redemocratization." Collier (1999, p. 165), in contrast, emphasizes that labor protest "continuing to the end of the transition rather than creating an authoritarian backlash, often kept the transition moving forward."

In this sense, then, the reduction in the level of contentious labor action in the course of the 1980s (which generally continued throughout the 1990s) had ambivalent effects on Latin American democracy, with Valenzuela's argument that labor restraint will facilitate democratization being only one part of the story. Overall, it seems fair to say that organized labor in Latin America in the 1980s and 1990s was not able to significantly push democratization further toward less low-intensity, more inclusive, or more social versions of democracy.[7]

This politico-economic/socio-structural argument also shows that the strength of labor movements, and as a consequence organized labor's impact on democratization, does not depend solely on actor constellations, structures, and dynamics at the intrastate level. In addition to the analytical frameworks and causal factors emphasized by Collier, Levitsky and Mainwaring, and Valenzuela, which all focus on domestic causes, international conditions, and the global political economy in particular, have clearly shaped both organized labor and its capacity to play a political role on behalf of some general interest of the working class. This international dimension includes the economic constraints (reinforced by the Latin American debt crisis), active international pressure (in particular, by the US government, the IMF, and the World Bank), and the emerging hegemony of neoliberal ideology (the "Washington Consensus"). Taken together, these factors contributed to the region-wide turn toward a market- and outward-oriented development model that weakened organized labor precisely at the time that the newly (re-)emerging democratic regimes took shape. In addition, the international dimension also concerns deliberate efforts on the part of external actors that supported democratization (such as, in particular, the US) and, in doing so, aimed at controlled, elite-centered transitions to rather limited, formal democracies that would not pose any serious threats to vital elite interests (nationally and internationally) and would leave the highly unequal social structures (again, at both the national and the international level) unaddressed (see Huber et al. 1997; Robinson 1996).

---

[7] This (potential) task of social movements—summarized by Rossi and Della Porta (2015, pp. 24–25)—has rather been fulfilled by more or less "new" social movements that, if in alliance with labor movements, were crucial in preparing the ground for the so-called leftist turn in the early 2000s (see later and Chap. 7).

4.3 The Consequences of Democratization for Organized Labor

One common expectation concerning democratization's effects on organized labor has been formulated by O'Donnell and Schmitter in their tentative conclusions on the ongoing transitions in Southern Europe and Latin America in the mid-1980s: They expected "the greatest challenge to the transitional regime [...] to come from the new or revived identities and capacity for collective action of the working class and low-ranking, often unionized, employees" (O'Donnell and Schmitter 1986, p. 52). With the reduction in repression and the opening of spaces for contestation, they speculated that the "enormous backlog of anger and conflict" that had accumulated during the authoritarian regimes will result "in an explosion of worker demands" (O'Donnell and Schmitter 1986, p. 53).

Valenzuela (1989), by contrast, argued that we should expect labor reactions to democratization to differ from case to case, with these differences being particularly shaped by the centralization and unity of the labor movement, the characteristics of the previous authoritarian regime and the type of transition. More specifically, Valenzuela suggested that decentralized and divided labor movements will not move from mobilization to restraint, but continue to engage in contentious mobilization (Valenzuela 1989, pp. 455–456); that democratization will produce more demanding and radical labor movements that do not join pacted transitions, especially when the prior authoritarian regime has been syndically harsh and/or politically closed (Valenzuela 1989, p. 458); and that an increase in labor mobilization and conflict is particularly likely when transitions follow the *ruptura* model, rather than a controlled path of gradual reforms (Valenzuela 1989, p. 463). With a view to his first "source of variation" (see above), Valenzuela argued that weak labor movements (because they are unable to shape the process of political change) "may well fail to develop firm commitments to the new regime" (Valenzuela 1989, p. 452).

With hindsight, it is generally acknowledged that democratization in Latin America has not led to an increase in labor protest. Rather than being strengthened and reactivated by democratization, organized labor "weakened throughout most of Latin America during the 1980s and 1990s." This weakening, however, was mainly due to "the economic crisis of the 1980s, the neoliberal economic reforms that followed it [...], and the rapid growth of the urban informal sector" (Levitsky and Mainwaring 2006,

p. 38; see also Birle 1999; Kurtz 2004; Oxhorn and Ducatenzeiler 1998; Portes and Hoffman 2003; Roberts 1998; Stillerman and Winn 2007).[8] Data on strike rates for a selection of Latin American countries clearly suggests that this type of labor protest was reduced as a consequence of economic, rather than political, liberalization (Kurtz 2004, pp. 300–301; see also Eckstein 2013, p. 87). In most Latin American countries, the first democratic governments after transitions were, in fact, frequently confronted with still relatively strong labor movements, and initial structural adjustment programs often met with significant labor resistance (Eckstein 2013, pp. 358–373; see also Cook 2007; Drake 1996). An exception are cases (such as, in particular, Chile) in which the implementation of neoliberal economic reforms—and, thus, the corresponding weakening of organized labor—preceded democratization (see Cook 2007, pp. 12–16).

As a result, even if in, for example, Brazil strike activity briefly rose (and significantly so) with the return to democracy, "there and elsewhere in Latin America, overall patterns of strike activity have been generally downward in the ensuing years" (Wickham-Crowley and Eckstein 2015, p. 32).[9] This politico-economic/socio-structural dynamic also, again, points to the relevance of the international context that, in pushing for privatization, deregulation, and liberalization, contributed to the weakening of organized labor (see Drake 2007; Hershberg 2007; Huber et al. 1997). Still, democratization arguably also contributed to these changes: first, to the extent that democratization along (neo-)liberal lines meant the dismantling of "corporatist labor laws" (Levitsky and Mainwaring 2006, p. 38; see also Drake 2007, pp. 161–162); second, because democratic elections lent legitimacy to economic reforms that, otherwise, would have probably required much more repression to push them through (see Wolff 2009); and third, because with the turn from authoritarian to democratic regimes, political parties and elections came to the fore at the expense of social organizations and protest (see Birle 1999, p. 202; Drake 1996, p. 182; O'Donnell and Schmitter 1986, p. 57; Oxhorn 1998, p. 208).

---

[8] As mentioned above, Drake (1996) also emphasizes this structural weakening of organized labor, but sees this as part of a broader set of legacies from the authoritarian past that continued to constrain labor movements even after the establishment of democracy.

[9] Still, besides the effects of economic crisis and neoliberal reforms, partisan dynamics also mattered, as Drake's comparative analysis shows: In contrast to Chile, where democratization led to the election of a coalition of parties that were closely related to organized labor, the return of civilian rule was followed by "significant strikes and [labor] demands," including general strikes, in Argentina, Brazil, and Uruguay (Drake 1996, p. 188).

In sum, democratization in the region generally meant "that labor recaptured its freedom to organize, negotiate, participate, and vote, but within the limits of an economy dedicated to the private sector and a political system dedicated to stability" (Drake 2007, p. 162). In this context, labor unions have certainly continued to organize strikes and other types of labor protests, but their numbers have generally been relatively low, as has the strength and impact of organized labor at the national level (see, for instance, Kurtz 2004). This situation, which, by and large, characterized the post-transition context in most Latin American countries, would only change several years, if not decades, after democratization. It was only after the turn of the century that scholars noted a "striking resurgence of organized labor as an important actor in national politics in several countries, such as Argentina, Uruguay, and Brazil" (Cook 2012, p. 269).

Generally speaking, this resurgence was the combined result of a period of economic growth between 2004 and 2013 and of a simultaneous "leftist turn" in the region, which led to a post-neoliberal turn in economic policies (see Burdick et al. 2009; Levitsky and Roberts 2011; Ruckert et al. 2017; Weyland et al. 2010). This also means that the strengthening of organized labor was a consequence, not a cause, of the political changes that characterized Latin America during the first years of the new century: While the leftist turn was a very diverse phenomenon, one common feature was that organized labor was not at the forefront of any of the protest movements that prepared the ground for the election of leftist governments (Drake 2007, p. 163; see Roberts 2008; Rossi 2017; Silva 2009; Silva and Rossi 2018). Still, this is certainly not to say that organized labor has been absent from the wave of social protest that preceded the leftist turn. A study on protests against neoliberal policies in Latin America between late 1995 and early 2001, for instance, found that "working-class groups" were by far the most important social actors (Almeida 2007).[10]

In terms of the leftist turn's consequences for labor movements, organized labor as well as salaried workers have mostly benefited from both the election of left-of-center governments and the post-neoliberal economic policies these have, by and large, pursued, as well as from the economic boom. As a result, "the still limited number of studies of unions and labor

---

[10] The quantitative analysis included protest events "related to a neoliberal policy, economic austerity measure, free-trade accord, or structural adjustment program (e.g., price hikes, new taxes, reductions in public budgets, privatization of public enterprises/utilities, etc.)" (Almeida 2007, p. 128). The category "working-class groups," however, includes labor unions but also other groups that, somehow, represent the working class.

policy under the Left point to increased levels of unionization, rising wages, and greater influence in policy debates in the 2000s as evidence of labor's resurgence" (Cook 2012, p. 267). Still, relations between left-of-center governments and organized labor have been far from smooth and have involved quite a few tensions and in part open conflict, while the increase in union strength and the improvements for workers have been only gradual (see Cameron and Hershberg 2010; Levitsky and Roberts 2011; Silva and Rossi 2018). In sum, the relative gains in socioeconomic well-being and political strength of organized labor across several Latin American countries have not meant that it has recuperated the status it had before the implementation of neoliberal reforms. Furthermore, given the reliance of left-of-center governments on the commodities boom of the early 2000s, falling prices in key export goods since 2014 have put increasing pressure on expansive economic and social policies.

4.4 Conclusion

The overall finding of existing research regarding the two questions posed at the outset of this literature review can be summarized with a quote from Paul Drake: "Organized labor played a big role in democratization but not in democracy" (2007, p. 162). In most Latin American countries, the labor movement played a significant role in pushing for and initiating processes of democratization, even if its role was much more diverse when it comes to actually shaping and negotiating actual regime change. At the same time, democratization was, by and large, accompanied by a structural weakening of organized labor. Driven by economic crises and the emergence of the "Washington Consensus," the dual transformation (political democratization and neoliberal restructuring of the development model) meant that labor organizations were hardly able to successfully push their socioeconomic claims at the national level, even if strikes and other labor protests certainly continued. It was only with a significant time lag—and facilitated by broader waves of social mobilization (see Chap. 7 in this book)—that organized labor in a series of Latin American countries could regain some strength and actually make use of the opportunity structure offered by democracy in order to bring the "social question" back on the agenda.

For the study of organized labor in times of political change, the literature reviewed also suggests that it is important to analyze and distinguish *socioeconomic* aims (on behalf of organized labor, the working class, or the population at large) and *politico-institutional* aims (related to the inclusion of organized labor, of the working class, or to democratization as such). To reach these aims, labor organizations principally make use of, and potentially combine, three types of strategies: *protest* (labor conflicts/strikes, political protests), *negotiation* (labor-related negotiations, political dialogue), and *political participation* (in and through parties or directly in government).

Finally, the scholarship on Latin America suggests four key dimensions that shape the relationship between organized labor and processes of political change. In terms of (1) *internal characteristics*, the strength or weakness of the labor movement, its unity or division, as well as the centralization or decentralization of labor organizations are important factors. In terms of (2) *political alliances*, linkages with political parties as well as with the government (before, during, and after the regime change) seem to matter most. With a view to (3) the *political context*, the type of the prior regime (repression, incorporation, etc.), the type of political change (abrupt, controlled, etc.), as well as perceived regime alternatives are crucial. Finally, (4) the *international context* also matters, and here, in particular, the general economic context (state of the global/regional economy) as well as the way in which external actors and/or transnational economic structures reward or constrain specific domestic policy choices and directions of political change.

REFERENCES

Almeida, P. D. (2007). Defensive mobilization: Popular movements against economic adjustment policies in Latin America. *Latin American Perspectives, 34*(3), 123–139.

Bellin, E. (2000). Contingent democrats. Industrialists, labor, and democratization in late-developing countries. *World Politics, 52*(2), 175–205.

Birle, P. (1999). Die südamerikanischen Gewerkschaften und Unternehmerverbände im Systemwechsel – Eine historisch-vergleichende Betrachtung. In W. Merkel & E. Sandschneider (Eds.), *Systemwechsel 4: Die Rolle von Verbänden im Transformationsprozeß* (pp. 181–219). Opladen: Leske + Budrich.

Burdick, J., Oxhorn, P., & Roberts, K. M. (Eds.). (2009). *Beyond neoliberalism in Latin America? Societies and politics at the crossroads.* New York, NY: Palgrave Macmillan.

Cameron, M. A., & Hershberg, E. (Eds.). (2010). *Latin America's left turns: Politics, policies, and trajectories of change.* Boulder, CO: Lynne Rienner.

Collier, R. B. (1999). *Paths toward democracy. The working class and elites in Western Europe and South America*. Cambridge: Cambridge University Press.

Collier, R. B., & Handlin, S. (2009). Introduction: popular representation in the interest arena. In R. B. Collier & S. Handlin (Eds.), *Reorganizing popular politics. Participation and the new interest regime in Latin America* (pp. 3–31). The Pennsylvania State University Press: University Park, PA.

Cook, M. L. (2007). *Politics of labor reform in Latin America: Between flexibility and rights*. University Park, PA: The Pennsylvania State University Press.

Cook, M. L. (2012). Labor. In P. Kingstone & D. J. Yashar (Eds.), *Routledge handbook of Latin American politics* (pp. 262–272). New York, NY: Routledge.

Drake, P. W. (1996). *Labor movements and dictatorships. The southern cone in comparative perspective*. Baltimore, MD: The Johns Hopkins University Press.

Drake, P. W. (2007). Organized labor's global problems and local responses. *International Labor and Working-Class History, 72*(1), 161–163.

Eckstein, S. (2013). The Latin American social movement repertoire. How it has changed, when, and why. *Moving the Social, 50*, 81–102.

Hershberg, E. (2007). Globalization and labor: Reflections on contemporary Latin America. *International Labor and Working-Class History, 72*(1), 164–172.

Huber, E., Rueschemeyer, D., & Stephens, J. D. (1997). The paradoxes of contemporary democracy: Formal, participatory, and social dimensions. *Comparative Politics, 29*(3), 323–342.

Kurtz, M. J. (2004). The dilemmas of democracy in the open economy. Lessons from Latin America. *World Politics, 56*(1), 262–302.

Levitsky, S., & Mainwaring, S. (2006). Organized labor and democracy in Latin America. *Comparative Politics, 39*(1), 21–42.

Levitsky, S., & Roberts, K. M. (Eds.). (2011). *The resurgence of the Latin American left*. Baltimore, MD: The Johns Hopkins University Press.

O'Donnell, G., & Schmitter, P. C. (1986). *Transitions from authoritarian rule. Tentative conclusions about uncertain democracies*. Baltimore, MD: The Johns Hopkins University Press.

Oxhorn, P. (1998). Is the century of corporatism over? Neoliberalism and the rise of neopluralism. In P. Oxhorn & G. Ducatenzeiler (Eds.), *What kind of democracy? What kind of market? Latin America in the age of neoliberalism* (pp. 195–217). University Park, PA: The Pennsylvania State University Press.

Oxhorn, P., & Ducatenzeiler, G. (Eds.). (1998). *What kind of democracy? What kind of market? Latin America in the age of neoliberalism*. University Park, PA: The Pennsylvania State University Press.

Portes, A., & Hoffman, K. (2003). Latin American class structures: Their composition and change during the neoliberal era. *Latin American Research Review, 38*(1), 41–82.

Roberts, K. M. (1998). *Deepening democracy? The modern left and social movements in Chile and Peru*. Stanford, CA: Stanford University Press.

Roberts, K. M. (2008). The mobilization of opposition to economic liberalization. *Annual Review of Political Science, 11*, 327–349.

Robinson, W. I. (1996). *Promoting polyarchy. Globalization, United States intervention and hegemony*. Cambridge: Cambridge University Press.

Rossi, F. M. (2017). *The poor's struggle for political incorporation. The Piquetero movement in Argentina*. Cambridge: Cambridge University Press.

Rossi, F. M., & Della Porta, D. (2015). Mobilizing for democracy: Social movements in democratization processes. In B. Klandermans & C. Van Stralen (Eds.), *Movements in times of democratic transition* (pp. 9–33). Philadelphia, PA: Temple University Press.

Ruckert, A., Macdonald, L., & Proulx, K. R. (2017). Post-neoliberalism in Latin America: A conceptual review. *Third World Quarterly, 38*(7), 1583–1602.

Rueschemeyer, D., Huber Stephens, E., & Stephens, J. D. (1992). *Capitalist development and democracy*. Cambridge: Polity Press.

Silva, E. (2009). *Challenging neoliberalism in Latin America*. Cambridge: Cambridge University Press.

Silva, E., & Rossi, F. M. (Eds.). (2018). *Reshaping the political arena in Latin America: From resisting neoliberalism to the second incorporation*. Pittsburgh, PA: University of Pittsburgh Press.

Stillerman, J., & Winn, P. (2007). Introduction: New studies/new organizations; labor organization in Latin America and beyond. *International Labor and Working-Class History, 72*(1), 2–17.

Valenzuela, J. S. (1989). Labor movements in transitions to democracy: A framework for analysis. *Comparative Politics, 21*(4), 445–472.

Weyland, K., Madrid, R. L., & Hunter, W. (Eds.). (2010). *Leftist governments in Latin America: Successes and shortcomings*. Cambridge: Cambridge University Press.

Wickham-Crowley, T. P., & Eckstein, S. E. (2015). "There and back again": Latin American social movements and reasserting the powers of structural theories. In P. Almeida & A. Cordero Ulate (Eds.), *Handbook of social movements across Latin America* (pp. 25–42). Dordrecht: Springer.

Wolff, J. (2009). De-idealizing the democratic civil peace: On the political economy of democratic stabilisation and pacification in Argentina and Ecuador. *Democratization, 16*(5), 998–1026.

CHAPTER 5

Proposals, Intermediation, and Pressure: The Three Roles of the UGTT in Tunisia's Post-revolutionary Constitutional Process

Bassem Karray

5.1 Introduction

Comparative research has shown that organized labor is often a relevant but usually not a decisive factor in processes of democratization (Collier 1999). The case of Tunisia is generally regarded as an exception to this rule. The Tunisian General Labor Union (Union Générale Tunisienne du Travail—UGTT) is widely considered to have played a key role during the country's recent transition from dictatorship to a democratic regime that is certainly still fragile but contrasts sharply with the experience in Egypt and other post-uprising trajectories across the region (Roy 2012; Beinin 2015, p. 7; see also Allinson 2015; Della Porta 2014; Bishara 2014; Netterstrøm 2016). Existing research on Tunisia's transition to democracy in general, and on the UGTT's contribution in particular, mostly focuses on the labor federation's (ambivalent) behavior during the revolution as well as on its role in the context of the so-called National Dialogue

B. Karray (✉)
University of Sfax, Sfax, Tunisia

© The Author(s) 2020
I. Weipert-Fenner, J. Wolff (eds.), *Socioeconomic Protests in MENA and Latin America*, Middle East Today,
https://doi.org/10.1007/978-3-030-19621-9_5

Quartet, which received the 2015 Nobel Peace Prize for contributing to solving the serious crisis of Tunisia's transition process in 2013 (see Beinin 2015; Yousfi 2018).[1] At the same time, scholars have studied the process of drafting Tunisia's new constitution as well as its result from a narrow legal perspective, but have generally failed to shed light on the role played by non-traditional actors such as the UGTT (see Al-Ali and Ben Romdhane 2014; Dubout and Baccouche 2015; Sfax Faculty of Law 2017).

Against this background, this chapter will focus on the UGTT's involvement in the process of constitutional reform that followed the revolution and was a key element in the country's transition to democracy. The involvement of civil society organizations such as trade union federations in processes of constitutional change is controversial, given that the drafting of a constitution is usually considered a matter for public institutions (governments, parliaments, or constituent assemblies). However, as this chapter will show, the UGTT made a significant contribution to the establishment of Tunisia's first democratic constitution. This includes both the union's indispensable role in facilitating a successful constitutional reform process and its more specific contributions in terms of the contents of the new constitution. The latter also implies that the UGTT's role as a political mediator in the post-revolutionary transformation process has not meant that it has given up its function as the national representation of organized labor.

During the first phase of the constitutional process that started with the election of the National Constituent Assembly (NCA) on 23 October 2011, the UGTT did not interfere formally in the drafting process. But unofficially it actively pushed for the legalization of social rights in the various drafts that were prepared by the NCA. Moreover, when the constitutional process was paralyzed in 2013 following the assassination of a leftist member of the NCA on 25 July, the UGTT officially intervened by pushing for, designing, and facilitating a national dialogue process that, ultimately, helped resolve the political crisis and culminated in the adoption of a new constitution in early 2014.

National dialogues are generally defined as "negotiating mechanisms intended to expand participation in political transitions beyond the political and military elites" (Papagianni 2013, p. 1). In the Tunisian case, however, the National Dialogue (October 2013–November 2014) was a forum for negotiation that deliberately encompassed political actors only.

---

[1] For accounts of the UGTT's involvement in the processes of political and socioeconomic change during previous regimes, see Bessis (1974), Chouikha and Geisser (2010), and Dot-Pouillard (2013).

Yet, the process was initiated and organized by four civil society organizations (the so-called "quartet") led by the UGTT. The aim of the national dialogue process was to enable consensus building between the government and opposition parties, in order to safeguard the transition by appointing a technocratic caretaker government, enabling the conclusion of the constitutional process, and moving toward general elections.

While this mediating role of the UGTT constitutes its best-known contribution to Tunisia's transition to democracy, a focus on this "political" dimension misses important parts of the picture. As the following analysis demonstrates, the UGTT has contributed to the constitutional reform process by adopting three roles that are intertwined but can be distinguished analytically:

- As a *force for proposals*, the UGTT announced its own project for a new constitution in October 2011, a few days before the election of the NCA. Although not officially taken account of by the NCA, the UGTT's proposal was a source of inspiration.
- As a *force of equilibrium*, the labor federation mediated between the ruling parties and the opposition by launching a national dialogue gathering all political and social stakeholders. The purpose here was to preserve the transition process from the political crisis triggered by the conflict between the ruling parties and the opposition after the assassination of the NCA member in July 2013.
- As a *force for political pressure*, the UGTT mobilized its members to defend democratic rights that were threatened by conservative and ultra-conservative groups. It also organized strikes and other forms of contentious action to counterbalance the ruling parties' hegemony over the constitutional drafting process.

This chapter starts with a brief historical overview and then analyzes the three roles of the UGTT in detail.

5.2 Historical Overview

5.2.1 *From the 1861 Constitution to the 2011 Revolution*

Constitutional thought is well entrenched in Tunisia, dating back to the middle of nineteenth century when the Tunisian Bey (the King) enacted a constitution providing several rights for both Tunisian and foreign people on 26 April 1861.[2] This constitution was adopted in the context of political openness, and the process was inaugurated upon publication of the emancipating act of the slaves (Decree 23 January 1846) and the security pact (9 September 1857). However, the 1861 constitution was written and adopted without any popular participation and it granted constitutional power to the Sovereign and not to the people, who were considered incapable of exercising such power. This first "liberal phase," however, did not last long, and in April 1864, a rebellion guided by Ali Ben Ghedahom led to the suspension of the constitution. This revolt against the Bey, which prematurely ended the political transformation, can be attributed to a rise in fiscal taxes and discrimination among regions. Thus, from early on, political change was deeply interconnected with socioeconomic crises.

In 1881 Tunisia became a French protectorate, but during the liberation movement against French domination, constitutional change again emerged as a popular slogan. Starting in 1920, the Tunisian people regularly called for the adoption of a constitution, the formation of a national government, and the election of a parliament responsible for managing national affairs. At that time, too, Tunisia's first political party was established by union leader Mohamed Ali Hammi. The Liberal Constitutional Party rallied Tunisians around the goal of gaining independence. Later, when UGTT was created as a national labor federation in January 1946, unionists and politicians joined together to remove the French authorities (Yousfi 2015). Following independence, the Tunisian people elected a constituent assembly to draft a constitution. For the 1956 elections to the constituent assembly, the UGTT, the Liberal Constitutional Party, the main business federation (the Tunisian Union of Industry, Trade and Handicrafts—UTICA), and the National Union of Tunisian Farmers (UNAT) formed joint electoral lists. This coalition, known as the National Front, won the election and thus gained control of the drafting process. As a result, unionists and politicians worked together in handling both the constitutional process and formulating the contents of the new basic law. After a three-year process (1956–1959), a liberal constitution was adopted on 1 June 1959 (see Amor 1987; Amor and Saied 1987).

Despite its close involvement in drafting the 1959 constitution, the UGTT would not mobilize against governments that acted against its liberal spirit. On numerous occasions, both President Bourguiba (1957–1987) and his successor Ben Ali (1987–2011) amended the constitution in order

---

[2] On the same day, the Bey enacted a new criminal code which formally prohibited corporal punishment.

to stay in power, to the detriment of the alternation principle and republican values. Still, while the UGTT rejected certain decisions—such as the appointment of Bourguiba as president for life or the periodic alteration of the constitution to keep Ben Ali in power—it never mobilized its supporters to denounce such actions, and thus indirectly contributed to the persistent violation of the constitutional rules. In general, Bourguiba and Ben Ali managed to keep the labor federation out of political affairs, and the UGTT in turn focused its activities on socioeconomic issues. As a consequence, the national leadership of the UGTT remained hesitant to join the revolution and joined the protests that, in the end, succeeded in toppling Ben Ali only very late in the process. However, the relative autonomy of the UGTT's subnational structures allowed its regional and local branches to play a much more active role in the run-up to the revolution.[3]

5.2.2 Overview of the Post-revolutionary Process

Following the toppling of Ben Ali in January 2011, controversies centered on different scenarios of transition. The government that was formed in January 2011—mainly by Ben Ali's ministers and supported by sections of the political elite—was favorable to a transition of power without constitutional change, and the first stage of the transition process was, indeed, conducted under the provisions of the constitution of 1959.[4] The opposition, led by leftist parties, as well as the main civil society organizations, UGTT included, rejected this scenario. Their stance was that the constitution was no longer legitimate and had already been replaced by revolutionary legitimacy.[5] As a consequence, they called for abrogating the 1959 constitution and replacing it by another one that would be drafted by a Constituent Assembly in the light of the "revolutionary message."[6]

As a means of counterbalancing the interim government and defending the goals of the revolution, on 20 January 2011 the UGTT—together

---

[3] For a detailed account of the UGTT's role in the 2011 revolution, see for example Netterstrøm (2016).

[4] The interim government itself held power pursuant to Article 57 of the constitution, which deals with cases of vacancy of the presidency.

[5] For more details, see Ben Achour and Ben Achour (2012).

[6] "Revolutionary message" refers to the slogan or values expressed and defended by protestors during the struggle against the authoritarian regime. In the Tunisian case, the revolutionary message around which all protestors rallied, regardless of their political affiliations, was freedom and dignity. See Ben Achour (2012, 2014).

with 28 organizations—formed the unofficial Revolution Protection Council. Together with the political opposition, the UGTT rejected the call for organizing presidential elections as provided for by the constitution of 1959 in the event of vacancy of the presidency (Kausch 2011). Instead, the labor federation pushed for the Revolution Protection Council's demand of convening a constituent assembly by mobilizing its members on the national and regional levels. Generally, the strategy of resistance included media campaigns, public protest, mobilization via social networks, and sit-ins (in front of the government square and regional public squares).

During this phase, the UGTT relied mainly on strategies of peaceful societal resistance to push for political change. The labor federation's regional branches also followed the central board's instructions and organized sit-ins and public demonstrations to resist the decisions of regional and central authorities. Interestingly, during the first months after the revolution, the national leadership of the UGTT itself remained unchanged. In turn, however, the central board decided to keep its secretary general, Abdessalem Jrad,[7] who was known for his loyalty to the Ben Ali regime, away from public events.

In the end, the Revolution Protection Council succeeded in establishing the goal of electing a constituent body in the public debate. In a famous speech delivered on 5 March 2011, the interim president backed down in the face of popular resistance and announced the decision to suspend the constitution and to convene an NCA to draft a new constitution. In December 2011, the 1959 constitution was finally abrogated by Constituent Law No. 6 (ATG 2013, p. 7).

5.3 The UGTT: A Force for Proposals

In order to assess the UGTT's role as an actor that brings forward proposals, this section analyzes the constitutional draft that was proposed by the labor federation (3.1) and compares it with the new constitution as finally adopted, in this way identifying the influence the UGTT has had on the contents of the new constitution (3.2). In line with the overall topic of this book, the focus is on socioeconomic issues.

---

[7] Following the General Assembly of the UGTT in December 2011 (Tabarka Assembly), Abdessalem Jerad was replaced by Houssine Abassi.

5.3.1 The UGTT's Constitution Draft

Early on, the UGTT showed its interest in influencing the constitution-making process. Well before the election of the NCA, its central board charged a group of constitutional experts with the task of drafting a proposal for a new Tunisian constitution.

When in January 2011 the interim government proposed charging a committee of experts with drafting a new constitution for the republic, the UGTT did not support this option, which it considered to be undemocratic. Yet, the labor federation's own drafting process was neither participative nor open to any kind of consultation or debate, not even within the UGTT itself. The UGTT's constitutional proposal was unilaterally written by a panel of experts. In the foreword to the proposal, then General Secretary of the UGTT, Abdessalem Jerad, explained that the proposal was not definitive but would be presented to trade unionists for consideration.[8] He also highlighted that the labor federation was undertaking this initiative based on its historical role as a defender of freedoms and liberties, especially those related to social justice and labor rights such as the right to strike (UGTT 2011, p. 2). In the events that followed however, the regional branches failed to respond to the call from the central board. Instead of participating in the debate on the constitution by providing suggestions to shape the proposal, they focused on concrete activities in defense of workers' rights and interests. This example clearly shows that the UGTT's central board focused strongly on influencing political developments at the national level, while the pursuit of socioeconomic demands was left to the regional branches.

The UGTT's proposal contains 124 articles divided into 11 chapters and a preamble. It envisages a semi-parliamentary regime in which the government obtains a vote of confidence and fulfills its policies under the supervision of the parliament. The president of the republic, who shall be directly elected by the Tunisian people, is vested with some delimited and specific powers. In these points, the proposal of the UGTT closely resembles the constitution that was adopted in 2014.

Social freedoms and rights are recorded in the second chapter. The right to bargain and to sign collective agreements is one of the main issues covered by the UGTT's proposal. In line with the UGTT's own organizational

---

[8] In the end, however, this proposal was not mentioned in the final declaration of the following UGTT General Assembly held in December 2011.

interests, this right is only granted to the most representative labor federation, a criterion that excludes the two other trade union federations that had been created in 2011 and 2013. The principle of trade union pluralism is completely absent in UGTT's proposal. As will be seen later, when it comes to the right to bargain and to sign collective agreements, the UGTT's proposal was not taken up by the NCA.

Article 24 of the proposal provides that the State shall guarantee social insurance for all citizens; the right to work is qualified as a fundamental right that the state shall offer on the basis of equality and justice. The right of training is also recognized for all, workers included, in order to improve their skills.

In addition to socioeconomic rights, the UGTT proposal also contains two key institutions that are charged with socioeconomic matters. First, it provides for the establishment of a Social Dialogue, which is to take place at the local and central levels under the terms of a social contract (Article 26). The key aims of this Social Dialogue, which was non-existent in Tunisia's former constitution, are to bring public authorities together with workers and employees when determining the main socioeconomic strategies and policies and to generate mutual understanding between workers and employers in both the public and private sectors. Together with the right to bargain and to sign collective agreements, the Social Dialogue constitutes a cornerstone of the UGTT's model of a social-democratic economic and political system.

The second institution included in the UGTT proposal—the Socioeconomic Council—did already exist. The constitution of 1959 had created an Economic and Social Council which focused, in accordance with Article 70, on social matters.[9] Throughout the following decades, this council was a pillar of public institutions and fulfilled an important role in drafting laws dealing with social issues. It also served as a kind of forum for gathering different social components which provided advice on executive and legislative powers. After the revolution, the council was dissolved by a decree-law dated 14 March 2011, which related to the provisional organization of public powers and was known as the "mini-constitution." Articles 108 and 109 of the UGTT's proposal provide for the re-establishment of a Socioeconomic Council which is to be comprised of experts, representatives from local authorities, and the most

---

[9] In June 1961, just a few months after enactment of the constitution, decree-law 61–23 was passed that established this council.

representative labor and business associations. This Council is to fulfill an advisory role and to propose bills relating to socioeconomic matters. Despite its importance, such a council was not included in the 2014 constitution.

5.3.2 The Socioeconomic Provisions in the Constitution of 2014

Although the NCA commission in charge of drafting the constitution started with a blank slate and did not officially recognize the UGTT's proposal as input for its deliberations, the ideas put forward by the labor federation did serve as a source of inspiration. On 14 March 2012, the NCA invited the UGTT experts to an inaugural hearing to present the content of the UGTT's proposal, especially its suggestions relating to socioeconomic rights. And when the NCA edited its second draft on 14 December 2012, the UGTT experts had attended five hearings. Still, Mohamed Guesmi, a member of the experts' panel, stated that this draft was disappointing and fell far short of meeting the expectations of the labor federation. He also stressed that the participatory method pursued by the NCA was not serious (Mokni 2014).

In general, four draft versions preceded the final draft: The first and second drafts were published in August and December 2012, respectively, the third in April 2013, and the fourth in June 2013. The first two drafts did not include primary socioeconomic rights, and principles of social justice, sustainable development, regional equality, social dialogue, bargaining rights, and the idea of a socioeconomic council were completely absent from the first two drafts. An exception concerns the freedom to form unions and the right to strike, which were included early on. In the third and fourth drafts, the constitutional contents were shifted on account of contributions from expert analyses and popular suggestions expressed during the popular consultation organized by the Assembly. Still, what the UGTT ultimately obtained in the final version of the new constitution was less than it had been hoping for, especially with regard to socioeconomic matters.

There are socioeconomic provisions interspersed within the 2014 constitution. Systematically, they can be divided into substantial norms that deal with rights and freedoms, on the one hand, and procedural ones, on the other, which establish institutions focused on socioeconomic matters.

Article 8 sets out that the state is bound by an obligation to provide due care and improve youth capacities.[10] According to Article 12, the state shall seek to achieve social justice, sustainable development, and balance among regions in reference to development indicators, based on the principle of positive discrimination, and it is to ensure the proper utilization of national resources.[11]

In addition to Articles 8 and 12, the constitution specifies several rights belonging to the so-called second generation of human rights, such as the right to health care (Article 38), social insurance (Article 38), and the right to be employed under just and favorable conditions (Article 40). Additionally, Article 35 links the freedom to organize and constitute unions with the freedom to form political parties and associations. Article 36 specifically addresses the right to join and form unions and the right to strike. From its first draft, the contents of this article were progressively shifted. The phrasing of these two articles in the final version is largely inspired by the UGTT's proposal.

In contrast to the UGTT proposal, the final version of the constitution does not recognize the right to bargain and to sign collective agreements. Similarly, the two institutional suggestions—the Social Dialogue and the Socioeconomic Council—were not taken up by the NCA. In stark contrast to the social-democratic model of the UGTT proposal, the 2014 constitution relegates institutions focused on socioeconomic matters to tenth place. In fact, the new constitution does not provide for any institution focusing exclusively on socioeconomic matters.[12]

---

[10] In the first and second drafts, no provisions dealt with youth conditions. Following the public consultation organized in different regions (December 2012–January 2013), the constituent assembly's sub-committees took into account popular propositions and inserted some rules dealing with youth. The third draft included Article 19 on this issue.

[11] Similar to Article 8, provisions relating to social justice, sustainable development, and balance among regions were inserted after the popular consultation (Article 8 of the third draft, 22 April 2013). Finally, the fourth draft (from 1 June 2013) reiterated this content on the basis of the consensual and coordinated committee proposal which added the reference to economic indicators.

[12] The 2014 constitution does, however, provide for five new independent constitutional bodies which are vested with the powers of adjustment and regulation. Matters that fall within their jurisdiction are elections, audiovisual communications, human rights, sustainable development, and the fight against corruption. Out of these five new constitutional bodies, at the time of writing, only the Elections Commission (called ISIE) has been established.

On 14 January 2013, however, the government, UGTT, and UTICA concluded a social contract which, among other things, provided for the establishment of a National Social Dialogue Council. More than four years later, on 11 July 2017, the Tunisian parliament finally approved Law 2017-54 that creates such a council.[13] According to Article 8 of this law, this advisory council is composed equally of members nominated by the government, the most representative labor federation and the most representative business association, respectively. Additional members are to be nominated based on their qualifications in legal, social, and economic matters. During the voting in the parliament's plenary session, many deputies criticized the exclusion of other federations representing businessmen, workers, farmers, and liberal professional unions, which had denounced the discriminatory criterion of "the most representative union" and called for enlarging the representation on the basis of proportionality to guarantee equity. Once established, the council can be consulted by the government on any draft law or decree that touches upon work conditions, professional relationships, training, or social protections, as well as on matters of economic budgets and socioeconomic promotion plans (Article 3). The council can also become active on its own on any affairs that fall within its scope. The Social Dialogue to be organized by this council is meant to reduce social conflicts. The partners are to launch a social partnership by implementing dialogue and bargaining. It is expected that this council will contribute to social stability and mutual understanding.

5.4 The UGTT: A Force of Equilibrium

In addition to acting as a force for proposals, in response to the escalating political crisis in 2013 the UGTT emerged as a powerful force of equilibrium (4.1). Its intervention in this crisis particularly included the push for National Dialogue and the proposal for a road map for the constitution-making process (4.2).

---

[13] The National Social Dialogue Council shall replace the Committee of Social Dialogue that has been established in accordance with Article 335 of the Labor Code, because the committee suffers from a lack of autonomy. In contrast, the council is provided with legal status as well as administrative and financial autonomy. Its internal organization is meant to obey the principle of separation between deliberative and executive organs.

5.4.1 The Political Crisis of 2013

As was to be expected, the constitution-making process faced several impediments. Among them were the vulnerability of the Troika government formed by the Islamist Ennahdha Party together with the secular center-left parties Congress for the Republic (CPR) and Democratic Forum for Labor and Liberties (Ettakattul), the splitting up of the party system, and the weak entrenchment of democratic values. The longer the deliberations over the new constitution lasted, the more doubts emerged in the population that the process would achieve its desired results, and the lower the trust in the NCA.[14] A first direct blow to the NCA was dealt by the assassination of the oppositional politician Chokri Belaid on 6 February 2013. While this first political assassination forced the government led by Hamadi Jebali (Ennahdha) to resign and led to a temporary interruption of the work of the NCA committees, it did not place the general work of the constituent assembly in question.

To ease the incipient political crisis, the government launched two initiatives. On 12 February 2013, Prime Minister Laarayedh (Ennahdha) convened a council of the wise at the Dar Ediafa Palace. Two months later, President Marzouki (Congress for the Republic) called for a national dialogue to be held at Carthage Palace from 15 April 2013 to 15 May 2013—and to which the UGTT was not invited. In response, the UGTT convoked political parties and some civil society organizations to a national conference on 16 May 2013.[15] The agenda mainly addressed the issue of finalizing the constitution and determining the ultimate date to submit a draft for discussions within plenary sessions. In this conference, the participants focused on constitutional issues, yet differences between the parties inhibited any agreement.

---

[14] Expected to last one year from the NCA election, the constitution-making process could not be accomplished by 23 October 2012. When this expected deadline was approaching, fixed by the decree that had convened the elections, it was clear that the assembly would be unable to finish its work.

[15] On 18 June 2012, that is, a year before the crisis, the UGTT had already called for creation of a National Council of Dialogue in order to bring together all political parties and social organizations with the aim of finding consensual solutions to the economic, political, and security crises. This initiative comprised six points and served as a basis for a National Dialogue Conference held on 16 October 2012. In all, 50 parties, 22 organizations, and more than 200 journalists took part in this conference. However, the Ennahdha party and Congress for the Republic, which had both confirmed their participation, decided in the end not to participate—a decision that interrupted the process. See M'rad (2015).

After the assassination of the constituent assembly member Mohamed Brahmi on 25 July 2013, the NCA underwent a deep crisis. Strong dissension arose between deputies with an allegiance to the government, dominated by the Ennahdha party, and those belonging to the opposition. In reaction to the assassination, the opposition group within the NCA decided to withdraw from the work in plenary sessions and committees. It also stressed redefining the competencies of the NCA and appointing a technocratic government.[16] This boycott was supported by a group of civil society organizations, including the UGTT, the main business association UTICA, the Tunisian Order of Lawyers, and the Tunisian Human Rights League (see Sect. 5.5). In response to this combination of internal boycott and external pressure, the president of the NCA, Mustapha Ben Jaafar, unilaterally decided on 6 August 2013 to suspend all parliamentary activities until a compromise was reached between the majority and the opposition. It was this unexpected and controversial decision that enabled the initiation of a process of reconciliation.

Because of its explicit support of the opposition's boycott, the UGTT was accused of acting as a political party.[17] While, including in previous years, the UGTT had not stayed aloof from leftist parties with whom it shares key interests and values, and left and center-left parties have frequently relied on the UGTT's support in their struggles, the labor federation did try to maintain a certain distance from all political parties represented in the NCA. Nonetheless, in the context of the constitutional crisis, the UGTT decided to join the opposition parties in their call for a boycott of the NCA and for the resignation of the government.

Paradoxically, the decision to take explicit sides in the political conflict over the NCA did not prevent the UGTT from proposing solutions when the political crisis escalated further. While it publicly supported deputies boycotting the NCA who accused the government of being lenient toward

---

[16] While calling for the government's resignation, the opposition suggested entrusting a constitutional expert group with helping the NCA with formulating the constitutional provisions and the electoral act.

[17] In spite of not being a signatory to "the salvation front declaration," approved by the boycotters and some political parties and social organizations on 26 July 2013, the UGTT shared a number of goals with the signatories. One of the assistant secretaries general, Bouali Mbarki, said in an interview that the UGTT approved the intention to replace the government in office by another composed of technocrats. He also stressed that, owing to its historical role, the UGTT had obtained a kind of popular remit to pilot the process. See Hakaeik online electronic newsletter, 10/08/2013.

the Salafist movement, the UGTT simultaneously offered to mediate between the parties of the Troika government and the opposition to diffuse their dissension that had dramatically deepened after the second political assassination of July 2013. This also reflected the acknowledgment that the Troika government would not simply give in to the opposition's demands. But it was in response to the NCA president's suspension of the work of the assembly that the UGTT launched the initiative of proposing a road map for concluding the remaining steps of the constitutional process. Without completely withdrawing its support for the opposition deputies, the UGTT partnered with the main business association UTICA, the Order of Lawyers, and the Tunisian League of Human Rights in searching for a compromise to start a National Dialogue.

5.4.2 The Contribution of the UGTT's Road Map

The UGTT urged the NCA to accelerate its work and frequently suggested to the political parties that a national dialogue should be launched to find a suitable outlet for the process. As has been shown, several attempts to initiate such a dialogue failed. It was only in the context of the open crisis of the constitutional process that the UGTT, together with its civil society allies (the so-called Quartet), succeeded in getting a serious process of negotiations started (Meyer-Resende and Weichselbaum 2014). When the deep polarization between the two political camps seemed to offer no way out, it was mainly the labor federation that emerged as a savior of national unity.

On 17 September 2013, the UGTT—together with the rest of the Quartet—proposed a road map, and on 5 October 2013 two parties of the ruling coalition (Ennahdha and Democratic Forum for Labor and Liberties) and almost all opposition parties (which had formed the salvation front) participated in the first official conference that launched the process of implementing the road map prescriptions. The mission of the Quartet was to conciliate between the positions taken by the ruling coalition and opposition parties. Operating with the objective of bringing the process to a conclusion, the road map was divided into three parts: governmental, electoral, and constitutional. The governmental part required that the government in office resign and be replaced by an appointed, technocratic government until the election of a new administration under the new constitution. The electoral portion of the road map consisted of approving the electoral act covering both presidential and parliamentary elections and electing the members of the Higher Independent Electoral Instance. As for the constitutional part, the NCA had to accelerate its work to approve the final version of the constitution.

The National Dialogue started officially on 25 October 2013, when the government agreed to resign, as set out in the road map. During the different phases of the dialogue, the UGTT was able to work through each stage and break the deadlock over constitutional issues. The labor federation managed to find mutual solutions which satisfied all parties and, in addition, applied pressure to further the process (see Sect. 5.5). Houssine Abassi, the secretary general of the UGTT, was undeniably the leader of the National Dialogue.[18] At critical moments, Abassi firmly declared that he would make public all the reasons behind the impasse and identify those who were responsible for delaying the process.[19]

Fifteen months after the beginning of the National Dialogue, the constitution was finally adopted, receiving the overwhelming support of 200 votes (with 12 abstentions and 4 negative votes).

5.5 The UGTT: A Force for Political Pressure

From the beginning of the constitutional process, the UGTT called upon its members to participate broadly in the election of the NCA in order to prevent the re-emergence of representatives of the previous regime and to exert pressure within the assembly. Without directly or officially participating in the election of the NCA by forming unionist candidate lists,[20] the UGTT exhorted its members to participate actively in the election as independent candidates or by using their personal name under the banners of their respective political parties. The unionists responded to this call in great numbers; however, no known unionist made a successful run. Since the electoral results did not permit the UGTT to shape the constitutional process from within the NCA, it exerted pressure on the constituent assembly from the outside. In addition to the UGTT's

---

[18] UGTT leaders are known for being experienced negotiators as well as patient and tireless activists. They have honed their skills over decades of settling disputes and negotiating deals (see Omri 2014).
[19] Interview, 5 September 2013.
[20] The UGTT's notification, 25/08/2011.

substantive proposals discussed earlier, a key strategy was also to influence the working methods of the NCA.[21]

A first point of divergence between the NCA and the UGTT concerned the question whether the assembly would be exclusively in charge of designing the process and writing the new constitution. As has already been stated, the assembly decided to start with a blank page. Relying on the Organic Law Organizing the Provisional Public Authorities from 16 December 2011 along with its Rules of Procedures, the NCA claimed its sovereignty over the constitution-making process. This decision was rejected by the UGTT, which argued that the electoral legitimacy of the NCA did not imply that it was exclusively responsible for framing and writing the constitution, as this matter should be shared with the main societal stakeholders, including the UGTT.

In response to this dispute, a group of civil society organizations including the UGTT decided to set in motion a Civil National Constituent Assembly on 3 November 2011. This unofficial assembly, which would run in parallel to the official NCA, fixed its own drafting framework based on an open, participatory method. This initiative, as their initiators emphasized, did not aim at competing against the NCA, but at exerting civil control over its work and furthering political awareness among citizens. This declared aim concealed the intention of counterbalancing the NCA, which was seen as predominately controlled by the Ennahdha party.

Whereas this civil society initiative generated misunderstandings and a certain degree of confusion, it clearly showed the interest of civil society organizations in participating in the constitutional process. As an unofficial council, it kept pressure on the NCA to draft a consensual text. It edited its own draft, composed of 155 articles which recorded numerous freedoms and liberties.

In this context, the drafting process faced many impediments (Zoglin 2013). After the agreement on the UGTT's road map, however, the drafting process rapidly achieved its desired purposes. The capacity to enforce

---

[21] These working methods—or the design of the constitution-making process—include the method of drafting or the general organization of the various steps leading to the adoption of the constitution's contents. They also refer to the way the Constituent Assembly works by drawing plans for discussing and approving the final version as well as setting the drafting method and the deadline to vote for the constitution. The design of the process also includes determining who is involved (and how) during the multiple phases of phrasing, discussing, and approving the text. See Ginsburg et al. (2009, p. 204).

such an agreement was not only due to the UGTT's powers of persuasion and its ability to act as a mediator. Together with allied civil society organizations, the labor federation also put direct pressure on the governing parties in order to push them toward accepting a compromise that included the resignation of the government.

As already mentioned, the political assassinations and the increasing polarization that ensued after them led the UGTT to explicitly support the boycott of the NCA by the opposition parties. Together with UTICA, the Order of Lawyers, and the Human Rights League, the UGTT staged a sit-in in front of the assembly at Bardo Square, known as the "sit-in to oust the government in office," which, in the eyes of the protestors, was responsible for the political crisis. In parallel, similar sit-ins that brought together many political figures, unionists, artists, and elites were organized in different cities. In response to the sit-in at Bardo Square, supporters of the ruling parties staged a sit-in at the other side of the square in support of the government in office. They called for respect for the electoral legitimacy of the NCA and blamed the boycotters for blocking the process.

In this context, on 5 August 2013, the central board of the UGTT called upon its members to protest in the streets on the night of 6 August 2013, in order to express their demand for dissolution of the NCA and the resignation of the government.[22] Because it was expected to refrain from taking sides, the UGTT was criticized by some political parties which denounced its interference in partisan conflicts. In the end, however, this external pressure was of key importance in pushing the president of the assembly to suspend the work of the NCA—a decision that, as described earlier, was crucial in enabling the later process of reconciliation. Therefore, in addition to the broadly acknowledged role of the UGTT as a mediator, it was also the pure sociopolitical weight of the labor federation that forced the political parties to come to terms with each other and advance the transition process. As Samir Dilou, a minister of the Troika government, emphasized, Ennahdha never had the intention of entering into an open power struggle with the UGTT.[23]

---

[22] UGTT, Press release 06/08/2013.

[23] Rabaa H, "Tunisie? Samir Dilou, ennahdha n'aurait jamais pensé rentrer dans un bras de fer avec l'UGTT," Tunisienumérique.com, 2 December 2012.

5.6 Conclusion

The Tunisian experience analyzed in this chapter confirms the first basic paradox of constitution-making processes that has been described by Jon Elster. According to him, this paradox

> arises from the fact that the task of constitution-making generally emerges in conditions that are likely to work against good constitution-making. Being written for the indefinite future, constitutions ought to be adopted in maximally calm and undisturbed conditions. Also, the intrinsic importance of constitution-making requires that procedures be based on rational, impartial argument. (Elster 1995, p. 364)

Given that the drafting of a new constitution was undertaken in the immediate aftermath of a revolution, the context in Tunisia was far from calm. Revolutionary fervor generally tends to foster passion rather than reason. Deep rifts between all the stakeholders had a negative impact on defining the procedures for drafting the constitution as well as the formulation of the contents of the new basic law.

In addition, the spread of democratic rights all over the world, especially those relating to public participation and the increasing role of civil society organizations, has progressively and profoundly shifted the core meaning of how a democratic approach for drafting constitutions should look. This encouraged the NCA to allow for participation and a certain degree of openness and inclusiveness. At the same time, however, this made the constitutional process even more complex and lengthy.

In sum, a constitution-making process is no longer regarded as a simple mechanism or set of procedures leading to the adoption of the supreme legal text (Tushnet 1986; Ghai 2012; Gluck and Ballou 2014; Gluck and Brandt 2015), but rather as a sociopolitical matter which interests and, therefore, should involve citizens and civil society organizations. Constitution-making should generate an environment favorable to fostering national unity, strengthening trust between government and non-governmental actors, enhancing reconciliation across competing ideologies, furthering consensus on controversial constitutional matters, and promoting awareness of the principles and practices of democratic society. These expectations clearly overwhelmed the capacity and the political will of the Tunisian NCA and of Tunisia's political parties in general. In the end, it was neither the constituent assembly nor political parties but civil society organizations—and the UGTT in particular—that facilitated a process of reconciliation that enabled a successful conclusion of the constitutional process.

As described in this chapter, the UGTT has been the essential non-traditional component of constitutional transformation in Tunisia. It served the critical roles of bringing a new figure to the constitution-making process and shaping constitutional content. The labor federation mobilized its own constitutional experts to contribute to shaping the constitutional content through participation in seminars and workshops organized by civil society organizations. It also organized public events for debating and assessing constitutional proposals made by NCA committees regarding social issues. Furthermore, it played a key intermediating role in avoiding the open failure of the constitutional process. In sum, the UGTT served as a cornerstone in the process. Its experience, therefore, offers insights regarding the ability of a social organization in general, and a labor federation in particular, to pilot political negotiations and facilitate compromise among different stakeholders.

Unquestionably, the UGTT is, in appearance, an impartial body. Ideologically, however, its stance is far from Islamist political parties and particularly close to leftist ones. Despite this, its contribution to the constitution-making process has mainly consisted of its facilitating a successful constitutional transition process (combining the UGTT's role as a force of equilibrium and as a force for exerting pressure) rather than in its actual shaping of the new constitution's content. This limited influence when it comes to the UGTT providing proposals for the constitution was related to the fact that—contrary to the first constitution-making process in 1956–1959—the labor federation could not directly interfere in the drafting process, because no unionist was elected to the NCA in 2011. It did, however, influence the process from outside the constituent assembly through consultations and by exerting pressure. But the UGTT really became a key actor only when it was called upon to find a way out of the stalemate—but then as a mediating force rather than as an actor with a particular political agenda.

The UGTT's historical legacy along with its unity and its strong organizational structure at the central and regional level are key comparative advantages which have enabled the labor federation to assume the prominent role it played during the post-revolutionary transition process. While some political parties were crippled by internal strife and others were newly created, the UGTT emerged as a unique organization capable of mediating between the competing political forces with a view to advancing constitutional change. Tunisia's experience, therefore, casts doubt on a key argument in the scholarly literature on democratic transitions: that "civil society" may be important in challenging and, eventually, toppling an authoritarian regime, but that it is "political society" that is needed to construct a democracy (see Stepan and Linz 2013, p. 23). In fact, the UGTT has managed to simultaneously act in both arenas, civil and political society, bringing the ruling parties and the political opposition together in the road map process while also proposing and pushing for its own draft constitution.

At the moment, a major challenge for the future of Tunisia's still fragile democracy concerns the way in which the government deals with the huge socioeconomic problems that face the country and that have hardly been addressed in the turbulent years since the revolution. Once more, the UGTT has called for a national economic dialogue to find a solution to the current socioeconomic crisis that threatens the transition to democracy. On 17 October 2016, the UGTT denounced the budget bill and the financial act of 2017; it called upon its members to focus their efforts on fighting for their rights, which it perceived as being threatened by the fiscal measures. In 2017, the UGTT also supported the socioeconomic protests in Kébili, Kef, and Kairouan. During the Tataouine protests in the same year, it intervened in the final phase as a guarantor of government involvement. It should not be forgotten that the constitution of 26 April 1861, which was adopted in the wake of Tunisia's first process of political liberation, was suspended precisely because the government decided to raise taxes.

References

Al-Ali, Z., & Ben Romdhane, D. (2014, February 16). Tunisia's New Constitution: Progress and Challenges to Come. *openDemocracy*. Retrieved November 5, 2018, from https://www.opendemocracy.net/north-africa-west-asia/zaid-al-ali-donia-ben-romdhane/tunisia%E2%80%99s-new-constitution-progress-and-challenges-to-.

Allinson, J. (2015). Class Forces, Transition and the Arab Uprisings: A Comparison of Tunisia, Egypt and Syria. *Democratization, 22*(2), 294–314.

Amor, A. (1987). *Précis de droit constitutionnel*. Tunis: Centre d'études, de recherches et de publication, Faculté de droit et des sciences politiques de Tunis.

Amor, A., & Saied, K. (1987). *Documents et textes politiques tunisiens. Précis de droit constitutionnel*. Tunis: Centre d'études, de recherches et de publication, Faculté de droit et des sciences politiques de Tunis.

ATG (Association Tunisienne de Gouvernance). (2013, November). Public Governance in Tunisia. Principles, Status and Prospects. Retrieved November 5, 2018, from http://pomed.org/wp-content/uploads/2013/11/Public-Governance-in-Tunisia-English.pdf.

Beinin, J. (2015). *Workers and Thieves. Labor Movement and Popular Uprisings in Tunisia and Egypt*. Stanford, CA: Stanford University Press.

Ben Achour, Y. (2012, September 17). Religion, Revolution and Constitution: The Case of Tunisia. Lecture at the Center for Middle Eastern Studies, Harvard University. Retrieved November 5, 2018, from http://www.leaders.com.tn/uploads/FCK_files/file/Harvard%20%20Anglais%20derni%C3%A8re%20version.pdf.

Ben Achour, Y. (2014, September 7). Le compromis historique entre Etat civil et religion dans le néo-constitutionalisme arabe post révolutionnaire. Retrieved November 7, 2018, from http://yadhba.blogspot.de/2014/09/le-compromis-historique-entre-etat.html.

Ben Achour, R., & Ben Achour, S. (2012). La transition démocratique en Tunisie: entre légalité constitutionnelle et légitimité révolutionnaire. *Revue française de droit constitutionnel, 4*, 715–732.

Bessis, J. (1974). Le mouvement ouvrier tunisien: de ses origines à l'indépendance. *Le mouvement social, 89*, 85–108.

Bishara, D. (2014). Labor Movements in Tunisia and Egypt. *SWP Comments*, 1. Retrieved November 7, 2018, from https://www.swp-berlin.org/fileadmin/contents/products/comments/2014C01_bishara.pdf.

Chouikha, L., & Geisser, V. (2010). Retour sur la révolte du bassin minier. Les cinq leçons politiques d'un conflit social inédit. *L'année du Maghreb, 6*, 415–426.

Collier, R. B. (1999). *Paths Toward Democracy. The Working Class and Elites in Western Europe and South America*. Cambridge: Cambridge University Press.

Della Porta, D. (2014). *Mobilizing for Democracy. Comparing 1989 and 2011*. Oxford: Oxford University Press.

Dot-Pouillard, N. (2013). *Tunisie, la révolution et ses passes*. Paris: L'Harmattan.

Dubout, E., & Baccouche, N. (Eds.). (2015). *Nouvelle Constitution tunisienne et transition démocratique*. Paris: LexisNexis.

Elster, J. (1995). Forces and Mechanisms in the Constitution-Making Process. *Duke Law Journal, 45*, 364–396.

Ghai, Y. (2012). The Role of Constituent Assemblies in Constitution Making. *International IDEA*. Retrieved November 7, 2018, from http://www.constitutionnet.org/sites/default/files/2017-08/the_role_of_constituent_assemblies_-_final_yg_-_200606.pdf.

Ginsburg, T., Elkins, Z., & Blount, J. (2009). Does the Process of Constitution-Making Matter? *Annual Review of Law Science, 5*, 201–223.

Gluck, J., & Ballou, B. (2014, May). New Technologies in Making Constitution. *United States Institute of Peace. Special Report*, 343.

Gluck, J., & Brandt, M. (2015). *Participatory and Inclusive Constitution Making. Giving the Voice to the Demands of Citizens in the Wake of Arab Spring.* Washington: United States Institute of Peace.

Kausch, K. (2011, October). Constitutional Reform in Young Arab Democracies. *FRIDE*, 101. Retrieved November 7, 2018, from https://www.files.ethz.ch/isn/133631/PB_101_Young_Arab_Democracies.pdf.

M'rad, H. (2015). *The National Dialogue*. Tunis: Nirvana Edition.

Meyer-Resende, M., & Weichselbaum, G. (2014, January 29). The Tunisian Art of Compromise. *openDemocracy*. Retrieved November 5, 2018, from https://www.opendemocracy.net/north-africa-west-asia/michael-meyer-resende-geoffrey-weichselbaum/tunisian-arts-of-compromise.

Mokni, N. (2014). *Al-Islam wa-l-dustur. Dirasa qanuniyya wa-fiqhiyya muqarana li-ʿalaqa al-din bi-l-dawla fi mukhtalif al-anzima al-dusturiyya.* [Islam and the Constitution. A Comparative Study of Secular and Islamic Law on the Relation of Religion with the State in Different Constitutional Systems]. Tunis: Al-Atrash.

Netterstrøm, K. L. (2016). The Tunisian General Labor Union and the Advent of Democracy. *The Middle East Journal, 70*(3), 383–398.

Omri, M.-S. (2014, January 22). The UGTT Labor Union: Tunisia's Powerbroker. *TunisiaLive*.

Papagianni, K. (2013). *National Dialogue Processes in Political Transitions.* Civil Society Dialogue Network Discussion Paper No. 3. Brussels: European Peacebuilding Liaison Office (EPLO).

Roy, O. (2012). The Transformation of the Arab World. *Journal of Democracy, 23*(3), 5–18.

Sfax Faculty of Law. (2017). *Qira'at dustur al-jumhuriyya al-thaniya.* [Readings of the Constitution of the Second Republic]. Tunis: Al-Atrash.

Stepan, A., & Linz, J. J. (2013). Democratization Theory and the Arab Spring. *Journal of Democracy, 24*(2), 15–30.

Tushnet, M. (1986). Constitution-Making: An Introduction. *Texas Law Review, 91*, 1983–2013.

UGTT. (2011, October 19). Draft of the Tunisian Constitution. [Mashru' al-dustur al-tunsi].

Yousfi, H. (2015). *L'UGTT, une passion tunisienne. Enquête sur les syndicalistes en révolution 2011–2014.* Tunis: Med Ali Editions – Institut de recherche sur le Maghreb contemporain (IRMC).

Yousfi, H. (2018). *Trade Unions and Arab Revolutions. The Tunisian Case of UGTT.* London: Routledge.

Zoglin, K. (2013). Tunisia at a Crossroads: Drafting a New Constitution. *American Society of International Law,* 17(18). Retrieved November 7, 2018, from https://www.asil.org/insights/volume/17/issue/18/tunisia-crossroads-drafting-new-constitution.

CHAPTER 6

From the Dream of Change to the Nightmare of Structural Weakness: The Trajectory of Egypt's Independent Trade Union Movement After 2011

Nadine Abdalla

6.1 Introduction

The neoliberal economic policies that were adopted under President Hosni Mubarak by the Ahmed Nazif government (2004–2011) ushered in the largest wave of worker protests in Egypt's recent history (Beinin and El-Hamalawy 2007). While achieving some progress in terms of economic growth, these policies produced immediate social hardship for many and dramatically deepened socioeconomic inequality. As a consequence, in the years before the 2011 uprising the number of labor protests increased to unprecedented levels. Given that the Egyptian Trade Union Federation (ETUF) was fully co-opted by the state, this wave of worker protests

N. Abdalla (✉)
American University in Cairo (AUC), New Cairo City, Egypt

Arab Forum for Alternatives (AFA), Beirut, Lebanon

© The Author(s) 2020
I. Weipert-Fenner, J. Wolff (eds.), *Socioeconomic Protests in MENA and Latin America*, Middle East Today,
https://doi.org/10.1007/978-3-030-19621-9_6

occurred outside the country's official union structure. Signaling the emergence of an independent labor movement, four new trade unions had already been established before the 2011 revolution: The foundation of the real-estate tax collector union in 2008 was followed in 2010 by the establishment of independent trade unions for teachers, health technicians and retired people.

When the protests of 25 January 2011 initiated the critical phase of what would become the Egyptian revolution, many workers as well as the majority of independent labor leaders participated, but they did so on an individual basis, as normal citizens and not as members of particular organizations. Yet, in early February, while the general protests decreased and the masses began to leave Tahrir Square, it was workers who began to strike, refusing to work until their rights had been duly recognized. Their protests quickly spread across the country.[1] Participants came from several sectors, from different companies and factories as well as from both the private and the public sectors. Their demands focused on improving living conditions, increasing wages and salaries, and bonuses. These labor protests paralyzed the economy, along with the main state facilities, and thus created an atmosphere of large-scale civil disobedience that prepared the ground for the revolution (Abdalla 2012a, 2015a, 2017). As a result, despite the fact that the independent labor movement was still lacking an organizational structure, labor protests outside the official union structure did play a crucial role in the 2011 uprising (Bishara 2012; Beinin 2011).

The uprising and the successful ouster of Mubarak initially led to rapid growth and incipient institutionalization of the independent trade union movement. In the immediate aftermath of the 2011 revolution, farmers, private-sector workers, public transport drivers and employees established new trade unions outside the official ETUF structure (Abdalla 2012a, 2015a). Hundreds of independent unions organized themselves under the umbrella of several new trade union federations. Two of them stand out: the Egyptian Federation for Independent Trade Unions (EFITU), whose establishment was announced by its founder, Kamal Abu Eita, at a press conference on 30 January 2011 at Cairo's Tahrir Square, and which was officially launched on 2 March 2011; and the Egyptian Democratic Labor

---

[1] According to the "Al-Masry Al-Youm" newspaper, labor protests increased from only a few protests on 7 February in a number of governorates to 20 protests on 8 February in 9 governorates, 35 protests on 10 February in 14 governorates, and to 65 protests on 11 February, that is, on the day President Mubarak stepped down.

Congress (EDLC), which was founded in 2011 by the head of the Center for Trade Union and Workers Services (CTUWS), Kamal Abbas, but which was formally established as a trade union federation only on 24 April 2013.[2]

After 2011, labor protests in Egypt generally continued at levels that have remained higher than during the pre-uprising period. Despite this, the independent trade union movement has not been able to establish itself as an organizing force able to support and coordinate labor protests and use such labor mobilization to exert influence on political decision-making at the national level. In fact, the new labor movement has been increasingly marginalized politically ever since the brief boom period in 2011. This marginalization is exemplified by two failures. On the one hand, the independent trade union movement was not able to push the successive governments after 2011 into passing a law that would have legalized the new structure of labor organization outside ETUF. On the other hand, the movement was also not capable of influencing the general political debate on economic policies and reforms in a direction that would have addressed workers' demands and grievances.

Against this background, this chapter sets out to answer the following research question: Why was the independent trade union movement unable to establish itself as a significant player in the post-uprising context and make its demands heard in the political arena?

The next section presents an overview of the labor protests before and after 2011, and summarizes the growth and marginalization of the independent labor movement. The remaining two sections identify key causes that help explain the weakness of the movement: Section 3 discusses structural and institutional causes, namely the movement's socioeconomic base and its organizational structure; Section 4, by contrast, discusses the ideational dimension by focusing on the collective action frame. Empirically, the following analysis relies on 30 semi-structured interviews with labor leaders and labor activists which were conducted between October 2011 and June 2017. It also draws on participant observation of internal union and federation meetings and debates as well as labor-related events such as CTUWS meetings and the celebration of the anniversary of the inauguration of new trade union federations. Additional information is provided by an analysis of government statements and newspaper articles on the topic.

---

[2] CTUWS, an NGO founded in 1990, has played an important role in providing legal and technical support for independent labor protests.

The main argument put forward in this chapter is that workers' protests, even if they have remained surprisingly high even after the increase in repression since Morsi's ouster in July 2013, are scattered and largely take place at the local or factory level without being either coordinated or supported by the independent trade union federations. This is so because the rise of new forms of labor mobilization in Egypt has led to an institutionally fragmented, organizationally weak and only partially representative movement which, at the national level, lacks the capacity to mobilize workers and/or exert significant political influence. In addition, the new trade union movement's predominant collective action frame is characterized by narrow and issue-specific economic claims. This frame reflects and reinforces both the movement's internal structural weakness and its external lack of reliable sociopolitical allies.

6.2   Egypt, 2004–2017: A Cycle of Labor Contention

The wave of labor protests that could be observed in Egypt between 2004 and 2017 generally follows the dynamic of a cycle of contention (see Tarrow 1998). This cycle of labor contention started in 2004. After the 2011 uprising, the number of labor protests increased further and reached a peak in 2012 and 2013. In the context of the closing of the political space that followed the military intervention against President Morsi in July 2013, labor protests declined significantly in 2014 and 2015. Still, the number of worker protests remained higher than in the pre-uprising period. But these remaining protests were scattered around the country, primarily organized at the local and factory levels, without being centrally coordinated or institutionally supported by the new trade union federations. As will be shown in this section, the formation after 2011 of hundreds of new trade unions, which were organized in two main independent trade union federations (EFITU and EDLC), did not lead to the emergence of a labor movement with the capacity to coordinate labor protests and act collectively at the national level.

In Egypt as elsewhere, neoliberal economic reforms have been a key trigger of labor protests. An example includes the wave of worker protests between 1998 and 1999 (Pratt 2001, p. 120). The strongest and longest wave of labor protests, however, emerged in 2004 in reaction to the acceleration of neoliberal economic policies under the government of Ahmed Nazif. Labor protests increased by 200%, from 86 in 2003 to 266 in 2004

(Beinin 2011, p. 191). Given the fact that the average number of annual labor protests between 1998 and 2003 was 118, the 266 labor protests in the year 2004 mean that workers' protests even doubled the 1998–2003 average. Along this line it should be noted that 190 labor protests in 2004—which means over 70% of the workers' collective actions of this year—occurred after the Nazif government took office in July 2004 (Beinin 2011, p. 190). Furthermore, after the labor strike in December 2006 at the Misr Spinning and Weaving Company in al-Mahalla al-Kubra, a huge public-sector firm with about 24,000 workers, the number of labor protests jumped from 202 in 2005 and 222 in 2006 to 614 in 2007 and 609 in 2008 (Beinin 2011, p. 191). These protests were mainly characterized by three types of concrete economic claim: (1) demands for unpaid bonuses or allowances, or profits, (2) claims related to the right to work, which included the rejection of dismissals, or forced retirement, and (3) demands for less precarious employment, which includes the rejection of temporary jobs (Ramadan 2012).

This wave of labor protests involved not only traditionally militant blue-collar workers, but also employees and workers from the public sector, including ministries and government agencies. This reflected the socioeconomic consequences of the economic reforms mentioned earlier. While the GDP grew, real wages did not increase, and for many white-collar employees and blue-collar workers in the public sector they actually declined (El-Naggar 2009, p. 49). The share acquired by wage earners decreased from 48.5% of GDP in the late 1980 to 28.6% in 1995 and less than 20% in 2007 (El-Naggar 2009, p. 49). According to El-Naggar, around 2008–2009, 95% of the 5.8 million civil servants in Egypt and their families could be considered "poor" by the standards of the World Bank (living on less than $2 per day per person) since an employee who worked for 30 years only earned a salary of about 730 EGP (41 dollars) (El-Naggar 2007, p. 179; 2009, p. 49). As a consequence, it is understandable why the state's employees joined the protests that started in 2004. Furthermore, neoliberal policies also affected workers in the private sector as they led to an increase in temporary contracts. At the same time, irregular and informal work expanded, which is generally associated with lower wages and thus worse economic conditions. Given that the official trade union federation, ETUF, was fully under the control of the state, these labor protests mainly emerged at the grassroots level and outside the official trade union structure. As a consequence, they were mostly isolated, with no structural ties or linkages. Every labor protest focused on demands related to the specific sector or, even, company. Consequently, before 2011 the wave of labor mobilization did not lead to the formation of an overarching social movement that would have connected the individual protest movements. Therefore, when the number of independent trade unions exploded after the 2001 uprising, the new labor movement could not rely on any organizational linkages (Abdalla 2012b, p. 3).

In the aftermath of the 2011 uprising, labor mobilization benefited from the temporary liberalization of the political system. In the revolutionary context, the number of labor protests increased dramatically from 530 protests in 2010 to 1400 in 2011 (ECESR 2015). The increase in strike activity in 2011 was also significant. In February 2011 alone, more episodes of strike action took place than during the entire previous year. Starting in September 2011, massive teachers' strike and other strikes brought an estimated 500,000 people out for a variety of social demands, including pay increases, the improvement of labor conditions, permanent contracts and the purge of former ruling party officials from public-sector institutions (Alexandar and Bassiouny 2017, p. 32). In 2012, labor protests further increased and reached a peak in the first half of 2013. More specifically, labor protests jumped from 1969 in 2012 to 2239 in 2013 (ECESR 2015). Even taking into account the historically high level of strike activity in the years before the 2011 uprising, the total number of strikes in 2012 surpassed the total number of strikes that had taken place over the previous ten years (Alexandar and Bassiouny 2017, p. 32). This increase responded to the neoliberal agenda, which was basically continued by the government of the Freedom and Justice (FJP), the political wing of the Muslim Brotherhood, between 2012 and 2013. This continuity was manifested by the negotiations that President Morsi pursued with the IMF in late August 2012, in return for a $4.8 billion IMF loan (Abdel Ghane 2012).

After the ouster of Morsi, the al-Sisi government decided to cut state subsidies and abandoned most currency controls. In July 2014, the government decided to reduce subsidies on fuel—a decision welcomed by the IMF.[3] In November 2016 the al-Sisi government started an IMF-backed reform effort that included a new round of subsidy cuts, which led to yet

---

[3] It is worth mentioning that the fuel subsidy has accounted for about 20% of total government expenditure since 2008, and has thus contributed to the increase of the state budgets deficit, which has reached 12–13% of GDP according to estimates by the current finance minister (see Adly 2014).

another increase in the prices of fuel and electricity as well as to an acceleration of Egypt's inflation rate.[4] Obviously, this has led to a further deterioration in the socioeconomic situation of the workers.[5] Still, because of the closure of the political space that followed the military intervention of July 2013, the number of labor protests has decreased since then: from 2239 in 2013 to 1655 in 2014 (ECESR 2015), 934 in 2015 (ECESR 2016a) and 726 in 2016 (ECESR 2016b). However, even with this significant reduction the number of labor protests remained higher than it was in the pre-uprising period, and large waves of strikes were also witnessed during this time. In February 2014, for instance, a series of strikes included workers from both the private and the public sectors, affecting textile companies, the postal service, the health sector, and the Ministry of Justice (Alexandar and Bassiouny 2017, p. 36).

These protests and strikes, however, remained fragmented and concentrated at the local level of specific workplaces. They occurred not only outside the state-corporatist structure of the official trade union federation ETUF, but also independent of the fragile structures of the newly established trade union federations EFITU and EDLC. A significant proportion of these individual protests were organized by independent trade unions affiliated to these new federations. However, these local collective actions did not receive the support of the central leadership or the cooperation of the executive boards of either EFITU or EDLC.[6] Due to their structural weaknesses, both federations, while expressing their full solidarity with these local protests, remained unable to centrally coordinate them and/or relatively incapable of providing the necessary legal and technical help for those among their affiliated union members who decided to go on strike. This was especially obvious in the governorates, where independent trade unions felt mostly disconnected and marginalized from the federations because of the weakness of their coordination mechanisms between the center and the periphery.[7]

---

[4] According to the state-run CAPMAS statistics agency, annual consumer prices in urban areas climbed 33%, up from 29.8% in June (see El Tanlawy and Feteha 2017).

[5] In order to bolster its fiscal position in late August 2016 the government also introduced value-added tax (13%), which has significantly increased the burden on consumers, workers included.

[6] These cases include protests by the local trade unions of real-estate tax collectors and teachers (both affiliated to EFITU) as well as of the local trade unions of the public transport workers, the post office workers and Telecom Egypt employees (all affiliated to EDLC). Interview with Mohamed Mostafa, ILO officer in Egypt, January 2016, Cairo.

[7] Ibid.

In sum, in the post-uprising context, labor protests became increasingly fragmented, and the independent trade union movement proved unable to coordinate, strengthen and capitalize on the (temporary) rise in labor mobilization. The following sections will identify both structural and ideational causes that help explain this weakness.

6.3 Structural and Institutional Features of the Independent Labor Movement's Weakness

Initially, the movement of independent trade unions made use of the space opened up by the 2011 uprising. As seen, early 2011 was marked by an impressive rise in the number of new trade unions outside the state-controlled federation. These new unions then quickly united under the roof of national trade union federations such as, most notably, EFITU and EDLC. Still, as will be seen in this section, the specific features of the independent labor movement's socioeconomic base as well as its internal organizational structures severely limited its capacity for collective contentious action.

6.3.1 The Independent Trade Union Movement's Socioeconomic Base

A high level of unionization and a strong presence of trade unions in key economic sectors have been identified as crucial variables that determine the political strength of organized labor during times of political transition (Valenzuela 1989).[8] However, in the case of Egypt, strong independent trade unions emerged mostly among civil servants and public service-sector workers, whereas Egypt's new labor movement remained weak among industrial workers (whether public or private) as well as, in general, in the private sector (Abdalla 2015a, 2017).

In Egypt, strongly representative independent trade unions exist among civil servants such as in the cases of the real-estate tax collectors (whose new unions are affiliated to EFITU) and the sales tax collectors (whose new union is affiliated to EDLC). In the public service sector, examples of strong new trade unions include post office workers (whose unions are affiliated to EDLC) as well as public transport workers and Egypt Telecom

---

[8] A case in point is Brazil's New Unionist movement that emerged in the 1970s and played a key role in the country's transition to democracy in the 1980s (see Abdalla and Wolff 2016).

employees (whose unions were affiliated to EFITU and joined EDLC in 2012 and 2016, respectively). These relatively representative independent trade unions emerged from the protests organized during the Mubarak era. Through these previous experiences of collective action, strong bonds were formed among the workers (Abdalla 2012b, 2017). A good example is the sit-in by the real-estate tax collectors in Hijazi Street in front of the Council of Ministers in December 2007, which lasted for ten days and involved 10,000 employees. During this sit-in, strong social ties and networks of solidarity were built among the participants. Even before the 2001 uprising, labor leader Kamal Abu Eita used this social capital to establish an independent trade union.[9] Another example concerns the strikes organized by employees of the Telecom Company and public transport drivers during the 2011 uprising, particularly in February 2011.[10] It was such collective experiences of mass mobilization that enabled the formation of representative, independent trade unions that were able to persist even in the context of the closing of political space following the ouster of Morsi in 2013. The majority of the independent unions, however, was established in the midst of the political opening that followed the 2011 uprising, and could not rely on such prior organizational and social structures.

This selective capacity to exert pressure was proven in January 2016, when civil servants managed to lobby and push parliament to reject the draft Civil Service Law No. 18 of 2015 (which was meant to replace the Civil Service Law No. 47 of 1976). This new law, in particular, aimed at significantly decreasing the salaries of state employees by reducing the rate of the annual increase in the civil servants' salaries. To prevent the parliament's approval of this law, a coalition named "Solidarity" (*tadamun*) was formed that united those independent trade unions whose members would be affected by the cuts. Despite the repressive context, the coalition succeeded in organizing several protests against the draft law. While this alliance was weakened by disagreements and splits, the new trade unions of the real-estate tax and the sales tax collectors succeeded, separately, in pushing the parliament's deputies toward rejecting the law.[11] For instance,

[9] Interview with Tarek Koaib, one of the leaders of the real-estate tax collector mobilization in 2007 and the current president of the Real-Estate Tax Collector New Trade Union, January 2016, Cairo.
[10] These strikes, by triggering a wave of strikes in other sectors, contributed to pushing the SCAF to oblige Mubarak to step down.
[11] Interview with Tarek Koaib, one of the leaders of the real-estate tax collector mobilization in 2007 and the current president of the Real-Estate Tax Collector New Trade Union, January 2016, Cairo.

through its 27 trade union committees (distributed across all 27 governorates of Egypt), the real-estate tax collectors exerted tremendous pressure on the respective parliamentary deputy in each governorate.[12]

In contrast to these exceptional cases from the public service sector, blue-collar workers in the public industrial sector mostly continued to remain organized under the ETUF umbrella. This is not only due to the historical linkages between this sector and the state but also reflects the material benefits that are associated with membership in the official union structure. ETUF, for instance, still holds a monopoly on the social funds that provide social security services to its affiliated unions. Contributions to these funds are part of the workers' membership fees for ETUF, which are usually deducted automatically from their salaries (Beinin 2012, p. 13). In addition, ETUF owns assets such as hospitals and clubs, and offers programs such as beach holidays to its members. These are important incentives which prevent workers from leaving ETUF despite its lack of responsiveness to workers' demands (Abdalla 2017, p. 18).[13]

The private sector employs 17.5 million workers and thus almost three-quarters of the 23.9 million workers in Egypt (CAPMAS 2013, cited in Abdel Moati 2015).[14] With the intensification of privatization since 2004, the private sector has come to play an increasingly important role in the Egyptian economy. Yet, it is characterized by a weak presence of independent trade unions. Exceptions include new unions that are affiliated to EDLC, namely in the textile sector in Sadat City and in the petroleum industry sector in the Suez Canal cities (Abdalla 2017, p. 19). The weak presence of new trade unions among workers in the private sector can be explained in various ways:

First, the weakness of the rule of law increases the costs of labor activism. In contrast to the public sector, 44.2% of the workers in the private sector have no legal contract and only 25% have health security (CAPMAS 2014, cited in Abdalla 2017). Moreover, according to a report by CTUWS, newly hired workers in the private sector are often obliged to sign an undated document in which they submit their resignation, giving the employer the liberty to fire them at any given moment. The same report

---

[12] Ibid.

[13] While these funds go mostly to the industrial workers, some civil servants also benefit from them.

[14] In Egypt, workers number 23.9 million according to the CAPMAS (see Abdel Moati 2015).

noted that many workers were in fact dismissed after engaging in contentious actions (CTUWS n.d.; see also Abdalla 2012b, p. 5; 2017, p. 18). This situation is reflected in the low level of mobilization in the private sector, when compared to the public and governmental sectors: In 2014, protests in the private sector represented 15.4% of all labor protests, whereas protests by civil servants and public-sector workers accounted for 63% and 21.3%, respectively (ECESR 2016a). Generally, the inability of the new trade union movement to defend those who lose their job because of their activism has reduced the movement's legitimacy among private-sector workers.

Second, the structure of the private sector, the legal framework and the way private companies are geographically spread hinder the capacity to organize among private-sector workers. Egypt's private sector is dominated by small and medium-sized companies. Very small firms with 1–4 employees account for the largest share of employment in the private sector, while only 4% of employment in the private sector in 2012 was with firms having 50–99 employees. As a consequence, wage work in the private sector is predominantly irregular and informal, and the share of irregular employment increased significantly after the economic reforms of 2004 (Assaad and Krafft 2013, pp. 9–10, cited in Abdalla 2017, p. 18). Furthermore, Labor Law No. 12 of 2003 encouraged employers to hire workers on temporary contracts. Moreover, the rapid turnover of temporary and irregular workers makes it more difficult for the latter to build strong relationships and connections, and therefore undermines collective action and organization.[15] Furthermore, the geographic distribution of private-sector factories makes it harder for workers to organize. In the large public-sector factories, workers often live in residences that are linked to the company and, as a result, remain strongly connected through social and familial ties.[16] By contrast, in industrial cities that are characterized by a high concentration of private-sector workers (such as the cities of 10th of Ramadan (*al-ʿAshir min Ramadan*) or 6th of October (*al-Sadis min October*)), workers often live in cities near to the city where they work.[17] An exception is the industrial city of Sadat City (*Madinat al-Sadat*) where

---

[15] Interview with Mohamed Mostafa, ILO officer in Egypt, June 2017, Cairo.
[16] This is the case, for instance, of the Egyptian Company for Spinning and Weaving in Mahalla al-Kubra, or the Iron and Steel Company Helwan.
[17] Workers of the 10th of Ramadan City live, for instance, in the cities of Belbeis and Ismailia.

private workers both live and work. Hence, it is not surprising that this city has witnessed the formation of the independent Sadat Union for Textile Workers that is part of EDLC, and contrasts with other private-sector-dominated industrial cities where new trade unions remain rare.[18]

Hence, it can be concluded that structural features of Egypt's political economy have imposed severe burdens on the independent trade union movement. When newly established trade unions had to respond to the rapid political changes after 2011, only those organizations that could rely on prior collective experiences were able to seize the opportunity of the brief political opening to build and strengthen their organizational structures. And it was only these individual organizations that were able to retain a certain capacity for collective contentious action that enabled them to defend their interests even after the closing of the public sphere under the al-Sisi regime. Still, even these instances of mobilization—such as in the case of the Civil Service Law—have been mainly defensive rather than proactive in pushing for more structural changes.

6.3.2 The Independent Trade Union Movement's Internal Organization

Building new trade unions was a complicated process for labor leaders that could not rely on any trade unionist experience outside the official structure. Administering and collecting regular membership fees was thus an obvious challenge. In addition, new trade unions lacked official recognition and legitimacy because of the state of legal limbo with regard to the freedom of association, which persisted after 2011. These problems are directly reflected in the situation of EFITU and EDLC, the main new labor federations that organized the independent trade unions. Both federations have generally suffered from two major structural deficiencies. First, the inability to establish effective mechanisms of horizontal coordination between the center (mainly in Cairo) and the periphery (mainly in the other governorates to the north and south of Cairo) has resulted in the marginalization of the latter. Thus, new trade unions in the governorates felt that their demands were not being considered by the federation's central leadership. This feeling was reinforced by the inability of the federations to provide the necessary (financial, legal, organizational or moral) support to these unions' members in times of strike, fire or arrest. Second,

---

[18] Interview with Mohamed Mostafa, ILO officer in Egypt, June 2017, Cairo.

the inability to establish effective mechanisms of vertical communication between the leaders at the federation level and rank-and-file members of trade unions within the federation has generated weak institutions and a perception of insufficient internal democracy. As this section will show, the organizational weakness, the lack of financial resources and the democratic deficit that has characterized both EFITU and EDLC have generally reduced their capacity to act effectively in the post-revolutionary period.

In terms of organizational weakness, the need to respond swiftly to the political changes initiated by the 2011 uprising posed difficult questions for the incipient movement of independent trade unions. Driven by labor leader Kamal Abu Eita,[19] EFITU decided to increase its political leverage by integrating as many of the newly founded trade unions as possible. However, most of the new unions which were incorporated into the federation were rather shallow organizations that represented only a small proportion of the workers in their respective sectors.[20] Moreover, EFITU's top-down approach created a lag between its institutional capacity for coordination and the rapidly increasing number of unions that had to be integrated within the new structure. Given EFITU's limited staff and resources, neither the federation nor its affiliated unions were able to build the necessary administrative capacities. This contributed to differences among EFITU's member organizations (Abdalla 2012b, 2017).[21]

While EDLC has similarly suffered from weak organizational and structural capacities, it proved better able than EFITU to survive in the context of the political closure after 2014. This can be traced back to the more bottom-up approach pursued by Kamal Abbas, the founder of EDLC and former president of the NGO CTUWS.[22] In the course of 2011, CTUWS broke with EFITU and established the EDLC. Yet, it was not until April

---

[19] Abu Eita was the founder of the independent union of the real-estate tax collectors, leader of the nationalist "Karama" party and member of the post-revolutionary parliament until it was dissolved in June 2012.

[20] Interview with Noha Roshdi, leader of the real-estate tax collector union and member of EFITU's executive board, January 2016, Cairo.

[21] In September 2013, one (of the 25 members) of EFITU's executive board left the organization to build a separate trade union federation: The General Federation for Egyptian Trade Unions (*al-iitihad al-'am li-l- niqabat al-misriyya*). By the end of 2015, several member organizations had left EFITU and joined EDLC, including the new trade union of Egyptian Telecom (*niqaba al-misriyya li-l-ittisalat*) and the Prosecutors and courts' new trade union (*niqabat al-niyabat wa-l-mahakim*).

[22] Before becoming president of CTUWS, Kamal Abas was a labor leader at the Helwan Iron and Steel factory.

2013 that EDLC was officially launched as a national trade union federation. Before integrating the individual unions into a national federation, CTUWS had worked on enhancing union capacities at the grassroots level and on coordinating joint activities of different unions (Abdalla 2017, p. 16). To enhance coordination between the center and the periphery inside the new national federations, Abbas adopted the idea of what he called "Regional Conferences" or "Regional New Trade Unions Federations" which were established in the center, north, south, east and west of Egypt. These new regional bodies were later merged into the national structure of the EDLC.[23] This approach of strengthening local unions and regional federations first has improved the capacity of EDLC to sustain itself despite internal differences and external pressure. Yet, it has not protected the organization from ongoing instability.

In this context, the lack of sustainable funding further undermined the capacity of the new labor federations. In general, EFITU and EDLC were not able to raise the funds necessary for covering basic costs.[24] This lack of financial resources limited the federations' capacity to defend their affiliated local unions in times of crisis and, as a consequence, local unions lost interest in financially supporting their national federations.[25] The direct financial support by a wide range of foreign institutions that became available after the 2011 uprising[26] offered immediate help, but ultimately hindered sustainable development of the independent trade unions because external funding weakened the main source of cohesion enjoyed by unions: the networks of solidarity among the workers. For example, the capacity-building workshops offered by foreign institutions to labor leaders contributed to the deepening of the splits between the leadership and the rank and file, and produced internal competition for travel and training oppor-

[23] Interview with Mohamed Mostafa, ILO officer in Egypt, June 2017, Cairo.
[24] Example of basic costs are the salaries of their administrative employees, the rents of their offices, costs for flyers and so on.
[25] Interview with Noha Roshdi, leader in the real-estate tax collector union and member of EFITU's executive board, January 2016, Cairo.
[26] Interview with Mohamed Mostafa, ILO officer in Egypt, January 2016, Cairo. These foreign institutions include international organizations (such as the International Labor Organization (ILO), the International Trade Union Confederation (ITUC), the International Transport Workers' Federation (ITF), Public Services International (PSI), and the Industrial Global Union (IGU)) as well as organizations affiliated to certain European countries (such as the Danish Development Assistance Programs (DANIDA), the Confederation of Professionals in Denmark (FTF) and the German Political Foundation Friedrich Ebert (FES)).

tunities (Abdalla 2017, p. 17). In general, rather than helping them to become autonomous actors, reliance on foreign support[27] made the newly established trade union federations dependent.

A lack of internal democracy further contributed to reducing the legitimacy of the national federations in their role as key representatives of the independent trade union movement at the national level. In contrast to the hierarchical official trade union structure, the independent labor federations provided wider powers to their general assemblies.[28] However, the weak mechanisms of vertical and horizontal coordination, on the one hand, and the limited financial resources, on the other, reduced the federations' capacity to act democratically in a way that would prevent the escalation of internal conflicts. Over time, this diminished the legitimacy of the national leadership of the federations in the eyes of their grass-roots members.

EFITU held its first internal elections on 28 January 2012, that is, only one month after officially being founded. This tight time frame favored those labor leaders who were best known to the members due to their extensive presence in the federation headquarters as well as because of their efforts to facilitate the paperwork and logistics for new unions that were seeking to join EFITU. These leaders were, however, not necessarily the most experienced or the most effective leaders. The resulting lack of experience and effectiveness of EFITU's executive board weakened the federation's legitimacy and quickly produced internal power struggles. These internal conflicts led to changes in EFITU's national leadership. Because these reshuffles were not the result of democratic electoral processes, they further reduced the internal legitimacy of the federation and generated a state of continuous instability (Abdalla 2017, pp. 16–17). This was especially the case when Abu Eita, whose charisma had contained internal crisis, left EFITU to assume the position of Minister of Labor in July 2013.

In EDLC, by contrast, the affiliated unions had much more time to get to know each other and even cooperate, before the official launching of the national federation. Still, this did not prevent power struggles—in particular, the presidency was seriously contested between competing factions (Abdalla 2017, p. 17). By contrast with EFITU, whose founder and president was the charismatic Abu Eita, who also had a strong social base among

---

[27] Or on support by local NGOs which were, for their part, funded by foreign institutions.

[28] Interview with Fatma Ramada, leader of the new trade union of the employees of the Ministry of Labor in Giza and ex-member of EFITU's executive board, Cairo, June 2017.

the workers, the founder of EDLC, Abbas, did not become its president. Given the relative structural weakness of the organization, this opened the door for struggles over the federation's presidency, in particular between the supporters of CTUWS and those who preferred to distance themselves from it. In February 2014, the general assembly supported by CTUWS took the decision to dismiss the elected EDLC president Yusri Ma'arouf and call for new elections. These elections—which occurred in a polarized context—were won by Saad Shaaban, the head of the group of new trade unions of private textile workers in Sadat City (Shonouda 2014).

In the context of the closing political space after 2014 and given the lack of funds, both federations have recently postponed or even canceled meetings of either their executive boards or their general assemblies.[29] Consequently, in recent years, decisions have mainly been taken in Cairo by the highest level of the federations. This has deepened the problem of both marginalization of other governorates and exclusion of the lower levels of the federation from the decision-making process, thus reinforcing the crisis of internal legitimacy.[30]

In summary, these organizational challenges help explain why the new trade union federations that emerged in the context of political opening after the 2011 uprising remained institutionally weak and fragmented, never developed significant capacity to act collectively at the national level, and were barely able to survive when the political space started to close again in mid-2013.

6.4 The Collective Action Frame of the Independent Labor Movement

Usually, the linkage between trade unions and political parties provides the former with the opportunity to have a channel for advancing their claims and ensuring access to the political arena. A key element that enables such linkages is a collective action frame that goes beyond narrow labor-specific claims and enables a dynamic of frame bridging[31] between

---

[29] The financial resources needed to organize these meetings include, for example, costs for large meeting rooms as well as for the travel of local trade union leaders coming from different governorates.

[30] Interview with Fatma Ramada, leader of the new trade union of the employees of the Ministry of Labor in Giza and ex-member of EFITU's executive board, Cairo, June 2017.

[31] Frame bridging is the "linkage of two or more ideologically congruent but structurally unconnected frames regarding a particular issue or problem" (Snow et al. 1986, p. 467).

the labor movement and its sociopolitical allies. However, as this section will argue, the adoption of a broader collective action frame by the independent trade union movement's leaders in the immediate context of the 2011 uprising remained a temporary phenomenon. The dynamic of frame bridging between the new trade unions and political organizations was thus short-lived. With the closing of the political space that followed the ouster of Morsi in 2013, most independent trade unions returned to a narrow collective action frame that was similar to the one being applied before the 2011 uprising.

The wave of labor protests that responded to the policies of economic liberalization under the Mubarak regime was characterized by a collective action frame that deliberately refused to challenge the political regime. On the one hand, labor protests at that time did not challenge the regime's legitimacy, rejected any politicization and, as previously mentioned, framed their claims in strictly economic terms. These claims mostly included tangible demands such as bonuses, allowances or wage increases. On the other hand, labor protests also refused to question the state-corporatist, patron-client relationship with the state. Thus, the existing structure of labor representation and the official trade union federation were not called into question. The only exception was the (successful) attempt by the real-estate tax collector movement to establish an independent trade union (Abdalla 2012a, b, 2017). This overall refusal to challenge the state arguably reflected both a fear of repression and the deep-seated, Nasserist belief among public and governmental workers in their partnership with the state.

In the aftermath of the Egyptian uprising, the labor leaders, who had carefully steered clear of politics during the Mubarak regime, found themselves thrust into the political arena, as the new trade union movement was obliged to take a stance with regard to the new authorities and the various political forces. In the years since 2011, the new trade union movement has chosen under specific circumstances to ally itself with political organizations—but only when communication and negotiation with the state have broken down entirely and/or when such alliances have been temporarily seen as mutually beneficial (Abdalla 2015a, b, 2017). As a result, the independent trade unions have sometimes chosen to broaden their agenda to include politico-institutional claims for labor to have the freedom to organize and a new, democratic structure of state-labor relations. While the new trade union leaders mostly focused on bread-and-butter demands in response to their rank and file, the demand for a new trade union law that would legalize independent unions as well as for a general minimum wage increasingly became parts of a broader collective action frame that united the new trade union movement.

These demands related to freedom of association and social justice, which flourished after the 2011 uprising, made it possible to bridge claims in concert with other oppositional organizations. In this sense, for example, the reluctance of the Morsi government's Minister of Labor, Khaled al-Azhari, to promulgate a new trade union law encouraged EDLC and EFITU to ally themselves with the National Salvation Front (NSF), an alliance of the non-Islamist parties, in order to ensure the latter's support for Ahmed El-Borei's draft law in the next parliament (which was, however, only elected after the ouster of Muhammad Morsi) (Abdalla 2015a, b, 2017). During the al-Sisi regime, the deadlock in negotiations with the state incited the new trade unions to establish a "Workers' Bloc" (*al-kutla al-'ummaliyya*) in July 2014. This bloc was coordinated by CTUWS with a membership of around 120 new trade unions, including members of both EFITU and EDLC. The new trade union leaders who are members of this bloc were supposed to support the electoral list of "Egypt Awakening" (*Sahwat Misr*) during the parliamentary elections of 2015. This electoral list was formed by a coalition of independent candidates as well as leftist political parties that supported the demands of the new trade unions. However, due to logistical complications, *Sahwat Misr* withdrew from the elections at the last minute (Abdalla 2015b, 2017).

However, despite the temporary political opening in the aftermath of the 2011 uprising and these moments of coalition building and frame bridging after 2011, the skepticism about becoming explicitly engaged politically remained the norm for labor leaders. This was particularly the case at the local level. Workers generally continued to mistrust political parties because of their potential for dividing them according to competing ideological approaches. In addition, the weakness of leftist parties meant that workers and unions could hardly benefit from such alliances.[32] As a consequence, the independent trade unions' collective action frame largely remained characterized by labor-specific demands and stopped short of openly challenging the political authorities. Hence, issue-specific

---

[32] For instance, in the 2011 and 2012 elections the leftist coalition "Revolution Continues" won only 8 of 508 parliamentary seats. The two remaining leftist parties that were not part of this coalition, Tagammu Party and the Egyptian Social Democratic Party, won 3 and 16 seats, respectively.

claims topped the list of workers' demands, while the new set of broader demands such as the claim to freely organize represented only a small share of worker claims. In 2014, for instance, material claims (e.g., for incentives or allowances) represented 49% of all demands made in workers' protests, whereas the improvement of working conditions represented another 16.9%, the improvement of contractual work relations 9.4%, and protests against arbitrary dismissal as well as arbitrary displacement to another geographical work site 9.4% and 5.7% of demands, respectively. By contrast, protests against corruption and bad management as well as the claim to freely organize represented only 4.5% and 1.5% of the claims made in labor protests in the same year (ECESR 2015).

Given the fragmentation of the new trade union movement at the national level, the unfavorable balance of power (in particular after the military intervention of July 2013), as well as the weakness of the political parties, the new local trade unions refused to openly break with the state. Thus, in the context of specific labor protests they have largely continued to frame their demands in ways that would not challenge the authorities. Examples include the unions of the real-estate tax collectors and of the sales tax collectors that both fought against a new civil servant law but refused to link up with any political force.[33] In order to prevent parliamentary approval of this law, these two unions organized protests against it and tried to exert pressure on members of parliament as previously mentioned, but they did so in far from confrontational ways. Rather, the leaders of these trade unions framed the employees' claims in a way that stressed their partnership with the state, and emphasized their refusal to challenge the latter. Thus, the banners which were held aloft during protests requested President al-Sisi to satisfy their claims and amend the law.

Such a narrow collective action frame focused on rather specific demands also reflected the thinking of important labor leaders and their relation to politics, as well as the relative lack of cohesion among different levels of trade unions within the labor federations. While the top level of the new trade union federations included politicized leaders such as Kamal Abu Eita in the case of EFITU, most local trade union leaders can instead be generally described as "service leaders" or "natural leaders": Their status as leaders is directly linked to their capacity to serve the short-term economic demands of the local rank and file. Contrary to the 1970s and 1980s, during which

---

[33] Interview with Noha Roshdi, leader at the real-estate tax collector new trade union, January 2016, Cairo.

politicized, leftist or Nasserite leaders led the labor movement, the new generation of leaders at the level of the local federations is largely depoliticized. These local labor leaders, therefore, hardly support the national federations' push for a more substantial change in state-labor relations, but are much more interested in achieving some tangible results for their social bases. In this context, the horizontal and vertical mechanisms of coordination within the new trade union federations have been too weak to generate consensus around a broader collective action frame.[34]

In sum, the broadening of the collective action frame and corresponding dynamics of frame bridging occurred only temporarily and sporadically in the post-revolutionary context. Particularly at the local level, independent trade unions have been characterized by a rather narrow framing of workers' demands. This narrow collective action frame adopted in an increasingly repressive political context both reflects and further reinforces the failure of the independent labor movement to establish reliable internal structures of coordination and representation as well as to build fruitful alliances with other sociopolitical forces. The latter have also remained weak, and thus unable to channel the movement's claims efficiently.

6.5 Conclusion

Although the 2011 uprising opened up an opportunity for the independent trade union movement to spread, institutionalize and struggle to assert its socioeconomic and organizational demands, the national federations that emerged out of this context were not able to seize this opportunity. Despite the role it had played during the revolution and the brief boom that was triggered by the political opening after the downfall of Mubarak, Egypt's new labor movement in the end was unable to develop a significant capacity to act collectively and become a relevant player at the national level. This chapter has identified three main reasons that account for this result:

First, the structural basis of the new labor movement severely limited its ability to exert organized pressure on the authorities that have ruled the country since 2011. While the number of workers' protests remained relatively high—by historical standards—even after the increase of repression since Morsi's ouster in 2013, they are scattered, mainly organized at the local and shop floor level, and mostly lack any central coordination or support from the new trade union federations.

---

[34] Fieldwork observation.

The second cause relates to institutional characteristics of the Egyptian new trade union movement. The national federations' inability to respond to the financial and organizational challenges it has faced during the post-revolutionary period has weakened their internal coherence and consequently hindered their capacity to exert a significant influence on the authorities. The analysis suggests that the change in political opportunities after 2011 overwhelmed the incipient independent trade union movement, because it had to respond collectively to the dramatic political changes while lacking any organizational structure and simultaneously experiencing a rapid emergence of new unions. The rapid explosion in the number of new trade unions after 2011 was not followed by a similar explosion in terms of quality. The consequence was deficits in internal coordination (both vertical and horizontal) as well as in internal democracy that undermined the legitimacy of the national leadership and reinforced splits between the central and the subnational levels of the federations. The result was an institutionally fragmented, organizationally weak and only partially representative movement that proved unable to resist the continuity, and even deepening, of repressive, state-corporatist state-labor relations.

Third, in the context of an increasingly repressive political context, the independent labor movement quickly returned to a rather narrow collective action frame. As a result, the dynamic of frame broadening and bridging which was temporarily favored by the political opening that followed the 2011 uprising did not last long. This narrow frame both reflected and consolidated the failure of the movement to establish reliable internal structures of coordination and representation as well as the weakness of its potential sociopolitical allies with whom it did not establish reliable ties.

In the light of this generally pessimistic analysis, it should be noted that despite all the shortcomings that have been identified in this chapter, Egypt's independent trade union movement is not doomed to disappear any time soon. On the one hand, in the context of the intensification of austerity measures and neoliberal structural adjustment, the socioeconomic grievances of the workers will certainly persist, if not increase. On the other, given the continuing co-optation of ETUF and the overall closure of the political system, workers lack any institutional channels for articulating these grievances. Therefore, it is unlikely that workers' protests will disappear, and independent labor organizations will probably remain crucial—if weak and informal—structures of labor representation, organization and coordination. At least, the door remains open for the emergence of new labor leaders who might benefit from considering organizational experiences and build upon both the positive and the negative lessons of the recent past.

References

Abdalla, N. (2012a). Social Protests in Egypt Before and After the 25 January Revolution: Perspectives on the Evolution of Their Forms and Features. *Mediterranean Yearbook Barcelona* (IEMed) (pp. 86–92). Retrieved November 27, 2018, from http://www.iemed.org/observatori-en/arees-danalisi/arxius-adjunts/anuari/med.2012/abdalla_en.pdf.

Abdalla, N. (2012b). Egypt's Workers – From Protest Movement to Organized Labor. *German Institute for International and Security Affairs.* Retrieved November 27, 2018, from http://www.swp-berlin.org/fileadmin/contents/products/comments/2012C32_abn.pdf.

Abdalla, N. (2015a). The Neoliberal Policies and the Egyptian Trade Union Movement: Politics of Containment and Limits of Resistance. In E. Akcali (Ed.), *The Limits of Neoliberal Governmentality in the Middle East and North Africa* (pp. 123–141). London: Palgrave Macmillan.

Abdalla, N. (2015b). The Labor and Politics in Egypt. *Middle East Insights*, 127. Singapore: Middle East Institute (MEI). Retrieved November 27, 2018, from https://mei.nus.edu.sg/publication/insight-127-labor-and-politics-in-egypt/.

Abdalla, N. (2017). *The Egyptian trade union movement in light of the 2011 uprising: Co-optation, containment, and limits of resistance. Research Report.* The Essam Fares Institute for Public Policy and International Affairs and Al-Asfari Institute for Civil Society and Citizenship, The American University of Beirut (AUB). Retrieved November 27, 2018, from https://www.aub.edu.lb/ifi/publications/Documents/research_reports/20170410_trade_union.pdf.

Abdalla, N., & Wolff, J. (2016). *From Driver of Change to Marginalized Actor: Egypt's New Unionism from a Comparative Perspective.* PRIF Working Paper 31. Retrieved November 27, 2018, from http://bit.ly/2d3O7qj.

Abdel Ghane, S. (2012). Morsi Discusses with the IMF the Conditions of the Loan of 4.8 Billion Dollars (Morsi yabhas ma' sanduq al-naqd al-dawli shurut iqtirad 4.8 billion dollars). *Al-Ahram Al-Masa'i.* Retrieved April 28, 2015, from http://digital.ahram.org.eg/articles.aspx?Serial=1000979&eid=1349.

Abdel Moati, A. (2015). The Egypian Labor Movement […]What's Next? (al-haraka al-'ummaliyya....ma al-'amal?). *Democratic Society.* Retrieved January 23, 2018, from https://dem-society.com/2015/10/22/الحركة-العمالية-المصرية-ما-العمل؟/.

Adly, A. (2014). Structural Crises That Have Become Urgent *(al-azamat al-haykaliyya allati asbahat muliha). Mada Masr.* Retrieved April 28, 2015, from http://www.madamasr.com.

Alexandar, A., & Bassiouny, N. (2017). *Bread, Freedom, Social Justice, Workers and the Egyptian Revolution*. London: ZED Books Ltd.

Assaad, R., & Krafft, C. (2013). *The Structure and Evolution of Employment in Egypt (1998:2012)*. Working Paper 805. Economic Research Forum (ERF). Retrieved November 27, 2018, from http://erf.org.eg/publications/structure-evolution-employment-egypt-1998-2012/.

Beinin, J. (2011). Workers and Egypt's January 25 Revolution. *International Labor and Working-Class History, 80*(1), 189–196.

Beinin, J. (2012). The Rise of Egypt's Workers. *Carnegie Endowment for International Peace*. Retrieved November 27, 2018, from http://carnegieendowment.org/files/egypt_labor.pdf#egypt_labor.pdf.

Beinin, J., & El-Hamalawy, H. (2007). Strikes in Egypt Spread from Center of Gravity. *Middle East Report Online*. Retrieved January 23, 2018, from http://www.merip.org/mero/mero050907.

Bishara, D. (2012). The Power of Workers in Egypt's 2011 Uprising. In K. Bahgat & R. El-Mahdi (Eds.), *Arab Spring in Egypt: Revolution and Beyond* (pp. 83–104). Cairo: American University in Cairo Press.

CTUWS (Center for Trade Unions and Workers Services). (n.d.). The Trade Union Structure Between New Labor Relation and Old Corporatist Structure (al-tanzim al-niqabi bayn 'ilaqat 'amal gadida wa tanzim niqabi qadim). *CTUWS Report*. Retrieved November 27, 2018, from http://www.ctuws.com/content/أوضاع-العمال-فى-مصر-بين-علاقات-عمل-جديدة-وتنظيم-نقابى-قديم-إعداد-كمال-عباس.

ECESR (Economic Center for Economic and Social Rights). (2015). Report on Workers' Protests in 2014. Retrieved January 23, 2018, from http://ecesr.org/?p=769983.

ECESR (Economic Center for Economic and Social Rights). (2016a). Report on Workers' Protests in 2015. Retrieved January 23, 2018, from http://ecesr.org/wp-content/uploads/2016/01/2015-Protests-interactive.pdf.

ECESR (Economic Center for Economic and Social Rights). (2016b). Report on Workers' Protests in 2016. Retrieved January 23, 2018, from http://ecesr.org/?p=775172.

El Tanlawy, T., & Feteha, A. (2017). Egypt Inflation Rate Surges to Record After Subsidy Cuts. *Bloomberg*. Retrieved November 27, 2018, from https://www.bloomberg.com/news/articles/2017-08-10/egypt-urban-inflation-rate-surges-to-record-after-subsidy-cuts.

El-Naggar, A. (2007). *The Economic Crisis in Mubarak era (al-inhiyar al-iqtisadi fi 'aqd Mubarak)*. Cairo: El-Mahroussa.

El-Naggar, A. (2009). Economic Policy: Form State Control to Decay and Corruption. In R. El-Mahdi & P. Marfeleet (Eds.), *Egypt, the Moment of Change* (pp. 34–51). London: ZED Books Ltd.

Pratt, N. (2001). Maintaining the Moral Economy: Egyptian State-Labor Relations in an Era of Economic Liberalization. *The Arab Studies Journal, 8/9*(1/2), 111–129.

Ramadan, F. (2012). A Reading of the Labor Movement in Egypt Between 2007 and 2009 (itala 'ala al-haraka al-'ummaliyya 2007–2009). *Al-Hiwar Al-Mutamaddin*. Retrieved January 23, 2018, from http://www.ahewar.org/debat/show.art.asp?aid=313257.

Shonouda, S. (2014). An Urgent Meeting for EDLC to Dismiss Its President Amid Accusation of Foreign Funding (ijtima' 'agil li-'ummal misr al-dimuqrati li-sahb al-thiqqa min ra'isuh bi-sabab tamwilat al-kharij). *Al-Shourouk Newspaper*. Retrieved November 27, 2018, from http://bit.ly/29droUh.

Snow, D. A., Rochford, J., Worden, S. K., & Benford, R. D. (1986). Frame Alignment Processes, Micromobilization, and Movement Participation. *American Sociological Review, 51*(4), 464–481.

Tarrow, S. (1998). *Power in Movement. Social Movements, Collective Action and Politics*. Cambridge: Cambridge University Press.

Valenzuela, J. S. (1989). Labor Movements in Transitions to Democracy: A Framework for Analysis. *Comparative Politics, 21*(4), 445–472.

PART III

Marginalized Groups

CHAPTER 7

Contention by Marginalized Groups and Political Change in Latin America: An Overview

Jonas Wolff

7.1 Introduction

In both academic studies on, and political debates in, Latin America, the peculiar concept of "the popular sectors" (*los sectores populares*) provides a key point of reference. This concept generally refers to "a heterogeneous category in the lower part of the socioeconomic hierarchy" that includes "both proletarians who sell labor and the self-employed in the lower strata of the income hierarchy" and thus covers not only "workers in the formal economy and a burgeoning group of earners in the informal economy" (Collier and Handlin 2009a, pp. 19–20) but also poor social sectors (peasants, indigenous peoples) in rural areas (Silva 2017, p. 116, note 1). In contrast to such a broad notion of "popular sectors," this book distinguishes between formally employed people, on the one hand, and marginalized groups, on the other (see Chap. 1, in this volume). This reflects the

J. Wolff (✉)
Peace Research Institute Frankfurt, Frankfurt am Main, Hessen, Germany
e-mail: wolff@hsfk.de

fact that, in the context of the Global South, those employed in the formal economy tend to represent a relatively privileged sector and therefore, in general, cannot be considered marginal(ized) (for Latin America, see Eckstein 1989, p. 13; 2013, p. 86).

While focusing on marginalized groups (as defined in the Introduction to this volume), this chapter follows the same logic and structure as the one outlined in Chap. 4, which focuses on organized labor. Consequently, in reviewing the state of research on collective contentious action of socioeconomically marginalized groups, it deals with the same overarching research questions. First, to what extent, how and determined by what factors have protests by marginalized groups shaped political change in Latin America, in general, and the processes of democratization between the late 1970s and the early 1990s, in particular? Second, to what extent, how and determined by what factors has the organization and contentious action of marginalized groups been affected by political change in Latin America?

7.2 The Role of (Protest by) Marginalized Groups in Democratization

It is widely acknowledged that the protest movements that helped to bring down authoritarian regimes in Latin America were, generally, broad, heterogeneous, and multi-class in nature.[1] Even if organized labor and upper- and middle-class-based organizations were normally the key elements in the bottom-up push for democratization (Rueschemeyer et al. 1992, pp. 167–168; Smith 2005, pp. 60–62), a "variety of forms of popular organization and mobilization" also contributed to that process (Vilas 1997, p. 4).[2] Still, in comparative studies on Latin American democratization, the mobilization and contentious action of marginalized groups do not feature as an important element.[3]

In analyses and overviews of the role of civil society and/or social movements during democratization in Latin America's "long 1980s,"

---

[1] See, for instance, Collier (1999, p. 13), Escobar and Alvarez (1992, pp. 1–2), Hipsher (1998, p. 149), and O'Donnell and Schmitter (1986, pp. 53–55).

[2] See also Alvarez and Escobar (1992, p. 326), Collier and Handlin (2009b, p. 55), and Peeler (2009, pp. 86–87).

[3] See O'Donnell and Schmitter (1986, pp. 48–56), Peeler (2009, pp. 69–89), Rueschemeyer et al. (1992, Chap. 5), and Smith (2005, pp. 60–62).

three individual types of organized social groups are frequently discussed in addition to the labor movement: (1) the human rights movement and, in particular, the organizations of victims of human rights violations (the most prominent case being Argentina's *Madres de Plaza de Mayo*); (2) religious, church-related groups and, in particular, the Christian base communities (CEBs) (with Brazil being the most discussed case); (3) urban shantytown movements and, in particular, the *pobladores* movement in Chile.[4] Given this book's interest in socioeconomic contention, the latter two are of particular interest.[5]

The protest movement of young shantytown dwellers (*pobladores*) in Chile in the 1980s represents one of the very few cases in the region in which contentious collective action on the part of "the socially and economically marginalized poor" came to play a "critical role" in destabilizing the authoritarian regime (Garretón 1989, p. 271).[6] According to Garretón, the aggressive protests staged by the shantytown dwellers "had great bearing on the dynamics and impact of the protest movement" that erupted in Chile in 1983, significantly weakened the Pinochet regime, and laid the groundwork for the negotiated transition via referendum at the end of the decade (Garretón 1989, p. 271; see also Hipsher 1998, p. 150; Schneider 1992, p. 261).

However, this is not to say that this movement had any direct influence on the overall process of political change. On the one hand, the "specific demands, such as land and housing" that motivated most urban *pobladores* and the failure to establish a common body that would collectively organize the shantytown dwellers meant that their protests "tended to be

[4] See Eckstein (1989, pp. 26–33), Kamrava and Mora (1998, pp. 901–902), and Peeler (2009, pp. 129–134).
[5] While the women who started the Argentine *Madres de Plaza de Mayo* in response to the forced disappearance of their children were mostly housewives "of working-class origin" (Navarro 1989, p. 249), the overall phenomenon represents "sources of grievances and targets of defiance independently of class- and market-rooted tensions" (Eckstein 1989, p. 27). In line with the broader human rights movement at that time, the *Madres'* focus during the time of the military dictatorship was clearly and narrowly on basic civil human rights (or, strictly speaking, specifically on the demand that those who had been detained/had disappeared should reappear alive) and only much later expanded to include broader goals, including aims related to social justice (see Borland 2006; Pereyra 2015).
[6] Rueschemeyer et al. (1992, p. 213) also mention Peru as a case where "mobilization of urban and rural workers and of urban squatters greatly increased and provided the basis for forceful protests against the military government's economic policies and for a return to democratic rule."

short-term" (Garretón 1989, p. 271). On the other hand, those groups of shantytown dwellers that organized more sustained resistance at the grassroots level had historic ties to the Communist Party, whose insurrectional strategy increasingly isolated them when the rest of the opposition parties, including organized labor and the middle classes, turned to a negotiating stance (Schneider 1992).[7] In general, competing attempts by the different opposition parties to organize the low-income neighborhoods contributed to dividing the shantytown dwellers (Garretón 1989, p. 271). As a result, by August 1986, "exhaustion had set in" and those continuing "to resist the dictatorship through direct confrontation had become isolated" (Schneider 1992, p. 261). In 1987, "only a small minority of *pobladores*" was "either organized or active," and when "the military was finally defeated in 1988, these *poblaciones*, along with the Communist Party, found themselves at the margins of political life" (Schneider 1992, pp. 261, 265).[8] This trend of demobilization consolidated when the center-left government elected in 1990 began to actively discourage and delegitimize contentious mobilization (Hipsher 1998, p. 159).

The most important example of the influence of Christian base communities is Brazil, where these so-called CEBs offered a crucial grassroots structure through which poor people from around the country had been mobilized since the 1970s and, in fact, became "leaders of neighborhood associations, labor unions, and peasant unions" (Levine and Mainwaring 1989, p. 216). According to Sandoval (1998, p. 177), both "the organized working-class" and "popular sectors" have to be considered "key actors" in Brazil's redemocratization process. When labor strikes resurged in the late 1970s, "unions were able to resist initial repressive measures, as church-based neighborhood organizations mobilized their members to collect food and strike funds, obstruct patrols by women and children at union headquarters, and open churches and parish halls to workers for union and strike meetings" (Sandoval 1998, p. 177; see also Moreira Alves

---

[7] The shantytown dwellers' aggressive protest tactics, which included the setting up of barricades, the burning of tires, and rock throwing, also contributed to this increasing isolation (cf. Garretón 1989, p. 271; Schneider 1992, p. 265).

[8] "Following 1987, when political events made a negotiated transition more possible, movement leaders began to re-evaluate their organizations' strategies and objectives to conform with those of the major opposition parties with which they had ties and to reflect their commitment to democratic stability. The result has been more moderate, institutionalized tactics and goals" (Hipsher 1998, p. 162).

1989, p. 286). This cooperation "was a precursor of later, more intense engagement of the labor and urban popular movements in the struggle for democratization" during the 1980s (Sandoval 1998, p. 179), which became institutionalized in the Workers' Party (Levine and Mainwaring 1989, p. 216; Keck 1992, pp. 78–79). With the formation of a pro-democracy coalition, the early 1980s were characterized by "a very significant increase in the mobilizations and collective action of urban social movements," which "made specific sectoral demands (food prices, housing, transportation, education, and health) but—more important—framed these demands around democratization as a means of achieving them and claimed these interests as part of a struggle in defense of human rights" (Sandoval 1998, p. 181).

While poor people thus played an important role in the wave of popular protest that from the late 1970s pushed for a return to civilian, democratic rule in Brazil, their role started to diminish with the gradual opening up of the authoritarian regime. In the end, popular grassroots movements were much less able to influence the shape of the democratic regime that gradually emerged during the second half of the 1980s (Levine and Mainwaring 1989, p. 221; see also Moreira Alves 1989).[9] Still, during the process of constitutional reform in the late 1980s, the popular social movements were able to regain a more autonomous and nationally oriented stance and to renew cooperation with the labor movement and, as a result, "achieved the adoption of many constitutional provisions on social issues" (Sandoval 1998, p. 193). Key factors that explain this relatively more successful role (as compared to the Chilean shantytown dwellers' movement) include the higher degree of autonomous organization on the part of Brazil's popular-sector movements (and the CEBs, in particular) as well as their close relationship and political alliance with other social movements, including the independent segment of the labor movement and the Workers' Party in particular (Sandoval 1998, p. 194).

---

[9] With a civilian government in power (even if not democratically elected), popular social movements contracted significantly after 1985: This demobilization was jointly driven by political party competition, the turn of social movement activists to participation in national politics, as well as the reduction in support of popular collective action on the part of the Catholic Church (Sandoval 1998, p. 185). As a consequence, "despite the increased opportunities for mobilization, many popular movement organizations opted for collaboration with governmental and party elites, which resulted in a major demobilization" (Sandoval 1998, p. 188). For a quite sobering assessment of Brazil's CEBs, see also Burdick (1992).

Adopting a broader perspective on democratization, Sonia Alvarez and Arturo Escobar, in a prominent volume on *The Making of Social Movements in Latin America*, identify contributions made by social movements related to "[s]maller transformations in power relations of daily life and in the practice of institutional politics" (Alvarez and Escobar 1992, p. 326). Such contributions can, of course, be manifold—challenging "authoritarian social relations," strengthening "the connection between civil society and institutional politics," bringing "previously suppressed or marginalized demands on the political agenda," or symbolically challenging "dominant discourses on politics and development" (Alvarez and Escobar 1992, pp. 326–327)—but generally they extend beyond the narrow question of politico-institutional regime change and are instead focused on the quality and substance of democratic participation and representation. As a consequence, in a subsequent volume (*Cultures of Politics/Politics of Cultures*), the editors explicitly focused on how the cultural politics of social movements foster social change, including the democratization of society broadly conceived (Alvarez et al. 1998). This, however, goes beyond the scope of the present volume.

7.3 The Consequences of Democratization for (the Protests of) Marginalized Groups

In general, scholarship on the development of social movements in Latin America suggests that democratization has shaped the mobilization and contentious action of marginalized groups in contradictory ways. The establishment of democracy (and the end of outright authoritarian rule), combined with economic crisis and subsequent neoliberal reforms, has tended to weaken (fragment and depoliticize) social movements as a political actor, but it has supported the flourishing of local, community-based associations (7.3.1). While this shift has, by and large, reduced the macropolitical role of collective contentious action on the part of the popular sectors, the political opportunity structure offered by democracy, combined with the grievances and the discursive opportunities implied by neoliberal reforms, has facilitated—if with a certain time lag—the organization and collective action of marginalized groups as well as the formation of broader protest alliances (7.3.2).

7.3.1 The Immediate Consequences

An important consequence of democratization in Latin American for contentious politics is suggested by the observation that democratic transitions were followed by a "decline of social movements" (Hipsher 1998, p. 152): In contrast to "the struggle against authoritarian regimes," which "had unified and coalesced movements," in the new democratic setting, demands became increasingly specific and divisive. In this context, many movements were either reduced to small groups or turned into professional nongovernmental organizations (NGOs) (Van Stralen 2015, p. 101). In general, the shift from the destabilization of an incumbent authoritarian regime to the conduct of negotiations on the future shape of a new (and more or less democratic) political order and, then, to democratic elections implied that elites, conventional actors such as political parties and politico-institutional issues had gained in importance, at the expense of popular-sector organizations, contentious actors, and socioeconomic issues.[10] As Huber et al. (1997, p. 331) summarize:

> The upsurge of mobilization of old and new social movements during the transition [to democracy in Latin America] was followed by a decline after the first democratic elections. In part, this decline was due to the disappearance of the common target of protest, in part to disenchantment with the failure of democratic rule to bring about significant improvements in the material situation of most citizens, and in part to the difficulties experienced by social movements in attempting to work with and through political parties. In addition, in those countries where economic stabilization and structural adjustment policies were continued and intensified after the transition (for example, Argentina, Brazil, and Peru), civil society, particularly labor, was weakened substantially.[11]

---

[10] As Hipsher argues, this trend, on the one hand, corresponded to popular-sector movements' own strategic reasoning: As popular sectors had "suffered the brunt of repression under dictatorships in Latin America and southern Europe," this had made "social movements and their members more likely to withhold demands, or to pursue strategies that will not threaten the democratic stability or the interests of authoritarian elites." On the other hand, the political opportunities for contentious action narrowed considerably with "opposition elites' decision to accept a limited democracy that, they believed, required protection from destabilizing forces" (Hipsher 1998, pp. 154–155).

[11] See also Chalmers et al. 1997, pp. 551–552; Oxhorn 1998, pp. 207–208; Pearce 1997, pp. 77–80.

Van Stralen (2015, pp. 100–101) briefly summarizes how the changing political context shaped the agendas pursued by social movements in Latin America. While in the 1970s and 1980s the experience of a military dictatorship caused urban social movements to focus increasingly on (basic, political, and civil) human rights, social movement agendas shifted with democratization, which caused organizations to formulate their demands in terms of "citizenship rights" (Van Stralen 2015, p. 101). Through this turn to "claims for rights," democratization contributed to the fragmenting of social movements, encouraging "the emergence of competing movements with specific demands" (Van Stralen 2015, p. 101).[12] At the same time, even under democratic regimes, the "ability to influence decision making through formal or nontumultuous informal political channels" on the part of "subordinate groups" has remained limited, "despite their strength of numbers" (Eckstein 1989, p. 28).

The consequence, across Latin America, has been a kind of retreat of popular movements to the local level, to everyday survival/self-help strategies (including contentious action) at the neighborhood/community level (see Collier and Handlin 2009a; Eckstein 2001; Oxhorn 1998), or what Federico Rossi (2017) calls a "territorialization" of poor people's movements. As with organized labor, it is, however, hard to disentangle the consequences of democratization, on the one hand, and economic crisis and neoliberal reforms, on the other, for the organizational strength and capacity of collective action on the part of marginalized groups in Latin America.[13] With a view to the latter, Marcus Kurtz has emphasized that the turn to "free market democracies" in Latin America "provoked social fragmentation, economic dependence, immiseration, and the near collapse of organization" in the countryside, while also contributing to "social decapitalization and demobilization" in urban areas (Kurtz 2004a, p. 14; see also Kurtz 2004b; Oxhorn and Ducatenzeiler 1998; Roberts 1998, 2002; Wolff 2009). The overall consequence, several scholars have noted, has been a retreat of popular mobilization and protests to the local, community, neighborhood, or grassroots levels:

---

[12] Even if with positive connotations, a prominent study edited by Arturo Escobar and Sonia Alvarez in the early 1990s also observed that since the 1980s, popular mobilization in Latin America has been increasingly characterized by a "mosaic of forms of collective action" and a "rich mosaic of identities" that has led the authors to doubt "whether a single label can encompass them all" (Escobar and Alvarez 1992, p. 2).

[13] For a brief summary of the debate on the complex relationship between social movements, democratization, and neoliberal reforms in Latin America, see Hochstetler (2012). For a related dispute between quantitative scholars, see Bellinger and Arce (2011) and Solt et al. (2014).

> Once elections are called [...] there is a dramatic demobilization of the popular sectors, as political parties come to dominate the political process. Intermediate levels of autonomous popular sector representation are disarticulated. The popular organizations that emerged throughout Latin America in recent years to help cope with unprecedented economic dislocations and demand greater political liberalization have ultimately remained confined to the community level after the initial impetus for political liberalization has run its course. (Oxhorn 1998, p. 208)[14]

To the extent that popular protests persisted in this context, they "tend[ed] to be erratic and reactive to specific events" (Portes and Hoffman 2003, p. 77). In the 1980s, the most important type of socioeconomic protest by popular sectors at the macrolevel concerned the so-called anti-austerity protests, sometimes also called "IMF riots." These protests, in many cases, had the immediate effect of forcing governments to partially retract or ameliorate their policies (see Walton 1989, p. 321; Wickham-Crowley and Eckstein 2015, p. 32). Yet, because they were rather short-lived outbursts of resistance, they prevented neither the implementation of austerity and macroeconomic stabilization policies nor the more far-reaching neoliberal structural adjustment programs in which they were embedded (Eckstein 2001, pp. 359–360; see also Almeida 2015).

What appears to be a retreat or decline of popular social movements—and protest on the part of the popular sectors—at the national level, takes on quite a different dynamic when attention is turned to what happens at the local level:

> Popular mobilization by no means disappeared during the 1980s [...]. From squatters to ecologists, from popular kitchens in poor urban neighborhoods to Socialist feminist groups, from human rights and defense of life mobilizations to gay and lesbian coalitions, the spectrum of Latin American collective action covers a broad range. (Escobar and Alvarez 1992, p. 2)

The combined effects of democratization and neoliberal reforms have significantly promoted what has been dubbed "the rise of urban associationalism" in Latin America (Collier and Handlin 2009b, p. 54; see also Chalmers et al. 1997).[15] On the one hand, democratization

---

[14] See also Lievesley 1999, pp. 101–130; Roberts 2002; Rossi 2017; Vilas 1997, p. 30.

[15] Again, the international context has also played a role in this regard, namely, "a supportive post-cold war international environment characterized by a new global convergence on the promotion of civil society" (Collier and Handlin 2009b, p. 57).

opened new possibilities for societal demand making and new expectations for the accountability of state officials [...]. In this context, new associations were founded, creating a more vibrant civil society than had previously existed in the region, including a proliferation of organizations around lower-class interests. (Collier and Handlin 2009a, p. 4)

On the other hand, economic crisis and the social hardships brought about by neoliberal reforms constituted "immediate stimulus for the new associationalism" (Collier and Handlin 2009b, p. 54).[16] As a result, "Latin America has witnessed an unprecedented proliferation of popular associations in urban areas over the last two or three decades"; these associations included "[n]eighborhood organizations, community soup kitchens, microcredit associations, street vendor unions, community policing and safety groups, women's groups, NGOs working on environmental or local development issues" (Collier and Handlin 2009b, pp. 53–54; see also Chalmers et al. 1997, p. 552).

Combined with the dramatic weakening of organized labor (see Chap. 4, in this volume), this has meant that the ways in which the popular sectors predominantly organize themselves and make collective claims have changed. In the terminology proposed by Collier and Handlin, "the dramatic changes in economic models and political regimes have been accompanied by a major shift in the *urban popular interest regime* in the region, the organizations through which the urban popular sectors, or the lower and lower middle classes, have sought to pursue their interests." Whereas in previous decades labor unions, usually in close association with labor-based political parties, have been the key instrument of popular-sector representation, this "union-party hub" has been replaced by an "associational network," in which "a diverse array of urban popular associations" constitutes a manifold and, at best, loosely coordinated set of organizations

---

[16] According to Chalmers et al. (1997, p. 551), the "twin processes" of economic restructuring and democratization, in an immediate sense, reinforced "the ongoing process of decomposition [of the traditional, populist-era structures of popular sector representation] [...], as major elite-dominated economic and political changes left the popular sectors more distant and disengaged from political decision-making than they ever had been since the onset of incorporation." From a long-term perspective, however, "the seeds for a new structure of popular representation were sown even in the midst of a terminal phase of decomposition of old structures." As Collier and Handlin (2009b, pp. 55–56) add, the shifts in social policies that accompanied both democratization and economic restructuring (partial privatization, reliance on public-private partnerships, and civil society as service providers, decentralization) also contributed to the "rise of associationalism."

through which members of the popular sector articulate and promote their interests and values (Collier and Handlin 2009a, pp. 4–5; see also Collier and Handlin 2009b, pp. 57–60; Chalmers et al. 1997).

From the perspective of marginalized groups, the major advantage of these popular associations is that they included the urban informal sector as well as peasants who were usually excluded from national labor organizations (see Collier and Handlin 2009b, p. 49). In fact, one key source of popular organization in contemporary Latin America is the neighborhood associations that "proliferated with the establishment of shantytowns on the urban peripheries" and which "sprung up as a means of demanding urban services as well as self-provisioning for collective neighborhood needs" (Collier and Handlin 2009b, p. 50).

Collier et al.'s comparative analysis of the working of this "associational network" (or "A-Net") shows that popular associations in this context continue to pursue "a significant amount of claim making within their repertoire of action" and that this claim making at times also target the state at the national level "through institutional channels and through protest." Still, in general, "the A-Net is characterized by a preponderance of provisioning, rather than claim-making strategies" (Collier and Handlin 2009b, p. 38). Furthermore, the level of coordination within the A-Net is mostly low and associations are predominantly local. This analysis, therefore, generally confirms the finding outlined earlier of an overall reduction in macropolitically relevant contentious collective action on the part of the popular sectors throughout Latin America since the 1980s (see also Chalmers et al. 1997).[17]

The same overall trend is implied by a reading of popular mobilization (in Latin America since the 1980s) that emphasizes the cultural or identity-related dimension of struggle (Escobar and Alvarez 1992; see also

[17] The "associative networks" that, according to Chalmers et al. (1997), have become the predominant type of popular representation in Latin America (largely replacing the "populist-corporatist" mode of popular sector incorporation) are clearly characterized by rather cooperative and deliberative modes of interaction between societal groups and the state (with a view to jointly shaping public policy in specific issue areas). The authors call this a "strong emphasis on [...] cognitive politics, involving debate and discussion of preferences, understandings, and claims, in addition to—and potentially transforming—more conventional bargaining over demands and interests" (Chalmers et al. 1997, p. 567). Furthermore: "Many associative networks create a serious potential for the splintering of political issues—and hence of organizations—into arenas that become disconnected, depoliticized, and narrowly circumscribed" (Chalmers et al. 1997, p. 580). In Chalmers et al.'s analysis, therefore, protest, contentious politics, or social conflict does not figure as a relevant dimension of popular sector representation in times of "associative networks."

Alvarez et al. 1998). The "transformative potential" that, from this perspective, is embodied in what are called "new social movements" relates to questions of "social recognition" and "the transformation or appropriation by the actors of the cultural field" (Escobar and Alvarez 1992, p. 4). To the extent that social movements' impact on democracy is addressed, democratization is understood in broad—and noninstitutionalist—ways as encompassing "the democratization of cultural, social, economic, and political life," in particular referring to "the terrain of 'daily life'" (Escobar and Alvarez 1992, p. 4; see also Alvarez and Escobar 1992, pp. 325–329; Alvarez et al. 1998, p. 14). Or, as Fernando Calderón and colleagues (in the same volume) put it:

> In sum, although they are characterized by 'small' social actors (that is, blacks, rockers, mothers, and so forth) compared to the protagonists in earlier movements who were 'grand' and more clearly visible (workers and peasants), the social movements of today nevertheless exhibit a marked political propensity. It is not impossible to imagine that these numerous small actors might communicate with each other and thereby connect their spaces, not in a simple aggregate manner, but organically. And this might provide one of the necessary conditions for reconstituting the institutional fabric of a type of democracy that is yet to come. (Calderón et al. 1992, p. 26)

While this last statement refers to the future, the contemporary assessment of the situation and the political impact of Latin American social movements in the late 1980s and early 1990s was much more pessimistic: Calderón et al. (1992, p. 28) identified what they called "a 'historical out-of-phase' between a diversity of social movements—fractioned, autonomous, monadic, and merely reacting to exclusion and crisis—and new patterns of domination." In this sense, then, the overarching assessment of the transformative impact that can actually be observed in terms of these diverse, heterogeneous, issue-specific, localized, and at best loosely coordinated (popular) social movements involved "[s]maller transformations in power relations of daily life and in the practice of institutional politics" (Alvarez and Escobar 1992, pp. 325–326). Examples of such transformations include the impact of feminist movements on mainstream discourses in the political sphere, the media and popular culture, or the addition of previously suppressed new topics, demands, and rights to the political agenda by movements of the urban poor (see Alvarez and Escobar 1992, pp. 326–327).

7.3.2 The Mid-term Consequences

The optimistic forecast concerning what might emerge from the myriad of small-scale "movements" on the ground (as represented by Calderón et al. and Escobar and Alvarez) has to a certain extent been confirmed over time. In line with social movement research, if with a certain time lag, the opportunity structure established by (however limited) democracy has indeed led to a new wave of social protest and social movements throughout the region (Almeida and Johnston 2006, pp. 11–15; see also Rossi 2017; Silva 2009; Wolff 2009, 2012).[18] All the limitations of Latin America's post-transition democracies notwithstanding, the reduction in state violence and the relative openness to popular demands that accompanied democratization have created "new opportunities and spaces for mobilization" (Almeida and Cordero Ulate 2015, p. 4; see also Almeida and Johnston 2006, p. 3; Bellinger and Arce 2011, pp. 691–692; Wickham-Crowley and Eckstein 2015, pp. 38–40).[19] An important example in this regard is the political rise of indigenous movements in a series of countries, which was clearly enabled by the (re)turn to democracy (see Van Cott 2005; Yashar 2005; Wolff 2007).[20]

While democratization created an enabling context for bottom-up dynamics of mobilization, it was "neoliberalism"—neoliberal adjustment

---

[18] Almeida and Johnston (2006, p. 15) explicitly note: "Democratization seems to have a 'lag effect' on mass contention in the region."

[19] This, in particular refers to the reduction in "state violence" (Almeida and Cordero Ulate 2015, p. 4) related to the incapacity of democratic regimes to rely on comprehensive political repression (Eckstein 1989, p. 46; Wolff 2009, pp. 1004–1005). Certainly, the repression of social protest in Latin America has remained an established state response also under democratic regimes, but research does not suggest that political repression, generally speaking, has been an effective means for preventing or quelling protests (see Ortiz 2015; Franklin 2009, 2015). Rather, violent state responses to protests have on many occasions provoked an escalation of protest (see Silva 2009; Wolff 2009).

[20] In this sense, Kurtz's above-mentioned analysis of rural areas, which focuses on the cases of Chile and Mexico, has to be qualified by taking into account the experience of indigenous movements in countries such as Bolivia or Ecuador. In Brazil it was possible to observe a roughly similar dynamic, where democratization meant expanding opportunities for the organization and contentious collective action of marginalized sectors in rural areas, namely, with the Landless Rural Workers' Movement (MST) (Bleil and Chabanet 2014; Carter 2010). But, apart from the indigenous movements, the Brazilian MST is really "an exception" to the overall trend; whereas, agrarian protests "were common in Latin America historically," in recent times, "they have been confined, in the main, to localized uprisings" (Eckstein 2013, p. 84). This is what Wickham-Crowley and Eckstein (2015, pp. 32–34) describe as "cost-of-subsistence protests."

programs and their socioeconomic consequences—that ultimately facilitated the emergence of broad alliances of popular organizations and movements. Neoliberal reforms, by constituting economic threats to broad parts of the population in the context of democratic regimes, tended to "increase the possibility of collective action with an alliance between traditional movements, NGOs, new social movements, and political parties," as suggested by the "massive campaigns against neoliberal reforms organized by NGOs, labor unions, new social movements, and oppositional political parties" (Van Stralen 2015, p. 105; see also Almeida and Cordero Ulate 2015, pp. 5–7). Still, this process came with a significant time lag. In the mid-1990s, Douglas Chalmers and colleagues could still conclude that, occasional protests "against particular anti-popular reforms or corrupt public officials" notwithstanding, "there are few signs of a sustained, broad-based popular movement against neoliberalism, and much less around an alternative project" in Latin America (Chalmers et al. 1997, p. 543). Since the second half of the 1990s, however, popular resistance to neoliberal policies and the political parties that sustained this agenda have not only grown in many countries in the region but they have also been key to the political changes associated with the much-discussed "leftist turn" (see Eckstein and Wickham-Crowley 2003; Johnston and Almeida 2006; Petras and Veltmeyer 2005; Silva 2009; Stahler-Sholk et al. 2014). The protests in the context of this recent upswing of social movements were, indeed, concerned quite explicitly with socioeconomic issues, motivated in particular by "perceived threats to economic benefits and social citizenship rights" (Almeida 2007, p. 124; see also Eckstein and Wickham-Crowley 2003; Johnston and Almeida 2006).[21] Almeida summarizes this reemergence of socioeconomic protest:

> Between 1996 and 2001, reports of popular protest against economic austerity and adjustment policies in Latin America increased. The cooling-off period brought about by the region's democratization in the 1980s and 1990s appeared to be over; the popular sectors returned with dramatic force to the public stage. If democratization had institutionalized earlier political

---

[21] According to Eckstein (2013, p. 89), "[u]nder neoliberalism," urban popular-sector protests in Latin America particularly "focused on anger with government cutbacks in subsidies that drove up the cost of everyday living." For an overview, and empirical assessment, of the different types of grievances and claims that have characterized social protests and movements against neoliberalism and/or for social rights in Latin America, see Eckstein and Wickham-Crowley (2003) and Johnston and Almeida (2006).

struggles, it now provides a more open context for civic organizations to mobilize against a reduction in government commitments to social welfare. An emergent incentive structure of austerity measures threatening economic and social benefits and citizenship rights was generating a Latin America-wide wave of contestation against the deepening of neoliberal reforms. (Almeida 2007, p. 135)[22]

Without going into any details of the complex processes of political change associated with the "leftist turn" in Latin America, the upsurge in contentious social mobilization since the second half of the 1990s—which has been characterized, to an important extent, by socioeconomic protests—ultimately initiated across the region a new period of struggles over the shape of both the democratic regimes and the economic order (see Arditi 2008; Rovira Kaltwasser 2011; Silva 2009; Wolff 2013). With a view to the popular sectors, this new period of struggle has plausibly been characterized as a "second historical process of mass incorporation" (Roberts 2008, p. 341; see also Rossi 2017; Silva and Rossi 2018), following up on the first such period that concerned the incorporation of the emerging working class in the early twentieth century (Collier and Collier 1991). In this sense, then, a broad and diverse set of marginalized groups in several Latin American countries has recently managed to use contentious collective action in order to successfully push for their socioeconomic and political incorporation. With the leftist turn, the turn to post-neoliberal policies, and the economic boom of the early 2000s, many marginalized sectors in Latin America have indeed benefited from gradual, but significant improvements involving both their socioeconomic inclusion and their political participation and representation (see Levitsky and Roberts 2011; Rossi 2017; Silva and Rossi 2018; Wolff 2012, 2018; World Bank 2015).[23] In the end, the leftist turn has not resolved the crisis of incorporation, and, as the years of leftist-dominated politics in the region

---

[22] See also Bellinger and Arce 2011.
[23] A particularly successful example in this regard concerns one of the traditionally most highly marginalized sectors: the indigenous population. Starting in 1990—that is, well before the leftist turn—indigenous movements in countries such as Bolivia and Ecuador have been able to mobilize significant numbers of indigenous people and by doing so were able to achieve significant victories in terms of recognition (of indigenous peoples and their collective rights), political participation (via their own movement organizations and parties), and socioeconomic improvements (via economic development projects, social programs, and social services) (see Lucero 2012; Van Cott 2005; Yashar 2005; World Bank 2015).

have clearly come to an end, it seems uncertain to what extent the progress in terms of socioeconomic and political inclusion of marginalized sectors will survive under right-wing governments and/or much more adverse economic conditions.

When it comes to explaining the emergence of strong popular-sector movements in Latin America that, in several cases, have proved successful in pushing for political and economic change, scholars have emphasized the necessary combination of macro- and micro-conditions. On the one hand, the overall political space offered by democracy as well as the mobilizing threats implied by neoliberal reforms and austerity policies have established the *opportunity* and the *motive* to mobilize. On the other hand, associational spaces and pre-existing societal networks at the local level as well as horizontal networks and communication across different local settings provided marginalized groups with the *capacity* needed to effectively seize the opportunities and respond to the threats (see Silva 2009; Wolff 2007; Yashar 2005).

7.4 Conclusion

This review of research on popular protest and social movements in Latin America since the late 1970s suggests the following four main features that have characterized (socioeconomic) contention by marginalized groups:

First, in some countries, the contentious collective action by grassroots organizations representing marginalized sectors as well as their participation in broader, multi-class protests contributed to the destabilization, opening up and/or toppling of authoritarian regimes, even if in a secondary role (behind organized labor, middle-class protests, and/or the activities of opposition parties). These protest activities by marginalized groups were, to a significant extent, driven by a combination of socioeconomic concerns with resistance to repressive, authoritarian regimes. In the cases in which the scholarship particularly emphasizes the role of protest by popular-sector groups outside the realm of organized labor, these were established and supported by different kinds of external actors (the Catholic Church in the case of Brazil's Christian base communities and the Communist Party in the case of Chile's movement of shantytown dwellers).

Second, with the turn from resistance to an authoritarian regime to the (contested) negotiation of regime change, marginalized groups generally played no significant role, neither as protestors continuing to push for change nor as participants at the negotiation table. Further driven by the economic crisis and the turn to neoliberal policies, the socioeconomic demands articulated by marginalized groups were largely ignored. Popular protests, in this context, were largely reactive and defensive (and, at times, successful in the short-term and in a concrete sense). A partial exception is Brazil where contributions by marginalized groups to the process of constitutional reforms depended on stable alliances and closely knit relations with a broad set of pro-democracy forces (in particular, with organized labor and in the context of the Workers' Party).

Third, overall, the dual transformation (political democratization and neoliberal restructuring) dramatically changed the structure of collective action among the popular sectors. These changes combined increasing diversity and reduced emphasis on classical—class-based—popular-sector claims, less hierarchical and centralized forms of organization and decreasing coordination, greater emphasis on the local, community, or grassroots level as well as on autonomy, self-help and self-organization, and less direct challenges to, and interaction with, the central state.

Fourth, with a significant time lag, the combination of democracy and neoliberal reforms made the emergence of broad anti-neoliberal protest alliances, in which organizations and movements of marginalized groups played an important role, possible. These protest alliances, which emerged from local associational structures and societal networks and were able to spread contentious collective action to the national level, brought the social question back onto the political agenda and facilitated the election of left-of-center governments that, at least partially, addressed a series of key socioeconomic concerns articulated by popular-sector movements.

Relating these findings to concepts in social movement studies, we can identify five key factors that have shaped protests by marginalized groups in Latin America:

- Socioeconomic *grievances* are key drivers of protest among marginalized groups, but the same kind of neoliberal policies that create or aggravate such grievances constrain the capacity of contentious collective action.
- In terms of *collective action frames*, resistance against some overarching "enemy" (dictatorship, neoliberalism) enables marginalized groups to overcome their internal fragmentation and sustain broader popular protests on a national scale.

- In terms of *resource mobilization*, sociopolitical allies are important in enabling broader dynamics of mobilization among marginalized sectors, but the relationship with such allies is, at the same times, ambivalent for marginalized groups because, in such alliances, they usually play the role of a junior partner.
- In terms of *mobilizing structures*, pre-existing local structures, associational spaces, and societal networks provide marginalized groups with the capacity to mobilize and facilitate scaling up to the regional or national level.
- In terms of *political opportunities*, marginalized groups tend to be disadvantaged vis-à-vis other social groups when it comes to making use of improving political opportunities. But, to the extent that the above conditions are present, a more democratic political context can make the emergence of significant movements of marginalized groups with impressive collective action capacity possible.

References

Almeida, P. D. (2007). Defensive Mobilization: Popular Movements Against Economic Adjustment Policies in Latin America. *Latin American Perspectives, 34*(3), 123–139.

Almeida, P. D. (2015). Democratization and the Revitalization of Popular Movements in Central America. In B. Klandermans & C. Van Stralen (Eds.), *Movements in Times of Democratic Transition* (pp. 166–185). Philadelphia, PA: Temple University Press.

Almeida, P., & Cordero Ulate, A. (2015). Social Movements Across Latin America. In P. Almeida & A. Cordero Ulate (Eds.), *Handbook of Social Movements Across Latin America* (pp. 3–10). Dordrecht: Springer.

Almeida, P., & Johnston, H. (2006). Neoliberal Globalization and Popular Movements in Latin America. In H. Johnston & P. Almeida (Eds.), *Latin American Social Movements. Globalization, Democratization, and Transnational Networks* (pp. 3–18). Lanham, MD: Rowman & Littlefield.

Alvarez, S., & Escobar, A. (1992). Conclusion: Theoretical and Political Horizons of Change in Contemporary Latin American Social Movements. In A. Escobar & S. Alvarez (Eds.), *The Making of Social Movements in Latin America. Identity, Strategy, and Democracy* (pp. 317–329). Boulder, CO: Westview Press.

Alvarez, S., Dagnino, E., & Escobar, A. (1998). *Cultures of Politics/Politics of Cultures. Re-visioning Latin American Social Movements*. Boulder, CO: Westview Press.

Arditi, B. (2008). Arguments About the Left Turns in Latin America. A Post-liberal Politics? *Latin American Research Review, 43*(3), 59–81.

Bellinger, P., & Arce, M. (2011). Protest and Democracy in Latin America's Market Era. *Political Research Quarterly, 64*(3), 688–704.

Bleil, S., & Chabanet, D. (2014). The Landless Workers' Movement in Brazil: The Emergence of a Militant Community. In D. Chabanet & F. Royall (Eds.), *From Silence to Protest. International Perspectives on Weakly Resourced Groups* (pp. 53–66). Farnham: Ashgate.

Borland, E. (2006). The Mature Resistance of Argentina's Madres de Plaza de Mayo. In H. Johnston & P. Almeida (Eds.), *Latin American Social Movements. Globalization, Democratization, and Transnational Networks* (pp. 115–130). Lanham, MD: Rowman & Littlefield.

Burdick, J. (1992). Rethinking the Study of Social Movements: The Case of Christian Base Communities in Urban Brazil. In A. Escobar & S. Alvarez (Eds.), *The Making of Social Movements in Latin America. Identity, Strategy, and Democracy* (pp. 171–184). Boulder, CO: Westview Press.

Calderón, F., Piscitelli, A., & Reyna, J. (1992). Social Movements: Actors, Theories, Expectations. In A. Escobar & S. Alvarez (Eds.), *The Making of Social Movements in Latin America. Identity, Strategy, and Democracy* (pp. 19–36). Boulder, CO: Westview Press.

Carter, M. (2010). The Landless Rural Workers Movement and Democracy in Brazil. *Latin American Research Review, 45*(Special Issue), 186–217.

Chalmers, D., Martin, S., & Piester, K. (1997). Associative Networks: New Structures of Representation for the Popular Sectors? In D. A. Chalmers, C. M. Vilas, K. Hite, S. B. Martin, K. Piester, & M. Segarra (Eds.), *The New Politics of Inequality in Latin America. Rethinking Participation and Representation* (pp. 543–582). Oxford: Oxford University Press.

Collier, R. B. (1999). *Paths Toward Democracy. The Working Class and Elites in Western Europe and South America*. Cambridge: Cambridge University Press.

Collier, R., & Collier, D. (1991). *Shaping the Political Arena. Critical Junctures, the Labor Movement, and Regime Dynamics in Latin America*. Princeton, NJ: Princeton University Press.

Collier, R., & Handlin, S. (2009a). Introduction: Popular Representation in the Interest Arena. In R. Collier & S. Handlin (Eds.), *Reorganizing Popular Politics. Participation and the New Interest Regime in Latin America* (pp. 3–31). The Pennsylvania State University Press: University Park, PA.

Collier, R., & Handlin, S. (2009b). Situating the Analysis: Analytic Approach, Cases, and Historical Context. In R. Collier & S. Handlin (Eds.), *Reorganizing Popular Politics. Participation and the New Interest Regime in Latin America* (pp. 32–60). The Pennsylvania State University Press: University Park, PA.

Eckstein, S. (1989). Power and Popular Protest in Latin America. In S. Eckstein (Ed.), *Power and Popular Protest. Latin American Social Movements* (pp. 1–60). Berkeley, CA: University of California Press.

Eckstein, S. (2001). Where Have All the Movements Gone? Latin American Social Movements at the New Millennium. In S. Eckstein (Ed.), *Power and Popular Protest. Latin American Social Movements* (pp. 351–406). Berkeley, CA: University of California Press.

Eckstein, S. (2013). The Latin American Social Movement Repertoire. How It Has Changed, When, and Why. *Moving the Social, 50*, 81–102.

Eckstein, S., & Wickham-Crowley, T. P. (2003). *Struggles for Social Rights in Latin America*. New York, NY: Routledge.

Escobar, A., & Alvarez, S. (1992). Introduction: Theory and Protest in Latin America Today. In A. Escobar & S. Alvarez (Eds.), *The Making of Social Movements in Latin America. Identity, Strategy, and Democracy* (pp. 1–15). Boulder, CO: Westview Press.

Franklin, J. C. (2009). Contentious Challenges and Government Responses in Latin America. *Political Research Quarterly, 62*(4), 700–714.

Franklin, J. C. (2015). Persistent Challengers: Repression, Concessions, Challenger Strength, and Commitment in Latin America. *Mobilization, 20*(1), 61–80.

Garretón, M. (1989). Popular Mobilization and the Military Regime in Chile: The Complexities of the Invisible Transition. In S. Eckstein (Ed.), *Power and Popular Protest. Latin American Social Movements* (pp. 259–277). Berkeley, CA: University of California Press.

Hipsher, P. (1998). Democratic Transitions and Social Movement Outcomes: The Chilean Shantytown Dwellers' Movement in Comparative Perspective. In M. Giugni, D. McAdam, & C. Tilly (Eds.), *From Contention to Democracy* (pp. 149–168). Lanham, MD: Rowman & Littlefield.

Hochstetler, K. (2012). Social Movements in Latin America. In P. Kingstone & D. Yashar (Eds.), *Routledge Handbook of Latin American Politics* (pp. 237–247). New York, NY: Routledge.

Huber, E., Rueschemeyer, D., & Stephens, J. D. (1997). The Paradoxes of Contemporary Democracy: Formal, Participatory, and Social Dimensions. *Comparative Politics, 29*(3), 323–342.

Johnston, H., & Almeida, P. (2006). *Latin American Social Movements. Globalization, Democratization, and Transnational Networks*. Lanham, MD: Rowman & Littlefield.

Kamrava, M., & Mora, F. O. (1998). Civil Society and Democratisation in Comparative Perspective: Latin America and the Middle East. *Third World Quarterly, 19*(5), 893–915.

Keck, M. E. (1992). *The Workers' Party and Democratization in Brazil*. New Haven, CT: Yale University Press.

Kurtz, M. J. (2004a). *Free Market Democracy and the Chilean and Mexican Countryside*. Cambridge: Cambridge University Press.

Kurtz, M. J. (2004b). The Dilemmas of Democracy in the Open Economy. Lessons from Latin America. *World Politics, 56*(1), 262–302.

Levine, D. H., & Mainwaring, S. (1989). Religion and Popular Protest in Latin America: Contrasting Experiences. In S. Eckstein (Ed.), *Power and Popular Protest. Latin American Social Movements* (pp. 203–240). Berkeley, CA: University of California Press.

Levitsky, S., & Roberts, K. M. (2011). *The Resurgence of the Latin American Left*. Baltimore, MD: The Johns Hopkins University Press.

Lievesley, G. (1999). *Democracy in Latin America. Mobilization, Power and Search for a New Politics*. Manchester: Manchester University Press.

Lucero, J. A. (2012). Indigenous Politics: Between Democracy and Danger. In P. Kingstone & D. Yashar (Eds.), *Routledge Handbook of Latin American Politics* (pp. 285–301). New York, NY: Routledge.

Moreira Alves, M. H. (1989). Interclass Alliances in the Opposition to the Military in Brazil: Consequences for the Transition Period. In S. Eckstein (Ed.), *Power and Popular Protest. Latin American Social Movements* (pp. 278–298). Berkeley, CA: University of California Press.

Navarro, M. (1989). The Personal Is Political: Las Madres de Plaza de Mayo. In S. Eckstein (Ed.), *Power and Popular Protest. Latin American Social Movements* (pp. 241–258). Berkeley, CA: University of California Press.

O'Donnell, G., & Schmitter, P. C. (1986). *Transitions from Authoritarian Rule. Tentative Conclusions About Uncertain Democracies*. Baltimore, MD: The Johns Hopkins University Press.

Ortiz, D. G. (2015). State Repression and Mobilization in Latin America. In P. Almeida & A. Cordero Ulate (Eds.), *Handbook of Social Movements Across Latin America* (pp. 43–60). Dordrecht: Springer.

Oxhorn, P. (1998). Is the Century of Corporatism Over? Neoliberalism and the Rise of Neopluralism. In P. Oxhorn & G. Ducatenzeiler (Eds.), *What Kind of Democracy? What Kind of Market? Latin America in the Age of Neoliberalism* (pp. 195–217). University Park, PA: The Pennsylvania State University Press.

Oxhorn, P., & Ducatenzeiler, G. (1998). *What Kind of Democracy? What Kind of Market? Latin America in the Age of Neoliberalism*. University Park, PA: The Pennsylvania State University Press.

Pearce, J. (1997). Civil Society, the Market and Democracy in Latin America. *Democratization*, 4(2), 57–83.

Peeler, J. (2009). *Building Democracy in Latin America* (3rd ed.). Boulder, CO: Lynne Rienner.

Pereyra, S. (2015). Strategies and Mobilization Cycles of the Human Rights Movement in the Democratic Transition in Argentina. In B. Klandermans & C. Van Stralen (Eds.), *Movements in Times of Democratic Transition* (pp. 186–205). Philadelphia, PA: Temple University Press.

Petras, J., & Veltmeyer, H. (2005). *Social Movements and State Power. Argentina, Brazil, Bolivia, Ecuador*. London: Pluto Press.

Portes, A., & Hoffman, K. (2003). Latin American Class Structures: Their Composition and Change During the Neoliberal Era. *Latin American Research Review, 38*(1), 41–82.

Roberts, K. M. (1998). *Deepening Democracy? The Modern Left and Social Movements in Chile and Peru*. Stanford, CA: Stanford University Press.

Roberts, K. M. (2002). Social Inequalities Without Class Cleavages in Latin America's Neoliberal Era. *Studies in Comparative International Development, 36*(4), 3–33.

Roberts, R. M. (2008). The Mobilization of Opposition to Economic Liberalization. *Annual Review of Political Science, 11*, 327–349.

Rossi, F. M. (2017). *The Poor's Struggle for Political Incorporation. The Piquetero Movement in Argentina*. Cambridge: Cambridge University Press.

Rovira Kaltwasser, C. (2011). Toward Post-neoliberalism in Latin America? *Latin American Research Review, 46*(2), 225–234.

Rueschemeyer, D., Huber Stephens, E., & Stephens, J. D. (1992). *Capitalist Development and Democracy*. Cambridge: Polity Press.

Sandoval, S. (1998). Social Movements and Democratization. The Case of Brazil and Latin Countries. In M. Giugni, D. McAdam, & C. Tilly (Eds.), *From Contention to Democracy* (pp. 169–202). Lanham, MD: Rowman & Littlefield.

Schneider, C. (1992). Radical Opposition Parties and Squatters Movements in Pinochet's Chile. In A. Escobar & S. Alvarez (Eds.), *The Making of Social Movements in Latin America. Identity, Strategy, and Democracy* (pp. 260–275). Boulder, CO: Westview Press.

Silva, E. (2009). *Challenging Neoliberalism in Latin America*. Cambridge: Cambridge University Press.

Silva, E. (2017). Reorganizing Popular Sector Incorporation: Propositions from Bolivia, Ecuador, and Venezuela. *Politics & Society, 45*(1), 91–122.

Silva, E., & Rossi, F. M. (2018). *Reshaping the Political Arena in Latin America: From Resisting Neoliberalism to the Second Incorporation*. Pittsburgh, PA: University of Pittsburgh Press.

Smith, P. H. (2005). *Democracy in Latin America. Political Change in Comparative Perspective*. New York, NY: Oxford University Press.

Solt, F., Kim, D., Lee, K., Willardson, S., & Kim, S. (2014). Neoliberal Reform and Protest in Latin American Democracies: A Replication and Correction. *Research and Politics, 1*(2), 1–13.

Stahler-Sholk, R., Vanden, H. E., & Becker, M. (2014). *Rethinking Latin American Social Movements. Radical Action from Below*. Lanham, MD: Rowman & Littlefield.

Van Cott, D. L. (2005). *From Movements to Parties in Latin America. The Evolution of Ethnic Politics*. Cambridge: Cambridge University Press.

Van Stralen, C. (2015). Introduction (to Part II: Latin America). In B. Klandermans & C. Van Stralen (Eds.), *Movements in Times of Democratic Transition* (pp. 91–107). Philadelphia, PA: Temple University Press.

Vilas, C. M. (1997). Participation, Inequality, and the Whereabouts of Democracy. In D. A. Chalmers, C. M. Vilas, K. Hite, S. B. Martin, K. Piester, & M. Segarra (Eds.), *The New Politics of Inequality in Latin America. Rethinking Participation and Representation* (pp. 3–42). Oxford: Oxford University Press.

Walton, J. (1989). Debt, Protest, and the State in Latin America). In S. Eckstein (Ed.), *Power and Popular Protest. Latin American Social Movements* (pp. 299–328). Berkeley, CA: University of California Press.

Wickham-Crowley, T. P., & Eckstein, S. (2015). "There and Back Again": Latin American Social Movements and Reasserting the Powers of Structural Theories. In P. Almeida & A. Cordero Ulate (Eds.), *Handbook of Social Movements Across Latin America* (pp. 25–42). Dordrecht: Springer.

Wolff, J. (2007). (De-)mobilising the Marginalised. A Comparison of the Argentine Piqueteros and Ecuador's Indigenous Movement. *Journal of Latin American Studies, 39*(1), 1–29.

Wolff, J. (2009). De-idealizing the Democratic Civil Peace: On the Political Economy of Democratic Stabilisation and Pacification in Argentina and Ecuador. *Democratization, 16*(5), 998–1026.

Wolff, J. (2012). Movimientos sociales y la lucha por la democratización de la democracia: experiencias recientes en América del Sur. In S. Kron, S. Costa, & M. Braig (Eds.), *Democracia y reconfiguraciones contemporáneas del derecho en América Latina* (pp. 297–322). Frankfurt: Vervuert.

Wolff, J. (2013). Towards Post-liberal Democracy in Latin America? A Conceptual Framework Applied to Bolivia. *Journal of Latin American Studies, 45*(1), 31–59.

Wolff, J. (2018). Political Incorporation in Measures of Democracy: A Missing Dimension (and the Case of Bolivia). *Democratization, 25*(4), 692–708.

World Bank. (2015). *Indigenous Latin America in the Twenty-First Century. The First Decade.* Washington, DC: The World Bank.

Yashar, D. J. (2005). *Contesting Citizenship in Latin America. The Rise of Indigenous Movements and the Postliberal Challenge.* Cambridge: Cambridge University Press.

CHAPTER 8

Unemployed Protests in Tunisia: Between Grassroots Activism and Formal Organization

Samiha Hamdi and Irene Weipert-Fenner

8.1 Introduction[1]

A key initial observation in connection with protests by the jobless in post-revolutionary Tunisia has been that mobilization of the unemployed is a quite significant factor. As demonstrated in Chap. 3, this has included massive outbursts of discontent, but it has lacked political leverage until today. In analyzing the two main types of mobilizing the jobless that can be observed in the country, the chapter offers an explanation for this puzzling

---

[1] We thank Johanna Faulstich and Giuseppe Campisi for their research support. An earlier version of this chapter was published as "Mobilization of the Marginalized: Unemployed Activism in Tunisia" (*Issam Fares Institute Working Paper*, 43, Beirut, the American University of Beirut: Beirut, 2017). The sections on the Union of Unemployed Graduates draw heavily on Weipert-Fenner (2018).

S. Hamdi
University of Sfax, Sfax, Tunisia

I. Weipert-Fenner (✉)
Peace Research Institute Frankfurt, Frankfurt am Main, Hessen, Germany
e-mail: weipert-fenner@hsfk.de

© The Author(s) 2020
I. Weipert-Fenner, J. Wolff (eds.), *Socioeconomic Protests in MENA and Latin America*, Middle East Today,
https://doi.org/10.1007/978-3-030-19621-9_8

observation: this focuses on the general lack of cooperation both among unemployed groups and with other societal and political actors. The first type of mobilization of the unemployed involves spontaneous, mostly disruptive contentious actions by unemployed people who operate outside formal organizations at the local level. These are studied here using the example of the Gafsa mining basin, a hotbed of protest by the unemployed since 2008. The second type is formally organized activism, found within the framework of the Union of Unemployed Graduates (*Union des Diplômés Chômeurs*—UDC), the only organization that advocates nationwide regarding this issue.

The chapter is based on participant observation, semi-structured interviews, and focus group discussions conducted in Tunisia between 2014 and 2016.[2] Based on this original empirical material, the two cases are analyzed and compared along three dimensions derived from social movement theory. First, from the point of view of collective action frames, the analysis finds substantial overlaps in how the two cases frame unemployment as injustice. There are only minor discrepancies, which cannot explain the lack of cooperation. Second, the study of mobilizing structures reveals a general lack of trust among societal actors and a predominance of the local level, even within the national UDC organization. This decentralized structure partly explains the weakness of the UDC at the national level. This perceived lack of power, in turn, reduces the incentives on the part of other unemployed people to join their ranks. Third, when it comes to political opportunities, the UDC has seized the opportunity offered by the political space opening up by joining forces with leftist parties, yet it has done so only cautiously due to fears about its own autonomy. At the grassroots level, being "political" or "politicized" is an outright negative attribute, which expresses a deeply felt mistrust of political institutions and parties, as well as social organizations such as the Tunisian General Labour Union (Union Générale Tunisienne du Travail, UGTT) and the UDC. Individual unemployed activists believe only in direct negotiations with officials, preferably from the national level, and reject any idea of

---

[2] Around 30 interviews with *Union des Diplômés Chômeurs* (UDC) activists, trade unionists, politicians, and journalists were conducted in Tunis, Sfax, Gabes, and Redeyef in November 2014, March 2015, and October and November 2016. Additional participant observation and group discussions were possible during the World Social Forum in Tunis in March 2015. The case study of Gafsa additionally builds on fieldwork conducted between 2015 and 2016 in Redeyef and Oum Larayes: 20 interviews, 5 focus groups with unemployed activists (graduates and nongraduates), and 4 interviews with members of the local and regional offices of the Tunisian General Labour Union.

another entity representing their interests. This difference in the perceived political opportunity structure has constituted a major obstacle to cooperation between autonomous unemployed groups and the UDC. In the conclusion, we summarize our key findings and discuss the interplay of the different forms of unemployed activism with the overall process of political change in Tunisia.

8.2　Overview of Unemployed Activism in Tunisia

In Tunisia, the lack of decent jobs is a particular problem for university graduates and people living in the marginalized interior regions of Tunisia, with graduates in the hinterland being worst off. This specific pattern of unemployment evolved slowly but steadily in the course of the economic policies that have been pursued since the 1950s and the structural adjustment attempts of the 1980s. After independence, Tunisia followed a state-centered development model, characterized by high levels of investment in higher education and the absorption of well-educated young people into the public sector. Like employment in large public sector companies, civil service employment came with a number of socioeconomic benefits, such as health services and pensions. As Hafaïedh (2000) stresses, the Tunisian regime presented university degrees as the key to social mobility. In the 1990s, however, this promise was broken when the government started to reduce the public sector to accommodate budgetary cutbacks. At the same time, the number of university graduates increased drastically, from 121,000 in 1997 to 336,000 in 2007 (Timoumi 2013, p. 118). Concurrently, the education budget was slashed, undermining the quality of university degrees. The consequence was a drastic rise in unemployment rates among university graduates: from below 5% in 1994 to 14% in 2005, jumping to 22.9% in 2010, and to around 30% since 2011 (Touhami 2012).

The extreme disparities between the coastal and interior regions in terms of demographic, economic, social, and infrastructural development have emerged since the colonial era and were deepened under President Habib Bourguiba (1957–1987) and Zine al-Abidine Ben Ali (1987–2011). State investment continued to flow to coastal cities according to the logic of clientelism: both presidents channeled resources into their areas of origin (Hibou 2015b, p. 124).[3] Regional imbalances were exacerbated by the

---

[3] At the same time, investment was channeled away from Tunisia's South, whose population largely supported Salah Ben Youssef, the great rival to Bourguiba during the fight for independence (Hibou 2015a, p. 125).

state's withdrawal from welfare provision and job creation that has already been mentioned.[4] In spite of politicians' promises of change,[5] until today, private and public investments continue to favor the coastal regions, in which 80% of Tunisia's industrial zones are located (African Manager 2016). Regional disparities are clearly visible in the area of unemployment: In Gafsa, which produces 80% of Tunisia's phosphate, the unemployment rate is among the highest in Tunisia; in 2013, it stood at 22%, the unemployment rate among university graduates stood at 52%. By comparison, in the governorate of Monastir, with its high level of tourism and almost complete lack of natural resources, only 9% of the population was unemployed in 2013. The unemployment rate of people holding a diploma stood at 25% (INS 2016b, p. 178). By comparison, the national unemployment rate remained relatively stable at around 15% between 2013 and 2016 (INS 2017).

In other cases of activism by the jobless outside the Middle East and North Africa (MENA) region, economic reforms that provoked dramatic job losses led to immediate protests by the people affected. In Argentina, for instance, massive layoffs during the mid-1990s led to the emergence of the *piquetero* movement, which became the biggest wave of mobilization among the unemployed ever witnessed worldwide (see Kaese and Wolff 2016, pp. 49–52). By contrast, activism by the unemployed in Tunisia and North Africa in general (see Chap. 1, in this volume) evolved slowly, with a growing number of people waiting to enter the labor market for the first time, more precisely the public sector or civil service. First protests erupted during the 1990s, when hiring processes brought fewer and fewer people into employment (Hibou 2015b). Yet, from the mid-2000s on, tensions increased and unemployed mobilization began to develop further. The UDC, as the first and only national organization of unemployed people, was founded in Tunis in 2006 after unemployed

---

[4] For an overview of this development in Gafsa, see Hibou 2015b.
[5] In 2014 and 2016, respectively, Tunisia's two major parties, *Nidaa Tunis* and *al-Nahda*, identified the development of marginalized regions and job creation in particular as a top priority. See, for instance, the speeches by Beji Caid Essebsi, "Speech of the Tunisian President Beji Caid Essebsi after his swearing in," Channel 9, December 31, 2014, https://www.youtube.com/watch?v=BIpfRh0bxbI (accessed January 23, 2019), and Rashid Ghanoushi, General Secretary of *al-Nahda* party, during the 10th Party Congress on May 21, 2016: "Speech of Rashid Ghanoushi at the opening of the al-Nahda's 10th conference," Tunisian News Network, May 20, 2016, https://www.youtube.com/watch?v=FN9BAptqCAA (accessed January 23, 2019).

graduates had staged a sit-in in front of the Ministry of the Interior, asking for employment. After being ignored by decision-makers, the former student union activists decided to found the Union of Unemployed Graduates. From the beginning and in spite of working clandestinely under the Ben Ali regime, the few hundred UDC activists established regional offices, one of them in the Gafsa mining basin. This allowed the UDC to participate in the 2008 Gafsa revolt that constituted the most important incident of mobilization among the unemployed before the mass uprising of 2011.

In January 2008, alleged manipulation of recruitment procedures at the publicly owned Gafsa Phosphate Company (*Compagnie des Phosphates de Gafsa*, CPG) caused contention in Redeyef, one of the mining cities, including demonstrations, sit-ins, and street blockades, that quickly spread to other cities in the mining basin. Local trade unionists and UDC activists also supported the protests, whereas the regional trade union level was accused of being involved in corruption and clientelism in regard to the hiring process. Demands quickly expanded to calls for regional development and job creation in general. These protests lasted over six months, and this could only be halted by the brutal intervention of the security forces (Gobe 2010; Allal 2010). Today, the Gafsa revolt of 2008 is considered a pivotal event that helped pave the way for the revolution (see also Chap. 1 in this volume). Indeed, less than two years later, the mass mobilization that ended the 23-year rule of Ben Ali began in Sidi Bouzid, another marginalized interior region, and quickly spread, first to other impoverished governorates in the Tunisian hinterland, including Gafsa, then to the coastal cities of Sfax and Sousse, and finally to the capital Tunis. One of the major slogans was "Work, Freedom, National Dignity" that was invented by the UDC in 2006 and had already been chanted in the Gafsa revolt in 2008. It made clear that, among the many grievances motivating the uprising, the lack of employment played a central role (Allal 2013; Chomiak 2011).

Since the ouster of Ben Ali, waves of unemployed protests have recurred (see Chap. 3, in this volume). Outbursts of discontent received widespread attention again when, in spring 2015, protesters in Gafsa blocked streets and railways, and pitched tents to bring the extraction and transportation of phosphate to a complete standstill, an unprecedented achievement given that even during the revolution of 2010–2011 mining had continued (La Presse de Tunisie 2015). In 2016, if only for ten days, mobilization of unemployed people spread from Kasserine to other marginalized regions including Gafsa, and even the capital Tunis. This episode made clear that five years after the end of authoritarian rule, socioeconomic contention could still rock the nation. It also made clear that patience was about to vanish and, instead, frustration over the outcome of the revolution was growing. Our interviews show that the impression that "nothing has changed" prevailed among all kinds of unemployed activists. Governments only tackle the problem of unemployment when protests become either too large or too disruptive to be ignored any longer. The responses to protests consist mostly of promises to carry out development and carry on dialogue that often remain empty words or limited in scope and means. The only tangible results so far have been the ad hoc creation of jobs without an overall plan for sustainable economic development (see Weipert-Fenner 2018).

Looking more specifically at the post-revolutionary dynamics of contention among unemployed people, our research reveals two divergent trajectories. The UDC used the opening up of politics since 2011 to expand its membership to 16,000 and managed to open regional offices in every governorate of Tunisia, while also increasing its levels of organization and professionalism. Contentious actions increased and also entailed more drastic forms of protest such as hunger strikes. Salam al-Ayari, the general secretary of the UDC, became a public figure representing unemployed youth in the media. In spite of all these developments, the press and the general public took little notice of UDC activism as such. The rank and file who autonomously initiated most protest events were often in dire need of the solidarity of the national office in trying to gain widespread attention for their fellow union members (Weipert-Fenner 2018). By contrast, the majority of unemployed protests, comprised of people with and without a university degree, have been staged without the support of any formal organization, often spontaneously and limited to a specific locality. Although protest actors raised limited claims, mostly demanding their own employment, they attracted more attention because, on the one hand, they made use of disruptive protests, such as street and railway blockages. On the other hand, local mobilization was relatively constant, making quick changes in the scale of protest possible. One trigger, such as the tragic death of an unemployed activist in January 2016, could be enough for single small protests to quickly stimulate broader, regional, or even national, protest waves.

Despite the greater political freedom that theoretically should have allowed unemployed groups to join forces, rally together, and build solid networks and in spite of occasional simultaneous episodes of contention, protests by the unemployed since 2011 have been characterized by growing fragmentation (see Joest 2017). Given these post-revolutionary dynamics of mobilization among unemployed people in Tunisia, we aim at explaining the puzzling combination of high levels of contention accompanied by low political leverage. In the following sections, we analyze the social meaning that activists attach to their grievances. Second, we analyze and compare the mobilization networks that have sustained and shaped protests by the jobless in the two cases. Third, we look at how activists have perceived political opportunities and threats since 2011.

8.3 Framing Grievances of the Unemployed

If we are to understand the dynamics of mobilization by the unemployed, it is not enough to look at the objective problem of unemployment as such. Instead, we need to study the social meaning of grievances as part of collective action frames, understood as "action-oriented sets of beliefs and meanings that inspire and legitimate the activities and campaigns of a social movement organization" (Benford and Snow 2000, p. 614). As Erica Simmons (2014, 2016) has recently argued, it is the social meaning with which grievances are imbued in particular times and places that shapes the emergence and dynamics of social mobilization. In contrast to earlier scholarship that focused on the quasi-objective severity of grievances, she argues for the need to understand their material and ideational dimension as well as the context in which these are embedded:

> When we understand grievances as meaning-laden we can begin to uncover some of the mechanisms at work in transforming political context into political opportunity and how group identifications are summoned by particular kinds of threats in particular ways. (Simmons, 2014, p. 518)

In the cases at hand, our interviews and focus group discussions reveal that activists frame unemployment as injustice in various ways,[6] demonstrating the existence of similarities and differences between the two types of unemployed activism. In both cases, activists sought jobs in the public sector (Gafsa) or the civil service (UDC) and thus saw the state as in charge of providing jobs. Both types of activists had never been employed, according to their notions of employment, although many of them worked

---

[6] For the concept of "injustice frames" see Gamson (1992, pp. 31–58) and Tarrow (2011, pp. 140–156).

in the informal sector and/or were formally employed in the private sector on limited contracts, in low-skilled and poorly paid jobs. All activists expressed the view that they were suffering while waiting for inclusion, with inclusion implying access not only to formal and secure public sector employment but also to the socioeconomic benefits that come with it. In more general terms, the lack of access to salaried jobs meant for them that they could not progress from adolescence to adulthood by moving into their own apartments, marrying, and starting a family. What is often described as "youth activism" is thus not defined by age but is a socially constructed category, better understood in terms of intergenerational relations. "Youth activism" in this sense means overcoming the state of "waithood" (Singerman 2007), which is perceived as undignified. This is the primary objective of unemployed activists.

Looking at how activists framed the general political causes of their grievances, we also found considerable overlap between the two types of activism. Both criticized the neglect of Tunisia's interior regions and the corrupt job distribution practices. However, with the exception of the UDC's national board, grievances were not translated into specific political demands. For the rank and file, the fundamental demand was state employment. Beyond these similarities, representatives from the two movements framed their situation in different ways.

Protesters from the Gafsa mining basin perceived their situation as unjust because (a) other regions have prospered, in particular, from resources extracted from Gafsa; (b) the socioeconomic situation in Gafsa has declined drastically; and (c) job distribution practices in Gafsa are corrupt and dominated by clientelist networks, which provoke feelings of injustice.

First, unemployed activists in Gafsa understood their situation as unjust due to the contrast between resource wealth and poverty. Seeing other regions prosper provokes feelings of being left behind (Chouikha and Gobe 2009; Chouikha and Geisser 2010). People who were interviewed referred to *hogra*, or "humiliation." As one young unemployed person explained:

> In the Gafsa mining basin, we produce richness, the CPG [Gafsa Phosphate Company] is the backbone of the Tunisian economy, but, to the contrary, richness accumulates on the coastal regions, and leaves us in unemployment, poverty, and disease.[7]

---

[7] Interview with autonomous unemployed activist, Oum Larayes, August 16, 2015.

The second dimension of injustice derives from Gafsa's relative deprivation over time, which provoked a notion of a "paradise lost." Its history has been bound to the fate of the CPG. Created in the late nineteenth century, the company was first owned by French colonialists, before it was nationalized after independence in 1956. The four mining cities of Redeyef, Oum Larayes, M'dhila, and Metlaoui came into being with the introduction of phosphate mining. Not only did the CPG ensure employment in the region, it also guaranteed the availability of basic social services (including drinking water and electricity, health services, education, grocery stores, and even golf courses). Starting in the 1970s, however, Tunisia embarked on a "modernization" process that went hand in hand with economic liberalization. The phosphate mining company had to undergo reforms, causing its retreat from service provision. In the mid-1980s, the World Bank and the International Monetary Fund (IMF) pushed Tunisia to speed up public sector reforms, resulting in a CPG labor force reduction from 16,000 in the 1980s to 6000 in the 2000s. At the same time, the quality of services and infrastructure in the region also dropped (Hibou 2015a, p. 305; see also Allal 2010).

In a region where job opportunities are limited, these reforms led to youth unemployment. However, the collective memory of a golden era, when the phosphate extraction industry was a workers' paradise, lives on. This is closely associated with the active developmental role of the state in the early postindependence era. As Jean-Claude Abric (1994, pp. 62–63) argued, it is important to understand the broad general outlook of activists to fully comprehend their mobilization dynamics. To that end, it must be acknowledged that adults passed on their memory of a golden age to the next generation for whom this vision continues to shape expectations. The idea of a well-off class and a stable working population is closely associated with the CPG. Identification with the company goes to the extent of one person who was interviewed explaining that "[the CPG] is part of our existence … it is my father … it is our history."[8] The sharp contrast between "the good old days," when the region was perceived as ahead of everywhere else, and its current miseries today was expressed by another activist:

> Here in Redeyef it was paradise. We lived here in a golden era, during and after independence. It was here that the first electric lamp was illuminated, here was the first golf course, [and] here we had the first supermarket. But they steal our richness and give us nothing. There is only poverty, deadly

[8] Interview with autonomous unemployed activist, Sfax, June 20, 2013.

diseases; even with drinking water we face enormous shortages. We are thirsty, and the water quality is very bad. We don't even have the right to laugh like the others because of the yellow stains on our teeth, caused by the quality of [our] water.[9]

This malaise is blamed on the state, whose perceived responsibility is to correct unemployment, poverty, and regional imbalances. In contrast to an efficient state that distributes goods and services fairly, the reality is seen as marked by a new form of clientelism and corruption—the third dimension of the injustice frame in Gafsa. Since the CPG was scaled back and its various services and functions outsourced, regional power holders, including the regional branches of the national labor federation UGTT, have manipulated recruitment procedures to favor their clients either by giving preferential treatment to relatives or through corruption (Allal 2010; Gobe 2010). In combination with the sharp reductions in job opportunities, this situation sparked the 2008 protests and, until today, continues to be a source of discontent.

In the case of the UDC, the primary grievances driving the mobilization of unemployed graduates were (a) the broken promise of social mobility via higher education; (b) a lack of development for marginalized regions; and (c) corruption in public recruitment procedures.

In interviews, UDC activists explicitly addressed the first problem, complaining about university education that did not qualify them for the labor market.[10] Interestingly, however, public demands for educational reform did not play any major role in the post-2011 context. This could be explained by the fact that the specific grievances that come with higher education do not offer a promising collective action frame that would also speak to unemployed people who do not have a post-secondary degree. Still, in the UDC's internal discourse, the past guarantees of state employment for university graduates underpin their perceived entitlement to state jobs.

Second, the marginalization of interior regions constitutes an issue that unites the perceived grievances of the UDC and the activists from Gafsa. The perceived injustice that can be observed in, for example, the Gafsa mining basin is in fact tied to the situation of unemployed university graduates. Right from the start, the UDC established two regional offices in the hinterland, in Jendouba and Redeyef. Local mobilization dynamics

---

[9] Interview with autonomous unemployed activist, Redeyef, August 17, 2015.
[10] Interview with Salam Ayari, group interviews, Tunis, March 2015.

have played an important role in the development of the UDC, which made it possible for the union to join broader protest alliances, increase its visibility, and expand its networks. This happened during the Gafsa uprising of 2008, which has already been mentioned, when local activists of the recently created UDC as well as local trade unionists supported the organization of the protests that had spontaneously emerged among unemployed people (Allal 2010). Furthermore, until today, local UDC activism has remained strikingly similar to autonomous unemployed protests in the way it connects the demand for individual employment with the general call for regional development. Given that the latter is not translated into claims for specific policies of how to develop Tunisia's interior regions better, the issue of regional marginalization serves more as a diagnostic rather than a prognostic frame for singling out solutions.[11] While the criticism is general and political, the specific demands remain focused on individual problem-solving.

Third, UDC grievances incorporate a criticism of recruitment procedures for the civil service, the *concours*. These annual exams are claimed to ensure that civil service jobs are distributed on merit. UDC activists contend that they are rife with corruption. Jobs are distributed either in exchange for money or along clientelist networks. The latter might be based on kinship or partisanship. Under Ben Ali, the ruling party distributed jobs to its own clients; for the activists, this persisted after 2011, when the *al-Nahda* party, heading the Troika government, distributed 18,000 jobs to its sympathizers.[12] Gafsa's protesters taking to the streets against rigged employment lists share this grievance. Additionally, the UDC criticized that the *concours* system distributed far too few jobs and therefore did not offer most applicants a real chance of being hired.[13]

Again, university graduates felt betrayed by the *concours* system, which promised prosperity as a reward for dedicated study. Behind this perceived injustice is the rebellion against waithood mentioned earlier. As Hafaïedh (2000) argued, the *concours* is another form of waiting for inclusion: Instead of being officially unemployed, the state gives university graduates the sta-

---

[11] On the different functions that collective action frames (can) serve, see Benford and Snow (2000).
[12] Focus group with UDC activists, Tunis, March 2015. See also La Presse de Tunisie (2014).
[13] See for example the criticism by the UDC of the recruitment of secondary-school teachers (*Certificat d'aptitude au professorat de l'enseignement du second degré*—CAPES). See Marzouk (2014).

tus of "waiting for another round of exams." Naming their struggle—as a protest against a state of being an unemployed university graduate—is, then, the first step in overcoming the perceived injustice. The second is reforming recruitment procedures. The UDC, for instance, proposed including one of its members on the *concours* supervisory board, to ensure transparency. The third step is expanding job availability, bringing us back to the question of economic development.

8.4 Mobilizing Structures of Organized and Autonomous Unemployed Activists

When trying to understand the patterns of protests by the unemployed, the specific shape of local mobilizing structures is a key factor to look at both in the Gafsa mining basin and in the case of the UDC. Scholars who have studied protest movements in Tunisia since 2011 have stressed the spontaneous character of these movements, with protests being carried out by societal actors without allegiance to political parties.[14] Our research generally supports this finding but with an additional twist: At least in the Gafsa mining basin, the landscape of protest actors has fragmented even further over the years. In 2008, the unemployed still coordinated their protests with different organizations, ranging from opposition parties and trade union federations to NGOs such as the *Association Tunisienne des Femmes Démocrates* (Tunisian Association of Democratic Women, ATFD) and the *Ligue Tunisienne des Droits de l'Homme* (Tunisian Human Rights League, LTDH), as well as individual journalists (Allal 2010; Gobe 2010). Additional support came from expatriates from Gafsa living in France, who organized solidarity marches, notably in Nantes. Since 2011, protests have been increasingly fragmented and disunited. Now primarily based on familial ties, they remain isolated from both political parties and trade unions. In some cases, even the claim to the right to work was derived from familial entitlements in a certain locality:

> We are all the cousins of 'Arsh Awlad Salem' [tribe of Salem's children]. We built the [sit-in] tent at the phosphate mine, because, by accident, this place was owned by our family once, before it was made available to the CPG, which gives us priority in getting employed.[15]

---

[14] See, for instance, Dakhli (2011), Bendana (2014), and Salmon (2016).
[15] Interview with autonomous unemployed activist, Oum Larayes, August 16, 2015.

A similar situation was found in Oum Larayes, where families organized sit-ins at CPG installations to support unemployed relatives. Although family and clan solidarities played a role in 2008, too, they have gained in importance in recent years. Economic insecurity has increased the dependence of individuals on their closest social linkages (Daoud 2011; Elbahi 2005). In the post-2011 context, mobilization in terms of these primary relationships is seen as the only way to overcome individual marginalization. Mobilization based on identities constructed in terms of local ties, such as family, neighborhood, or tribe, has replaced other mobilizing networks that were still effective in 2008.

Furthermore, the ambivalent nature of the UGTT has driven the unemployed to mobilizing locally. The UGTT has historically played the double role of a political actor at the national level and a societal actor at the local level. This dates back to the first years after independence, when UGTT leader Ahmed Ben Salah was undecided whether to form a union or a political party (Chouikha and Geisser 2010). The UGTT leadership (e.g., Farhat Hached, Ahmed Tlili, Ahmed Ben Salah, and Habib Achour) long played a political role, as the UGTT remained militant, mobilizing for protest movements such as the general strike of 1978 (peaking on "Black Thursday," January 26, 1978) or the bread riots of January 4, 1984. Security crackdowns on large protests restricted the freedom of movement of the national leadership. Yet, at least at the local level, the UGTT served as an umbrella for different kinds of opposition forces, integrating political rivalries, social and ideological conflicts, and protest movements (Beinin 2016). Within this loose structure, local cadres could remain militant and act with relative autonomy.

This dynamic was evident in Gafsa, in 2008, when local trade unionists, the rank and file of the primary and secondary education unions as well of the health unions, supported the movement. This is why young activists staged their sit-in and hunger strike at the UGTT facilities.[16] Adnan Hajji, a local UGTT activist, eventually even became the unofficial leader of the protest movement. At the same time, the regional branch of the UGTT, and the mining unions in particular, opposed the protest. The general secretary of the regional UGTT unit Amara Abbassi condemned the protesters and the trade unionists who supported the movement. Abbassi was simultaneously a Member of Parliament for the then ruling Democratic Constitutional Rally (Rassemblement Constitutionnel Démocratique,

[16] Interview with one of the initiators of the 2008 uprising, Redeyef, June 25, 2013.

RCD) and allegedly had manipulated the recruitment lists in favor of his clientelist networks. The regional UGTT office even organized a protest march against the movement.[17] At the national level, the UGTT did not adopt a position in 2008.

Despite these mixed UGTT strategies prior to 2011, a young unemployed activist, in 2013, stressed the memory of betrayal: "The unions of the mines only take care of their interests. They are the profiteers, and the corrupted. They have always sided against the protest movements."[18] This rift worsened when the UGTT's national and regional leaderships repeatedly reject the unemployed protests. As one representative of the regional UGTT in Gafsa put it:

> We are in favor of the right to work, that the young unemployed demand, but we condemn the halt of phosphate production. In fact, the UGTT has not organized the protest movements; 90% of the protests are spontaneous, and not within the framework of UGTT.[19]

According to this union representative, the UGTT also endorsed the action plan for Gafsa, which was presented in May 2015 by then Prime Minister Habib Essid in response to a new wave of protests in the region. This plan combined the usual set of promises: the creation of new jobs; consultations between the national and regional level as well as between political and civil society actors; activation of environmental organizations to reduce pollution; an audit of the CPG according to environmental protection standards; and an evaluation of those responsible at the regional level, followed by replacement of inefficient employees (Tunisie Numerique 2015). In contrast to the UGTT at the regional level, local UGTT offices criticized the plan and responded with a general strike on May 20, 2015.

This episode illustrates a general dilemma that characterizes relations between trade unions and unemployed movements: The UGTT prioritizes the interests of CPG workers, who cannot afford frequent work stoppages and the resulting bonus reductions. This applies not only to Gafsa's workers, who tend to support the protests because of their strong ties to the region's unemployed, but also to workers in other cities, such as Gabes and Sfax, where downstream phosphate processing installations are located. A standstill in Gafsa means no work in Gabes

---

[17] Interview with trade unionist, Oum Larayes, August 16, 2015.
[18] Interview with autonomous unemployed activist, August 16, 2015, Oum Larayes.
[19] Interview with a member of the UGTT regional office in Gafsa, August 2015, Gafsa.

and Sfax.[20] Additionally, the new UGTT leadership carefully balances the social demands of its local base against gains to its political position, while maintaining good relationships with regional and national authorities. Supporting protests, in particular those organized by non-members, comes at a price. As the earlier quote shows, unemployed protesters are aware of the UGTT's balancing act.

Interestingly, not even the UDC is regarded as an ally by local unemployed activists in Gafsa. They consider the UDC to be part of the political parties and civil society organizations that are generally perceived to support only the claims of politicized youth, not of ordinary Tunisians: "We only trust our group," one unemployed graduate said, explaining that:

> The UDC, for instance, only defends the interests of its politicized members. I was a member of the UDC and I know very well that [for] those who are politicized, their parties will support them. They always seek to manipulate the protests for political reasons. We refuse to be pawns.[21]

To understand this lack of trust that impedes cooperation, we must also look at the UDC's mobilization networks. The union is clearly associated with the left camp, linking student union activism within the General Union of Tunisian Students (*Union Générale des Étudiants de Tunisie*, UGET) to labor activism within the UGTT. Former student unionists founded the UDC in 2006, and until today former members of the leftist student federation UGET are the core network of people engaging within the UDC. This provides the unemployed union with high organizational skills and a shared worldview. As soon as their status as unemployed is remedied, former UDC activists usually join the ranks of the UGTT. The three unions—UGET, UDC, and UGTT—are regarded as natural steps in an activist's career. This explains the UDC's traditionally close ties with the labor federation. From the very beginning, for instance, the UDC has usually benefited from the space the UGTT provided for opposition to be voiced during the dictatorship. Staging protests in front of the UGTT's local offices was a key element in the repertoire of contention in authoritarian Tunisia (Beinin 2016). In the post-revolutionary context, staging protests inside UGTT headquarters has been an important strategy employed by the UDC, as the increasing number of hunger strikes (up since 2014) held at UGTT buildings illustrates (Weipert-Fenner 2018).

---

[20] Interview with a member of the UGTT executive board, Tunis, November 2014.
[21] Focus group with unemployed graduates, Redeyef, January 2016.

While the UGTT publicly supports many UDC protests and is considered a natural ally, like the autonomous unemployed activists, UDC members see the UGTT's role as ambivalent. Fear of being exploited by the trade unions prevails: The UDC might be good enough to mobilize and build up pressure on the street, but as soon as the trade union representatives sit at the negotiating table with the government, they care more about workers' interests (mainly salaries) rather than job creation.[22]

When considering the UDC's mobilizing networks, it is important to differentiate between the local and national levels—the former being relatively independent of the latter. Decisions about protests are taken at the grassroots level and then carried out with local allies (such as the local UGTT cadres). There is thus no overall strategy of mobilization coordinated by the national office. Instead, many, often small, contentious actions are carried out that are quite similar to autonomously organized protests by the unemployed. Since 2014, there has been an increase in hunger strikes, in which UDC activists demand jobs for themselves. No political claims beyond the demands for job creation and regional development are made (Weipert-Fenner 2018). This is clearly at odds with the UDC's national agenda, which includes explicit demands for sweeping policy changes in the country. Yet, given the union's limited material resources, the national level often tries to provide support for fellow activists at the local level, especially through media attention. That the decentralized network absorbs resources without pursuing political goals also contributes to explaining the UDC's lack of political influence. In combination with the low levels of trust among unemployed activists and social organizations, the union's own weakness makes cooperation with the UDC even less attractive.

8.5 Opportunity and Threat Perception: The Interplay with the New Political Order

The 2011 uprising opened up the political space, enabling new forms of contentious action. Gafsa activists perceived this new freedom as state weakness, encouraging disruptive forms of protest motivated by personal interests, without the shelter of civil society institutions or political support. For the Gafsa activists, even an informal leader of the 2008 uprising, the local UGTT activist Adnan Hajji (elected to parliament in 2014),

[22] Interview Salam al-Ayari, Tunis, March 2015.

ceased to be a unifying figure when he tried to stop the regional protest wave in 2015. This contrasts with the uprising of 2008, when most opposition parties were illegal and weak, vis-à-vis Ben Ali's repression. At that time, the Tunisian Communist Workers Party (now the Workers' Party, and member of the Popular Front) and the Tajdid Movement were able to support the protests in the mining basin, mainly through the latter's newspaper *al-Tariq al-Jadid*, which covered the security crackdowns as well as the lawsuits against activists. Party support also helped unify the movement so that negotiations were offered. The result was the release of imprisoned activists and some measures favoring the young unemployed and regional development.[23]

One explanation for why cooperation in the Gafsa region was feasible with certain political actors under authoritarian rule but not in post-2011 Tunisia is that, while facing competition from an influx of new parties and associations, established parties have remained paralyzed by restrictions inherited from the Ben Ali regime. As a result, the former lost influence on young protesters, contributing to the fragmentation of the protest movement. Still, it is striking that activists overwhelmingly mistrust political parties and the trade union federation: In interviews, the unemployed activists recurrently expressed such skepticism. One activist, for instance, asserted that "the political parties and the UGTT only pursue their own interests. We only see them during their electoral campaigns. They use us for the affairs of the politicians."[24] By enabling opposition parties and societal organizations to officially engage in electoral politics, democratization thus led to increasing distance between these formal organizations and the autonomous unemployed.

This crisis of trust, which influenced the perception of opportunities and threats (of exploitation) in the post-revolutionary context, is plausibly also exacerbated by the general disappointment with politicians, who are perceived as not delivering anything more than empty promises to take care of unemployment. Furthermore, the instability of governments—with six successive cabinets since 2011—has intensified frustration with an ineffective political system and politicians incapable of solving the country's major challenges. Activists from Gafsa explicitly said that their relationship to political parties is solely pragmatic. "I only look for employment," one

---

[23] At that time, the governorate made promises to create 2700 jobs and encourage the private sector to invest in the region. However, sustainable development was never achieved (Hibou 2015b, pp. 317–319).

[24] Interview with autonomous unemployed activist, Redeyef, August 2015.

explained, "nothing else is of interest for me. I do not have any other worries, neither politics nor political parties are of interest to me."[25] As elaborated in the previous section, autonomous activists similarly refuse to cooperate with the UDC because they consider it politicized and thus more part of a political—leftist—camp than a societal ally.

Given the obvious crisis of political representation among unemployed activists, we find a trend toward unmediated negotiation with the state. Unemployed activists in Gafsa feel that political parties and civil society organizations support politicized youth only, rather than ordinary Tunisians, and therefore prefer direct interaction with state officials. "We have the capacity to negotiate with the authorities ourselves," said one unemployed graduate, adding that "we do not have any trust, neither in political parties, nor in the UGTT or UDC."[26] By the same token, this plausibly also reflects the strategies of the political authorities themselves. It is usually the governor who selects the most active protesters and starts negotiating job distribution, thereby splitting protesters into small groups. This creates incentives for the mobilized unemployed to adapt their strategies by organizing around more resilient units, such as the family. From their perspective, this increases their individual chances of employment. In contrast to 2008, when six trade unionists were selected to negotiate with the government on their behalf, young protesters now negotiate with the local (and occasionally national) authorities without intermediaries.[27] Simultaneously, they try to build pressure through disruptive and at times violent forms of protest: blocking roads and railways, halting phosphate production, hunger strikes, and suicide (attempts).[28]

The preference for direct negotiations with state representatives is not the result of a perceived opportunity but rather of a lack thereof: unemployed protesters have generally struggled to gain direct access to the state. State institutions do not function properly or are simply absent. One interviewee claimed that, "in Redeyef, the state does not exist.

---

[25] Interview with autonomous unemployed activist, Oum Larayes, August 2015.

[26] Focus group with unemployed graduates, Sit-in in Redeyef, January 2016.

[27] Ministerial delegation to Gafsa, April 23, 2015; meetings of Kamel Jandoubi, Minister for Relations with Constitutional Institutions, Civil Society, and Human Rights; as well as interviews with protesters, May 26–27, 2015, in Tunis.

[28] Houssem Ben Azaz from Oum Larayes committed suicide by self-immolation on February 4, 2016. The most unconventional protest form was a march toward Algeria with participants threatening to give up Tunisian citizenship.

The delegate[29] exercises his function from a distance, from the headquarters of the governorate at Gafsa city."[30] The absence of the state is also felt indirectly in the lack of state functions performed on the ground such as the miserable state of infrastructure. In the city of Redeyef, for instance, no police station can be found, youth clubs lack basic equipment, and protesters occupy municipal properties. "The only project implemented in Oum Larayes, since 2015, was the closure of the factory Yasaki," said another person interviewed.[31]

In summary, despite formally greater political opportunities and potential political allies, autonomous unemployed activists in Gafsa feel that the political system de facto does not provide improved access, or realistic chances of realizing their aims. Therefore, they resort to contentious actions, especially through disruptive protests, with very specific and tangible aims and the goal of directly negotiating with the highest levels of government, circumventing dysfunctional local and regional authorities.

The UDC generally shares this disappointment with the incapacity of the successive governments that have ruled Tunisia since the fall of Ben Ali. Yet in contrast to autonomous unemployed, UDC activists used the newfound freedoms post 2011 to expand its organization. Now a legal entity, there has been an increase in its membership and number of regional offices (see Sect. 8.2). Internal elections were held and Salam al-Ayari—the long-time informal leader of the UDC—became its first official general secretary. Al-Ayari took to the media, speaking on behalf of unemployed graduates. Internal and external communication is now openly carried out via new social media, mainly Facebook. Thus, while the increased political freedom encouraged the fragmentation of the protest movement in Gafsa, it broadened and improved the level of organization of the UDC.

Looking for potential political allies to support unemployed demands, the UDC allied itself with the left-wing Popular Front (*Jabha Sha'abiyya*) bloc, led by Hamma Hammami. Yet, the Popular Front has remained a weak partner, holding only 15 of the 217 parliamentary seats (2014–2019).

---

[29] This is an appointed state official responsible for a subregional "delegation" serving as the intermediary between the governorate and the smallest administrative unit, the so-called sector (*imada*).

[30] Interview with autonomous unemployed activist, Redeyef, August 2015.

[31] Focus group interview with unemployed graduates and demonstrators at the delegation of Oum Larayes, February 5, 2016.

The party has not joined any government since 2011, and it actually refused to cooperate with the ruling *Nidaa Tunis* for fear of co-optation. Its seemingly natural alliance with the leftist camp garners the UDC support from the Popular Front—mostly through displays of solidarity in public but also in the form of legal support from the party for UDC activists facing state repression. Yet the UDC also shares a fear of being exploited by political actors: first as a way to create pressure on the street, then being neglected during policymaking (Antonakis-Nashif 2016, p. 139). Cooperation with the major ruling parties, *Nidaa Tunis* and *al-Nahda*, is unthinkable, as they are regarded as too neoliberal. Additionally, the division between Islamist and secular forces makes any cooperation with *al-Nahda* impossible for the UDC.[32]

Similar to the autonomous unemployed activists, local UDC members have also engaged in direct negotiations with state authorities following a protest. This was always on an ad hoc basis, and meetings were often canceled or postponed by state officials. Other state responses involved ignoring or repressing UDC protests through the imprisonment of protesters and violent dispersals of sit-ins. However, this only caused more protests staged in solidarity for fellow UDC members (Weipert-Fenner 2018). All in all, this has led to growing frustration with state representatives in the new democratic order.

8.6 Conclusion

Despite greater opportunity to articulate grievances, the two types of unemployed activists studied in this chapter express increasingly acute frustration. "Nothing has changed" is how most sum up their assessment of the political transformation process since 2011. From the state, they experience neglect and repression, which provokes increasingly dramatic protest events, such as hunger strikes. This stands in sharp contrast to the Tunisian democratization process's novel resolution for a number of social justice questions. Article 12 of the 2014 constitution, for instance, obligates the positive discrimination of marginalized regions. The transitional justice law covers economic crimes and violations of social and economic rights, in unprecedented ways. For example, not only individuals but also

---

[32] Interview with both UDC and *al-Nahda* members. For more on the Islamist versus secularist cleavage that dominated the Tunisian transformation process until late 2013, see Boubekeur 2016.

entire regions can be regarded as victims (Almajdoub 2017). Employment has also been recognized as a top priority. Around 90,000 new state jobs were created in 2011 alone (INS 2016a, p. 7). In Gafsa's state-run phosphate company, employment increased from 5000 in 2007 to almost 30,000 today. Politicians, thus, did respond. At least regarding the latter figure, it is clear that the spike in employment at the CPG was a short-run maneuver to assuage protesters. This is demonstrated by the fact that the increase in personnel did not result in a corresponding increase in phosphate production—which, in fact, dropped from 8.8 million tons/year in 2010 to a mere 3 million tons annually after 2011. The addition of CPG employees thus ought not to be considered as part of any genuine effort to fulfill the obligations of Article 12 of the new constitution. Instead, state resources are used—in this case, by creating unsustainable jobs—as an instrument for stabilizing rule, continuing the political economy logic that characterized the Ben Ali regime (see Chap. 2, in this volume).

When President Beji Caid Essebsi took his post in 2014, he asked for patience. Unemployment would not be solved "within 90 days," he said.[33] In 2015, during the Gafsa protests—and after terrorist attacks on tourism hot spots—Essebsi portrayed the protesters as instigators of chaos and threats to national security, enabling terrorists to further destabilize the country (Marzouki 2015). During the massive mobilization of January 2016, he made the same suggestion, but then asked the government to "prepare a program to deal with the crisis of unemployment, and improve the situation of the interior regions."[34] Concurrently, he blamed parties for "agendas aiming at exploiting the demands of the young unemployed in order to destabilize the country,"[35] suggesting that the Popular Front was using unemployed activists for its own cause. This diverse set of discursive strategies reflects the indecisive handling of unemployment, by both types of unemployed activists. The government asks for time, promising changes without implementing them, and then delegitimizes protesters as either political puppets or permissive causes of terrorism.

[33] See "The President of the Republic on the Program Today al-Yom al-Thamin the Tunisian Dialogue Channel," Tunisian Dialogue Channel, May 11, 2015, https://www.youtube.com/watch?v=_o_YjbDjrbQ (accessed January 22, 2019).

[34] "Baji Caid Essebsi: Tunisia is targeted," Qafsa Broadcasting, December 22, 2016, http://www.radiogafsa.tn/الباجي-قائد-السبسي-تونس-مستهدفة-في-أمن/ (accessed January 22, 2019).

[35] "Address to the nation by President Essebsi after stoppages in a number states," Hannibal TV, January 22, 2016, https://www.youtube.com/watch?v=BErtI5wuRo8 (accessed 22 January 2019).

How can political actors continue to ignore, repress, or halfheartedly engage with the massive discontent of the unemployed? Part of the answer seems to lie in two dynamics uncovered in this chapter. Though protests in marginalized regions, at times, mobilize huge numbers of people, they remain fragmented and thus have no capacity to push for broad-based change. In contrast, the only organized actor, the Union of Unemployed Graduates, has strengthened its capacity as well as its internal cohesion since 2011. Still, the UDC has remained comparably small and has lacked capacity to build political pressure. Both types of unemployed mobilization struggle with a lack of trust, a fear of being exploited, and a perception that the most promising opportunities are protests limited to apolitical demands for individual employment.

The negative consequences of this strategy include waning support from a public that has grown tired of disruptive protests hampering their daily lives. This not only facilitates the strategy of delegitimization used by the political authorities, it also makes it difficult for politicians to engage in genuine negotiations with "the unemployed." In fact, only the UDC's central office could be regarded as a possible negotiating partner at the national level. Yet, it is clearly not able to plausibly represent the fragmented range of unemployed activists, not to speak of unemployed people as such. The mistrust of the autonomous unemployed activists vis-à-vis the UDC as well as the decentralized structure of the union itself limit its capacity to negotiate on behalf of a broader movement of the unemployed. The current state of affairs thus seems to constitute a missed opportunity, given that there is much common ground between the two movement types. Clearly, a comparable set of grievances and a joint desire to find paths toward sustainable regional development, increases in job opportunities, and fair access to employment are not enough to enable the emergence of a unitary unemployment movement.

References

Abric, J.-C. (1994). *Pratiques sociales et représentations.* Paris: PUF.

African Manager. (2016, February 17). Tunisia: Only 20% of industrial zones are located in interior regions. Retrieved January 18, 2019, from https://african-manager.com/site_eng/tunisia-only-20-of-industrial-zones-are-located-in-interior-regions/.

Allal, A. (2010). Réformes néolibérales, clientélismes et protestations en situation autoritaire. *Politique africaine, 117*(1), 107–125.

Allal, A. (2013). Becoming revolutionary in Tunisia, 2007–2011. In J. Beinin & F. Vairel (Eds.), *Social movements, mobilization, and contestation in the Middle East and North Africa* (pp. 185–204). Stanford, CA: Stanford University Press.

Almajdoub, S. (2017). Addressing inequality in Tunisia: Victim regions and transitional justice. Retrieved January 18, 2019, from http://www.ewinextgen.com/africa/2017/6/13/addressing-inequality-in-tunisia-victim-regions-and-transitional-justice.

Antonakis-Nashif, A. (2016). Contested transformation: Mobilized publics in Tunisia between compliance and protest. *Mediterranean Politics, 21*(1), 128–149.

Beinin, J. (2016). *Workers and thieves: Labor movements and popular uprisings in Tunisia and Egypt*. Stanford, CA: Stanford Briefs, an imprint of Stanford University Press.

Bendana, K. (2014). Entrer dans l'histoire de la Révolution tunisienne. *L'Année du Maghreb, 10,* 49–58.

Benford, R., & Snow, D. (2000). Framing processes and social movements: An overview and assessment. *Annual Review of Sociology, 26*(1), 611–639.

Boubekeur, A. (2016). Islamists, secularists and old regime elites in Tunisia: Bargained competition. *Mediterranean Politics, 21*(1), 107–127.

Chomiak, L. (2011). The making of a revolution in Tunisia. *Middle East Law and Governance, 3,* 68–83.

Chouikha, L., & Geisser, V. (2010). Retour sur la révolte du bassin minier. Les cinq leçons politiques d'un conflit social inédit. *L'Année du Maghreb, VI,* 415–426. https://doi.org/10.4000/anneemaghreb.923.

Chouikha, L., & Gobe, E. (2009). La Tunisie entre la "révolte du bassin minier de Gafsa" et l'échéance électorale de 2009. *L'Année du Maghreb, V,* 387–420. https://doi.org/10.4000/anneemaghreb.623.

Dakhli, L. (2011). Une lecture de la révolution tunisienne. *Le Mouvement Social, 236*(3), 89–103.

Daoud, A. (2011). La révolution tunisienne de janvier 2011: Une lecture par les déséquilibres du territoire. *echogeo*. https://doi.org/10.4000/echogeo.12612.

Elbahi, M. (2005). *La tribu en Tunisie à l'époque moderne (XVI–XIX siècles)*. Sfax: Faculté des Lettres et Sciences Humaines de Sfax.

Gamson, W. A. (1992). *Talking politics*. Cambridge: Cambridge University Press.

Gobe, E. (2010). The Gafsa mining basin between riots and a social movement: Meaning and significance of a protest movement in Ben Ali's Tunisia. Retrieved January 22, 2019, from https://halshs.archives-ouvertes.fr/halshs-00557826.

Hafaïedh, A. (2000). Trajectoires de diplômés chômeurs en Tunisie: l'attente, l'ailleurs, et la conversion. In V. Geisser (Ed.), *Diplômés Maghrébins d'ici et d'ailleurs. Trajectoires sociales et itinéraires migratoires* (pp. 122–136). Paris: CNRS Édition.

Hibou, B. (2015a). La formation asymétrique de l'État en Tunisie. Les territoires de l'injustice. In I. Bono, B. Hibou, H. Meddeb, & M. Tozy (Eds.), *L'État d'injustice au Maghreb. Maroc et Tunisie* (pp. 99–150). Paris: Karthala.

Hibou, B. (2015b). Le bassin minier de Gafsa en déshérence. Gouverner le mécontentement social en Tunisie. In I. Bono, B. Hibou, H. Meddeb, & M. Tozy (Eds.), *L'État d'injustice au Maghreb. Maroc et Tunisie* (pp. 301–343). Paris: Karthala.

INS (Institut National de la Statistique). (2016a). Caracteristiques des agents de la fonction publique et leurs salaires, 2010–2014. Retrieved January 18, 2019, from http://www.ins.tn/sites/default/files/publication/pdf/Rapfonct-pub2-site.pdf.

INS (Institut National de la Statistique). (2016b). Enquête nationale sur la population et l'emploi 2013. Retrieved January 18, 2019, from http://www.ins.tn/sites/default/files/publication/pdf/emploi2013%20avec%20lien.pdf.

INS (Institut National de la Statistique). (2017). Annuaire statistique de la Tunisie 2012–2016. Retrieved January 18, 2019, from http://beta.ins.tn/sites/default/files/publication/pdf/annuaire-2016%20avec%20lien_1.pdf.

Joest, P. (2017). *Work, freedom, dignity—Once more? Contentious politics, emotions and organizational constraints in Tunisia since 2011*. Unpublished Master Thesis, Universität Tübingen.

Kaese, F., & Wolff, J. (2016). Piqueteros after the hype: Unemployed movements in Argentina, 2008–2015. *European Review of Latin American and Caribbean Studies, 102*, 47–68. https://doi.org/10.18352/erlacs.10112.

La Presse de Tunisie. (2014, January 30). Union des diplômés chômeurs. Appel à une stratégie nationale de lutte contre le chômage. Retrieved January 18, 2019, from http://lapresse.tn/component/nationals/?task=article&id=78236.

La Presse de Tunisie. (2015, May 27). CPG. Reprise du travail au siège social, après 21 jours d'arrêt. Retrieved January 23, 2019, from http://www.lapresse.tn/?option=com_sport&task=article&id=99968.

Marzouk, H. (2014, February 18). UDC: chômage et système éducatif sont intimement liés. *L'Économiste Maghrébin*. Retrieved January 23, 2019, from https://www.leconomistemaghrebin.com/2014/02/18/udc-chomage-systeme-educatif-lies/.

Marzouki, N. (2015). Tunisia's rotten compromise. *Middle East Report Online*. Retrieved September 23, 2016, from http://www.merip.org/mero/mero071015.

Salmon, J.-M. (2016). *29 jours de révolution. Histoire du soulèvement tunisien, 17 décembre 2010–14 janvier 2011*. Paris: Les Petits matins.

Simmons, E. (2014). Grievances do matter in mobilization. *Theory and Society, 43*(5), 513–546. https://doi.org/10.1007/s11186-014-9231-6.

Simmons, E. (2016). Market reforms and water wars. *World Politics, 68*(1), 37–73.

Singerman, D. (2007). *The economic imperatives of marriage: Emerging practices and identities among youth in the Middle East.* Middle East Youth Initiative Working Paper 6. Washington, DC and Dubai: Wolfensohn Centre for Development and Dubai School of Government.

Tarrow, S. (2011). *Power in movement: Social movements and contentious politics. Cambridge studies in comparative politics.* Cambridge: Cambridge University Press.

Timoumi, H. (2013). *Ben Ali et ses 23 ans de règne sur la Tunisie. La tromperie du "despotisme doux".* Sfax: Med Ali Editions.

Touhami, H. (2012, December 2). Disparités sociales et régionales et chômage des diplômés du supérieur. *Leaders.* Retrieved January 23, 2019, from http://www.leaders.com.tn/article/9988-disparites-sociales-et-regionales-et-chomage-des-diplomes-du-superieur.

Tunisie Numerique. (2015, May 15). Tunisie—Gafsa: Les décisions du conseil ministériel pour débloquer la situation dans le bassin minier. Retrieved January 18, 2019, from https://www.tunisienumerique.com/tunisie-gafsa-les-decisions-du-conseil-ministeriel-pour-debloquer-la-situation-dans-le-bassin-minier/.

Weipert-Fenner, I. (2018). Unemployed mobilisation in times of democratisation: The Union of Unemployed Graduates in post-ben Ali Tunisia. *The Journal of North African Studies.* https://doi.org/10.1080/13629387.2018.1535317.

CHAPTER 9

Mobilized Along the Margins: Survival Strategies of Tuktuk Drivers in Egypt

Nayera Abdelrahman Soliman

9.1 Introduction

Egypt is not a poor country in resources (Farid 2017), but most of its population is. According to a survey of income and expenditures by the Egyptian Central Agency for Public Mobilization and Statistics (CAPMAS) (Aswat Masreya 2016), in 2015, 27.8% of Egypt's population of nearly 90 million were living below the poverty line, which is equivalent currently to $55 per month per person.[1] According to the same survey, if a full family is spending $473 monthly,[2] which means $5682 per year,[3] it belongs to

---

[1] The poverty line according to Egyptian Central Agency for Public Mobilization and Statistics (CAPMAS), in 2015, is E£428 per person per month which was equivalent in July 2016 to $54.70. At the current floating exchange rate between the Egyptian pound and the American dollar, it is equivalent to $23.60.

[2] This corresponds to the July 2016 exchange rate. At the current exchange rate, it is equivalent to $229.30 per month.

[3] This corresponds to the July 2016 exchange rate. At the current exchange rate, it is equivalent to $275.70 per month.

N. Abdelrahman Soliman (✉)
Freie Universität Berlin, Berlin, Germany

© The Author(s) 2020
I. Weipert-Fenner, J. Wolff (eds.), *Socioeconomic Protests in MENA and Latin America*, Middle East Today,
https://doi.org/10.1007/978-3-030-19621-9_9

the richest sector of Egyptians, representing only 15.7% of the population in 2015 (Abou El Gheit 2016). Given these numbers, it was far from surprising that in the mass uprising of 2011, the call for social justice was predominant. However, compared with the large number of poor people in Egypt, the small numbers of socio-economic protests after 2011 presented in Chap. 3 are even more striking. Obviously, public protests have not been a common way of dealing with socio-economic discontent after the mass uprising of 2011, yet there is sporadic contention. The aim of this chapter is to take a case study of one specific group, tuktuk drivers, in order to develop an understanding of how poor people in Egypt deal with their precarious way of life and at what point they choose to mobilize and protest.

In 2015, there were about half a million tuktuks, three-wheeled vehicles, in Egypt, used daily by almost 30 million persons (N Gage 2015). Tuktuks are a means of transportation used in disadvantaged urban or rural areas: they are a means of transportation for the poor, driven by poor operators and in poor areas. The tuktuk phenomenon thus combines different dimensions of marginalization such as low-paid, insecure work, poor education and services, and a lack of infrastructure. After appearing for the first time in Simbalyuun, one of the villages in the Nile Delta, in 2000,[4] tuktuks gradually spread to most cities and villages of the Nile Delta between 2000 and 2005 (Tastevin 2012, pp. 220–229). It was not until 2005 that tuktuks entered Cairo for the first time through the disadvantaged quarter Imbaba (Tastevin 2012, p. 258); the use of tuktuks was transferred from rural to urban spaces, from the "margins" to the center. In 2008, the state recognized their presence, especially in rural areas, through amendments to traffic law. This resulted in mobilizing taxi drivers against tuktuk drivers in some areas, as explained by Tastevin (2012). However, he did not mention protests by tuktuk drivers themselves. Based on reports on tuktuk drivers' protests in different Egyptian newspapers,[5] I found that the mobilization of

---

[4] There are different narratives about the first importer of tuktuks from India to Egypt. During his field research on the origin and development of this trade in Egypt through India, Tastevin found that it was a businessman, originally from *Simbalyuun* and married to an Indian woman, who was the first importer of tuktuks in this area (Tastevin 2012, pp. 155–157).

[5] I checked for news related to tuktuks on the websites of the main Egyptian newspapers, including *Al Ahram, Al Masry Al Youm, Al Watan News, Al Shorouk, Mada Masr, Al Wady News, Youm7*, and *Daily News Egypt*.

Fig. 9.1 Belqas, Egypt; October 18, 2017; taken by researcher

these drivers appeared after the 2008 law in demand of further recognition and formalization. Until today, however, most tuktuks remain illegal or have ambiguous legal status, as discussed later in more detail. This directly influences the working conditions of their drivers and their daily interactions with state representatives. There is no professional association or trade union for tuktuk drivers. Until today, Egypt has witnessed only sporadic protests, organized by drivers outside any formal organization, which are generally spontaneous, local, and limited in duration. They were always an ad hoc reaction to a specific decision taken by the government or confiscation of their vehicles (Fig. 9.1).[6]

---

[6] See Table 9.1.

In order to understand the collective action of tuktuk drivers, I argue that we need to understand their social position. Tuktuk drivers are regarded by the mainstream culture and even by themselves (Kaddah 2016) as "'outsiders', as people who do not fit into the prevailing social fabric" (Bayat 2012, p. 16). They belong to the "margins"—defined as the periphery, away from the center or the mainstream where people enjoy "the position of power, comfort, respect, security, protection and recognition" (Bayat 2012, p. 26). Drawing on Bayat (2012) and Saad (2012), I argue that poor people are not marginal but "marginalized." Yet, instead of being passive victims, tuktuk drivers have developed tactics and strategies for dealing with their marginalization and informalization because margins can also "provide a space for alternative norms and lives, a place of respite and counter-power, for the very excluded and self-excluded" (Bayat 2012, p. 14).

This chapter thus pursues two related aims: to understand the tuktuk drivers as marginalized actors and to analyze their response to this situation of marginalization. It supports the argument of Piven and Cloward (1977), Ismail (2006), and Bayat (2010) that marginalized people, in this chapter tuktuk drivers, try to avoid direct conflict with any authority (people from the center) and that they survive on the margins. However, this chapter's main argument is that sometimes they try to break out either physically or through laws, but they face resistance from the center, which pushes them back to their place, the margins. This is when and where contentious acts of the marginalized appear: at the borders between the margins and the center. In line with the special issue of *Current Sociology* on informality (Boudreau and Davis 2017), I attempt to go beyond the dichotomy of formal and informal sectors by focusing on the process of informalization of tuktuk drivers. Inspired by feminist epistemology, the chapter produces knowledge from the "margins": "marginal subjects produce different, more reliable, knowledge because of conditions of inequality that mean they know dominant frames of legitimation in order to survive or thrive, and generate local knowledges for the same reason" (Hemmings 2012, p. 155). This means that the chapter aims at understanding the positionality of marginalized people in relation to different factors and actors in their specific context.

To understand the processes of marginalization, I first of all collected news related to tuktuk laws reported between 2004 and 2017. For an overview of contentious actions by tuktuk drivers, I used a database of tuktuk drivers' protests and mobilizations since 2004 gathered by the research team of the Egyptian Center for Economic and Social Rights. An additional media analysis was carried out to gain further insights into these protests. The result was a mapping of protests held by tuktuk drivers in Egypt, since 2008, when the first protests occurred (see Table 9.1). Based on this overview, I chose two different areas for ethnographic fieldwork—one urban area, which includes the neighboring quarters of Imbaba and Ard El Lewa in the Giza governorate, where no protest was ever monitored, and one rural area, Belqas in the Dakahliyya governorate in the Nile Delta, where the last protest of tuktuk drivers was observed (see Table 9.1). I conducted 12 interviews with drivers and an interview with a tuktuk garage manager in Ard El Lewa in August 2015, and 13 interviews with drivers and an interview with the owner of a tuktuk supplies tool shop in Belqas in October 2016. For security reasons, field trips had to be short, a few days only per trip. During this time, I conducted semi-structured interviews with tuktuk drivers. The drivers interviewed were chosen on the spot: those available and ready to share their experience with me. The interviews were about the reasons for driving a tuktuk, their working conditions, their interactions with police in the streets, and how they responded to different laws related to tuktuks. I also asked for their opinions on any collective actions organized by tuktuk drivers.

The first part of this chapter examines the process of marginalization and informalization of tuktuk drivers by considering their socio-economic conditions: level of education, access to work, and their work context and conditions. The second part analyzes the impact of these factors on their interactions with the center (mainly governmental authorities, either street police and/or traffic administrations). It focuses on their tactics—contentious or not—for facing their degrading socio-economic conditions in the marginal state they are forced into and the borders separating the margins and the center. What becomes clear is that tuktuk drivers are experiencing a continuous process of marginalization, from their education to their daily working conditions. The marginalization of tuktuk drivers is taking place through law, discourse, and practices, without any chance of escaping. This chapter focuses on laws and how they represent the main factor the drivers tried to negotiate to escape from the margins, either by not accepting their position without direct confrontation or by participating in contentious acts sporadically, depending on the particular situation.

Table 9.1 Laws and protests related to tuktuks from 2008 to 2016

Year	Month	Type of act	Claim	State response	Governorate
2008	June	Law 121 for 2008 which recognized tuktuks as vehicles to be driven on in Egyptian streets[a]			
	December	Self-immolation	Policeman wanted to take his vehicle. He put gas on himself. Protests against this act took place in the street	Denial and use of force against the protests	Alexandria
2010	February	Strike by dozens of drivers	Against the local unit because of fees being collected without any real reason	Denial of what the drivers were saying and statements that they were not respecting regulations	Qalyubia
		Threat of sit-in	Against not allowing them to license their tuktuks and confiscating them	They offered them the solution of replacing the tuktuks with microbuses, but the drivers refused because they are more expensive and less practical in this area	Suez
		Hunger strike of seven drivers	Against not completing the procedures of licensing their tuktuks although they had paid what they were required to pay	They sent an inspector to the hospital to follow the case	Ismailia
	May	Protest in front of the parliament	Against not allowing licenses for tuktuks		Cairo

(*continued*)

Table 9.1 (continued)

Year	Month	Type of act	Claim	State response	Governorate
2011	September	Protest in front of cabinet of dozens of drivers	Against the confiscation of tuktuks in Maadi, Dar Al-Salam, and several other districts of the capital		Cairo
	December	15% import tax on tuktuks imposed by the Ministry of Finance[b]			
2014	February	Strike in front of state council	Against setting E£1500 as the fee for the annual license of a tuktuk		Gharbeya
	March	Protest	Against not permitting them to license their tuktuks as in the rest of Egypt	The officials in the local unit promised to facilitate the licensing procedures	Qena
	May	Cut off road	Against killing one of the drivers for not paying off a policeman in Matareya		Cairo
	May	Decree 105, 2014 of Ministry of Industry and Trade "Country's state commissioners authority (SCA) issued a non-binding decision to courts to halt the import of tuktuks, claiming that auto rickshaws posed a security threat in several areas nationwide, particularly slums"[b]			
	July	Amendments to traffic law: Tuktuks should be licensed[a]			
2015	February	Protest plus sit-in	Protest in front of traffic unit and then state council against the confiscation of their tuktuks and the requirement that they should pay E£2500 to get them back. After they paid, they announced they would sit in if they did not get their tuktuks back	The governor promised to solve the problem and then didn't want to return the impounded tuktuks although they had paid E£2500	Dakahaleya (Belqas)

[a]Amendments to traffic law
[b]Ministry of Finance decrees

9.2 Tuktuk Drivers: On the "Margins" with No Way Out

While I was sitting in a tuktuk tool shop in Belqas, a 52-year-old driver told me: "You are for him (the government) a fly, the latter has a dignity more than you and me. Let us live in *halal*."[7]

The 25-year-old shop owner added: "They are treating tuktuk like the trash of society."

This small three-wheeled vehicle—"treated as the trash of the society" as the shop owner put it—helps to transport people inside their neighborhoods, especially in narrow streets: some streets are not accessible except by tuktuk. In Belqas, for instance, tuktuks offer the only means of transportation in town: there are no taxis, and microbuses do not operate inside the town but only between villages and cities. They are present everywhere in Egypt: small and big streets in big cities, in villages, and between them.

Kaddah (2016) in her ethnography about the presence of tuktuks in Maadi, one of the bourgeois neighborhoods of Cairo, showed how tuktuks as mobile objects "disturb the social geographies of power." She describes how the presence of tuktuks in the streets of this bourgeois neighborhood is considered by its residents to disturb its purity and cleanliness (Kaddah 2016, p. 61). The same argument is advanced by some Ard El Lewa tuktuk drivers when explaining why they are not supposed to circulate in the streets of Mohandessin, the middle-class neighborhood closest to Ard el Lewa. Furthermore, it is actually stated in law that tuktuks should not circulate in big cities or main streets (Human Rights Public Library 2014). Although becoming an important form of transportation and visible almost everywhere in Egypt, tuktuks are supposed to stay away from the main big clean streets. They are supposed to stay out of sight on smaller streets and in disadvantaged areas, along the margins.

This section argues that tuktuk drivers are marginalized: they are not confined to the margins because they have specific features but because of socio-economic conditions relegating them to an inferior social position. Bayat (2012) defines being marginalized as being "economically exploited,

---

[7] *Halal* is an Arabic word meaning permissible or lawful according to Islam. It is used by the drivers to describe their work as tuktuk drivers in opposition to other *haram* work, which is the opposite of halal. Haram describes any act or object that is not permitted by Islam, something illegal or unacceptable on the grounds of religion, customs, and values, such as dealing drugs.

politically repressed, socially stigmatized and culturally excluded from a closed social system" (Bayat 2012, p. 18). By analyzing their socio-economic conditions in terms of access to education, access to work, work conditions, and legal status, this section argues that tuktuk drivers are not exploited like the proletariat in Marxist terms, but they are pushed to the margins (Adly 2017).

Of 15 tuktuk drivers interviewed in Imbaba and Ard el Lewa, only one had studied beyond secondary school and one was aiming to continue his secondary education.[8] In Belqas, 8 of 14 drivers had a vocational secondary diploma or aimed at continuing their diploma.[9] The rest did not intend to continue their education or did not mention it. Most of them had not received any education, which is one of their basic rights according to the Egyptian constitution. This is the first pillar of their marginalization process: they had not received an education qualifying them for "productive" work.[10] Furthermore, those who had completed vocational or secondary school had not found a job in their specialty or preferred to be a tuktuk driver. In Belqas, most drivers had prior experience working in a trade.[11] A 19-year-old driver and former butcher explained: "any artisanal work brings money to its owner, not for us (workers) […] and the work is really hard and consumes all my energy. For what?"[12] Thus, they had not chosen to be tuktuk drivers: there was no other suitable option, no other rewarding work that was also *halal*.

> It solved many problems. Those who can't find a job and want to work, they simply start driving a tuktuk.[13]

> It has been four years now that I've been driving a tuktuk because I couldn't find another job. Something that I own is better than working for other people.[14]

---

[8] See profiles of tuktuk drivers, *in* https://docs.google.com/spreadsheets/d/1WGhEIKOEpK2RG95vKRyireBkYP_btcbT1gqGmHNsZzY/edit?usp=sharing.
[9] Ibid.
[10] More research should be done on the reasons for and the conditions of their (non)education. This is an important question for understanding and analyzing one of the main pillars of the marginalization process of many Egyptians.
[11] See profiles of tuktuk drivers, *in* https://docs.google.com/spreadsheets/d/1WGhEIKOEpK2RG95vKRyireBkYP_btcbT1gqGmHNsZzY/edit?usp=sharing.
[12] Interview with driver B8, Belqas, October 19, 2016.
[13] Interview with driver AL6, Ard el Lewa, August 3, 2015.
[14] Interview with driver AL9, Ard el Lewa, August 4, 2015.

A 57-year-old driver in Belqas summed it up by saying: "Tuktuks came as a gift from God for unemployed people."[15]

Since its appearance, driving a tuktuk has established itself as a good *halal* job, not only for young men but also for any unemployed male[16] regardless of his age: children to help their families, educated and noneducated young people unable to find any other job, and old men who left their jobs or who have handicaps. One of the main remarks in interviews was that, after the 2011 revolution, many businesses, especially small ones, were closed because of the poor economic conditions. As a result, more young people found themselves without work, and driving a tuktuk was their way of getting out of this situation.[17]

Tuktuk driving is presented as an entrepreneurial project (Tastevin 2012, pp. 238–240), a good "project" for those who cannot find jobs. This is confirmed by the N Gage report, which estimated that tuktuk driving has created 1.7 million jobs since its appearance, including 200,000 indirect jobs for technicians and providers of tuktuks and their parts. In 2015, it is estimated to have provided around 261,000 jobs (N Gage 2015). It is a way for unemployed males to escape unemployment, badly paid jobs, or poor treatment from a business owner, but they still suffer from a precarious work situation, depend on many factors to meet their daily expenses, work without any insurance, and, additionally, have an "inferior" social position in the mainstream culture (Kaddah 2016) as well as in the eyes of the authorities.

---

[15] Interview with driver B6, Belqas, October 19, 2016.

[16] In Ard el Lewa and Belqas, I heard that one or two females are driving tuktuks. The drivers knew them by name. It is not common but they exist. There is a video report about female tuktuk drivers that can be viewed here http://www.bbc.com/arabic/media-37775153.

[17] This was the case of Kamal who worked for more than 15 years in a workshop making parquet flooring, but after the revolution and the tourism crisis, the owner had to shut down his business. Kamal and his colleagues found themselves without work. His savings and the savings of his mother-in-law helped him to buy a tuktuk, and he has been driving it since then. He is one of the two interviewed who had continued his education, and he considers this job humiliating and said that it is "affecting his psychological health," but he cannot find other work. It is humiliating because he is always obliged to deal with many challenges in the streets, mainly those imposed by the authorities, and is treated badly.

N: Did you try to find another job?
F: It is not about searching. All who offer jobs demand certificates and if I go and work for someone, I will earn less than I am earning now. So why torture myself as long as I am working on a tuktuk.[18]

The income of tuktuk drivers depends mainly on how many trips they make per day and also on the ownership of the *makana*[19]: if they own it, do they pay installments for the tuktuk or to the bank? In Belqas, most drivers depend on loans from banks to be able to buy a tuktuk.[20] If they do not own it, how much do they pay the people they are renting from. Their income also depends on the price of fuel and the expenses they have for repairing or doing anything to their *makana*. This is how one of the drivers expressed how it is hard to pay his expenses from the income earned with the tuktuk: "I am fed up and all are fed up because there is nothing. I spent three hours in streets and worked only for E£8 (equivalent to 50 cents). Now I want to change oil (for the tuktuk) for E£40 (2 dollars). All people are fed up and those who speak up, they accuse them of being with the Muslim Brotherhood."[21] Another driver added: "Any trip by tuktuk in Belqas costs E£2. Say that I will do 20 trips which means E£40, what can I pay for with that, rent or bank installments or tuktuk installments or school for children."[22] Furthermore, tuktuk drivers are not insured: if they have an accident, there is nothing to pay for repairs: "If something happened to me, I am without any value."[23] Drivers do not feel they have any value because if they are injured, they will not be compensated or receive any support from the state.

Schumacher (1973) analyzed the situation of unemployed rural workers in developing countries moving to the city to find jobs: they end up not being able to escape the misery because "their work opportunities are so restricted." This applies to unemployed Egyptian males who become tuktuk drivers. They not only search for work in their own cities, but they try to obtain work in bigger cities, especially Cairo, and they also end up as tuktuk drivers. This is the case with most Ard el Lewa drivers: they come from different governorates, especially those of Upper Egypt, and, even

---

[18] Interview with driver Imb2, Imbaba, June 1, 2015.
[19] Makana is an Arabic word for machine, it is the word used by drivers to designate their tuktuk.
[20] Interview tuktuk supplies shop owner, Belqas, October 18, 2016.
[21] Interview with driver B3, Belqas, October 18, 2016.
[22] Interview with driver B8, Belqas, October 19, 2016.
[23] Interview with driver B6, Belqas, October 19, 2016.

spatially, they are grouped by their city of origin. In Belqas, 6 drivers out of 15 mentioned that they had gone to Cairo or traveled to other countries seeking work, but they had returned and found that tuktuk driving was the only work they could get in their city. When I asked the rest of them why they did not go to Cairo or leave the country, they expressed the view that it makes no difference. This means that their "work opportunities" are becoming more and more limited and, unlike in previous generations, they have only limited prospects of finding a "way out of misery." They go to cities (or remained there) and take up tuktuk driving as a job, but it is a marginal, weak, unproductive, uninsured, and low-paid job. That is why Adly (2017) argued that driving a tuktuk, among many other informal labor activities, is regarded as underemployment or unemployment—based on Schumacher's (1973) definition.

These weaknesses and the precariousness of their situation are maintained by their unclear legal status. In 2008, tuktuks were recognized for the first time in traffic law (121/2008), seven years after their first appearance. This recognition came in the same article defining what is a motorcycle:

> Tuktuk should not be used for other purposes than transporting people for a fee according to the technical and manufacturing conditions decided by the minister of Trade and Manufacturing. Taxes and fees are collected from them as prescribed in the law. Deciding the places, routes and numbers of these vehicles are the prerogative of the governor [...] They are prohibited to circulate in the capitals and to them, in highways and outside of the places they are registered in it, and this is decided according to the executive regulations of this law.[24] (Human Rights Public Library, 2014, article 7)

Thus, the law came to legitimize the circulation of tuktuks only in rural areas. Out of 15 interviews conducted in Ard el Lewa, only one driver had licensed his tuktuk. Unlike Belqas, where the majority of tuktuks are licensed, I did not observe any licensed tuktuks in Cairo. Recently, operators have started skipping licensing because it is becoming more and more expensive. "We took two pounds from the client, one pound for the government and the other one for us, but not net."[25]

According to the interviews, the average cost is between E£2000 and E£3000 ($100–$150). Officially, it should be less than this. The only

---

[24] Translated by the author.
[25] Ibid.

driver in Ard el Lewa who was licensed said it costs around E£1000 ($50). In Belqas, the position is also ambiguous: the cost varies from E£700 ($35) to E£2000 ($100). According to the N Gage report, licensing costs around E£1200 ($60). Although not able to state the exact cost of licensing, all agreed that they paid "money for people to finish things," which means bribes. My first interview partner in Belqas in August 2016 summarized the licensing issue: "it's all about collecting money," a statement that was repeated in different ways by drivers in Ard el Lewa and Belqas. In 2014, the 2008 law was amended and the recognition of tuktuks is clearer and states that they should be licensed (Zalat 2014). However, it does not specify a penalty for those who do not have a license or drive on highways or in places they are not registered to circulate in. There are one or two main articles related to tuktuks in traffic law at the national level. Many local regulations exist, depending on the governorate. Drivers in the field do not know the exact details.

From the perspective of government authorities and economists, all these vehicles circulating without a license are part of the "informal" labor market; as they are not monitored, drivers do not pay taxes to the state and are not insured. However, this chapter seeks to "discuss informality in relational context, examining the connections established between informal groups and other actors and institutions, including the law" (Boudreau and Davis 2017). The dichotomy of formal and informal labor is not as clear and simple as it is represented to be in most of the literature: formality is what is regulated by the rule of law, and informality is any activity not regulated by law and the state (Boudreau and Davis 2017). Here, the borders between formality and informality are blurred: local regulations on licensing are not clear. They do not satisfy the needs of the drivers as shown in the second part of this chapter, and, moreover, even licensed drivers are threatened with being stopped by officers for any reason. Furthermore, the argument that the "legal" is what comes from and/or is related to the "state" is questionable: all drivers mentioned the bribes policemen took to let them go or the people working in the traffic department took to process their documents. In this case, the "state" represented by these employees is itself acting illegally. Adding to the blurriness of informality, the drivers interviewed considered that driving tuktuks stops them from carrying out illegal or *haram* activities such as drug dealing or stealing. For them, it offers a legal job:

> The problem of tuktuk is that it is attracting all the unemployed. (…) Everyone is now on tuktuk. It is not bad. You can make good money, for example one can earn E£50 in a shift. […] E£50 *halal* is better than earning the money *haram*.[26]

Consequently, driving a tuktuk cannot be classified as belonging to either the formal or the informal sector. However, in order to understand the status of the tuktuk, it is important for each actor to be able to analyze its power dynamics. From the perspective of governmental authorities, tuktuk drivers are informal workers and therefore particularly vulnerable to the arbitrary exercise of state power, as they have no legal means of defending their business. However, from another perspective, they are young and old men living in poor rural\urban areas in Egypt who do not have a job or obtain adequate resources from their public or private jobs. They do not wait for the government or enterprises to employ them, but they carry out direct action working at anything they find, and satisfy their direct and immediate needs in this way: driving a tuktuk becomes an act of empowerment. For at least the drivers I interviewed, it is not important whether it is managed by the government or not, as long as it is not *haram*. It could be understood in the context of what Bayat calls the art of presence: "The courage and creativity to assert collective will in spite of all odds, to circumvent constraints, utilizing what is available and discovering new spaces within which to make oneself heard, seen, felt, and realized. The art of presence is the fundamental moment in the life of nonmovements, in life as politics" (Bayat 2010, p. 26).

Tuktuk drivers carried out an action to solve their major problem—unemployment. They became "seen" by driving their tuktuks in every street in Egypt. The history of introducing tuktuks to the Egyptian market was *art of presence*: it was introduced by individuals living in the Delta to increase their income and has since enjoyed great success among young unemployed people (Tastevin 2012, pp. 296–306). Ghabbour—one of the biggest car sales companies in Egypt—became interested in importing them and then became their main provider. This is when the state started to make regulations to control their presence in the streets. They became *heard* and *seen* despite being on the margins.

However, I would not go so far as to see this as an *act of resistance* to the control by the state of the means of production. Rizzo (2011) promi-

---

[26] Interview with driver AL3, Ard el Lewa, June 29, 2015.

nently argued in the case of informal transport workers in Tanzania that interpreting the growth of the informal sector as a process of poor people's empowerment is *romanticizing* reality and ignoring working conditions such as the work environment, working hours, remuneration, and lack of any socio-economic rights such as health insurance or the right of organization. Although driving tuktuks might represent a way for people to earn a living, it places them in a position where marginalization is reproduced and reaffirmed. Consequently, Rizzo (2011) argues that applying class analysis helps to deconstruct this theory of empowerment: it helps to understand transport workers' "lack of voice and political quiescence vis-a-vis bus owners and the state" (Rizzo 2011).

> I am trying to find another job because this one doesn't have a future [...] I want to be a driver on a private car to deal with respected people better than this chaotic work.[27]
>
> I was searching for job in a company. So, there are fixed working hours and a salary at the end of the month.[28]
>
> I am an old man, those who are my same age should take pension and stay at home. They are not supposed to work at night, so the traffic officers don't confiscate my vehicle. How can I live?[29]

These quotes confirm that tuktuk drivers are on the "margin" not because they choose to be there but because they did not have a chance to obtain a proper education which would make them able to obtain productive legal work, while even those who have an education did not manage to get work for a variety of reasons. They are on the margin because when they chose to work as tuktuk drivers, this is what they encountered; the regulations do not help them to obtain proper working conditions (a decent income and social insurance). Moreover, they are regarded as part of the "informal sector," which is directly threatening the source of the income they manage to obtain. As a result, they are forced to remain on the "margin" by socio-economic conditions and policies (unclear laws). They are not exploited in the way the "proletariat" of Marx are said to be exploited, but they are marginalized (Adly 2017). Being marginalized

---

[27] Interview with driver AL8, Ard el Lewa, August 3, 2015.
[28] Interview with driver Imb1, Imbaba, June 1, 2015.
[29] Interview with driver B8, Belqas, October 19, 2016.

gives them the freedom to achieve a sort of "autonomy, both cultural and political from the regulations, institutions and discipline imposed by the state and modern institutions" (Bayat 2012). However, they have no chance of accessing "the benefits of being in the centre, enjoying the position of power, comfort, respect, security, protection and recognition" (Bayat 2012). They are vulnerable: they are economically and socially insecure and exposed to repression at anytime and anywhere.

Although on both the "margin" and marginalized, tuktuk drivers are symbolically challenging the authority of the state by not licensing their vehicles. However, they are at permanent risk of having their vehicles impounded or being stopped for not being licensed, for driving in certain streets, or for any other reason according to the mood of the police officer. Between having a free space on the margin and trying to get out, interactions between tuktuk drivers and authorities (especially street police and traffic administrations) take place along this continuum. It is a conflict over space, over the boundaries between the margins and the center.

9.3 Conflict Over Space Within Margins: Tuktuk Drivers' (Contentious) Interaction with the State

I am not a billionaire to participate in protests

This is what a 30-year-old tuktuk driver in Ard El Lewa said when asked if he would participate in protests organized by other drivers against their work conditions. It clearly shows that protests are not regarded as something poor people can afford. Yet, as my research has shown, there have been acts of contention by tuktuk drivers. The challenge is to understand why these protests occur. In media analyses (see Table 9.1), the major reason for conflict is access to the formal sector of the economy (via licensing) and about formal property rights (against the confiscation of tuktuks). From my interviews, I learned about an additional, spatial dimension: attempts to get out of informal and/or poor neighborhoods. What they all have in common is that they represent conflicts with state institutions and representatives, although the state is regarded as being absent from the drivers' lives. Yet, what they experience is that its representatives (here, street police or traffic administration) perform illegal actions against them by using the coercive power of the state. It is "the elusive state: the state that does not exist, but is everywhere" (Ismail 2006). In her fieldwork in a popular neighborhood in Cairo, during the 1990s, Ismail (2006) heard repeatedly that there is no state. The same happened with me in 2015–2016 after the uprising of 2011 that led to the fall of Mubarak (1981–2011). *Mafish hukuma*[30] (there is no government) was the answer of many drivers when asked about the role of the state/government in ameliorating their work and living conditions. The government *does not exist* to implement better conditions for drivers, but it is always present to limit the space—legal and physical—of drivers, which limits their chance of obtaining better working conditions.

The following table includes the dates, types, claims, places, and state responses to any contentious acts performed by tuktuk drivers in Egypt, monitored by the team of the Egyptian Center for Economic and Social Rights and the researcher. It also includes the dates of national traffic laws, including articles related to tuktuks and the dates of the Ministry of Finance decrees related to the import of tuktuks.

In *Moga Hara*,[31] a 2013 Egyptian TV show discussing social and political status in Egypt in 2010, a policeman named Sayed Al Agati says "the laws are not being enforced. When laws are not enforced, this is the result: chaos, only chaos." This sums up the status of laws and its implications in real life in Egypt, including those of tuktuk drivers. Different laws, regulations, and local decrees exist and are issued to organize the status of tuktuks and their drivers in Egyptian streets, as explained in the first part of this chapter. They are trying to *order the disorderly* (Abdelrahman 2013). However, drivers do not respect these laws, whether they know them or not, not as agency but because they are not beneficial to them. The question of licensing determines the relationship between drivers and authorities.

[30] *Hukuma* is the Arabic word for government and *dawla* is the word for State. In Egypt, in common language, there is confusion between government and state and sometimes they are both designated by *hukuma* or *dawla*. This difference became more and more after 2011 revolution when a discourse was developed that it is *hukuma* (government) that should fall, not *dawla* (State). For tuktuk drivers, they used more *hukuma* to talk about those in power or the state apparatus in general.

[31] *Moga Hara* means hot wave. It is a TV series based on a novel written by Osama Anwar Okasha, one of the prominent Egyptian TV-series writers. He is the writer of one of the most famous TV series called Nights of Helmeya, which was a five-season (1987–1995) series deconstructing the Egyptian society with its different classes before and after the 1952 revolution. *Moga Hara* was produced and shown in Ramadan in 2013 and is one of the few contemporary TV series which present a deep and realistic understanding of the social, economic and political transformations in Egyptian society during the Mubarak era: the rise of corruption, control of the police, the rise of social problems, political oppression, the use of religion in politics.

In Ard el Lewa and Imbaba, only one driver licensed his tuktuk. There is a consensus that registration is not important and not beneficial to them. The act of consciously not registering their vehicles involves questioning the power of the law and the state. But it also exposes drivers to an ever-present threat of being harassed by any official representative in the streets at any time and according to law. For instance, in Belqas, if an unlicensed tuktuk is caught by police officers, it will be confiscated without the driver being able to get it back, which is regarded by the drivers, but also in comparison with what is happening in Ard el Lewa, as "exceptional." This was the main reason people protested in February 2015. It is one of the extensively reported tuktuk protests because it lasted many days, and it was recent. During my fieldwork there, I tried to reach drivers who had participated in this protest, but I failed. When I asked about it, most of them answered that they knew nothing about it: I do not know if this was out of fear because they had forgotten it because two years had passed, or whether they really had not heard about it.[32] The only clear testimony I got is the following:

> They protested because tuktuk are confiscated without being able to get them again and the license isn't regulated yet. So, they protested to try to have a solution. With the protest, some drivers got their tuktuk back and others not. Now, no tuktuk is getting out.[33]

Although they protested, nothing changed, and drivers are still suffering. Three out of my interview partners had their tuktuks confiscated, although they were still paying their installments, and they have not been able to get them back. "I licensed because I don't want my tuktuk to be confiscated. If it is taken, it won't come out and all its parts will be stolen. Those who say that they are not stolen, they are liars."[34] Police officers brought impounded tuktuks to a place on the Mediterranean coast called *Gamasa*, but they also—according to the stories of most of the

---

[32] The only remaining memory of contentious acts that took place in Belqas is when a citizen was killed by a policeman in 1998. It was narrated to me by young and old men in Belqas, and this is also mentioned by Ismail in her book. The people marched to the police station and even burnt it and the court (Ismail 2006, pp. 161–163). It was mentioned in order to make plain to me that if the people of Belqas "do a revolution," it will be a violent one. However, currently, this has no meaning, and they cannot afford its costs.

[33] Interview with driver B13, Belqas, October 20, 2016.

[34] Interview with driver B7, Belqas, October 19, 2016.

drivers I interviewed—stole any valuable parts from the vehicle such as sound systems or other parts. The state representatives take bribes and "steal" the drivers' vehicles.

The licensing question is related to the spatial dimension of conflicts: licenses limit the geographical space in which drivers can circulate. For instance, the only benefit of licensing for Ard el Lewa drivers is to be able to circulate in the main streets. Geographically, Ard el Lewa is separated from the "bourgeois" neighborhood of Giza El Mohandessin by Sudan street. In addition to this street, there is a railway that was easily crossed by people and vehicles until a bridge was built that created a physical barrier between the two neighborhoods. The same driver would praise and criticize "going out" (*barra*) in the same interview: the fares are more rewarding. At the same time, one of them said: "but the government is right, we should not go out because we are unorganized and drivers could harass people there" (Fig. 9.2).

The law indicating the limits of tuktuk circulation in the city or in villages is not clear and does not correspond to the realities of the street plan. However, virtual barriers, as in the case of Maadi (Kaddah 2016), or real ones as in the case of the Ard el Lewa bridge, exist between *barra* (out) and *gowa* (in) and "limit" the circulation of tuktuks. In the case of the Ard el Lewa drivers, once out, they are directly threatened: if police officers are

Fig. 9.2 The view after crossing the bridge over the railway "Mazlaa'an," taken by the researcher, June 29, 2015

present, the drivers are stopped and their tuktuks confiscated. In this case, there are two main solutions. The first is that the vehicle is sent to a place outside the city called *kilo 10 w nos*, and then the driver must go to the traffic office to license the tuktuk and go back to this place to get it back. According to the drivers, this process is too long and costs too much money. They also sometimes "pay something" to the police officer to let them go and try to establish good relations with him by promising not to drive in this street again, and\or that it was the first time and/or it was urgent.

> When I went out in Sudan Street. I got caught with another one. We said we were lost. They let go the other one because he paid a bribe but they took mine. I paid E£315 and I spent 10 days searching for my tuktuk in kilo 10 w nos[35]
>
> [...] this bridge was done and everything changed. We used to cross this *mazla'an* (barrier) but now we don't go out. They gathered us all here, they restricted our movement.[36]

This statement sums up the interaction between tuktuk drivers and authorities in Egypt: it is a conflict over space. The drivers are trying to escape from the margins, and the latter are pushing them back; consequently, they develop tactics to survive "inside." Sometimes their attempts to get out, either physically or legally, result in contentious acts (protests, sit-ins, burning themselves) against authorities. This spatial dynamic is not present in Belqas because tuktuks are the main form of transportation there, and they can circulate in all streets. Nonetheless, authorities try to control who is working, where, and from where. During my second visit to Belqas in October 2016, the traffic department decided to color licensed tuktuks blue, to differentiate between those from Belqas and those from surrounding villages. Most of the drivers interviewed described this decision as useless or meaningless because they will simply paint their tuktuks blue without licensing them. This decision is only making the licensing process more expensive because of the additional documents and the costs of painting paid by the drivers. Here, the conflict over space is more obvious: drivers are trying to enlarge the real space they can circulate in. Furthermore, it is not only the state that is pushing them to stay in "rural" or "poor" areas but also the inhabitants of "rich" neighborhoods

---

[35] Interview with driver AL11, Ard el Lewa, August 4, 2015.
[36] Interview with driver AL2, Ard el Lewa, August 3, 2015.

(Kaddah 2016). In September 2011, there was a protest by Maadi and Dar el Salam tuktuk drivers in front of the Ministry Cabinet against the confiscation of their vehicles because they were circulating in streets they were not supposed to drive in.

While the everyday interaction with the state (and its representatives), on the one hand, is marked by conflict, it was fascinating to see that, on the other hand, the drivers generally desire a strong state that actively regulates traffic, infrastructure, and licensing procedures. Some of them confirm how licensing could be beneficial for controlling crimes by or against tuktuk drivers, and have an "imagination" of how tuktuks should be regulated and organized in the streets in order to uphold their rights and ensure their security:

> The government is good. It is letting us go out of the bridge. They will be better if they make for us a station and that to be under the supervision of the government. They take from each tuktuk E£5, they will collect monthly 150 from 20, 30 or 40 tuktuks. It is not free and it will be beneficial for the state and the state will be beneficial for us all. If they let the station random as it is now, it won't be useful.[37]

> The system will come from above. There are different problems for tuktuk. The governor of Giza should permit to license tuktuk locally for a bigger zone. I want a route where I can circulate freely. When law meets me, I will be straightforward with my license. No one comes here.[38]

> If the procedures of license are easier, more people will do it. People don't have E£1500 each year.[39]

Thus, there is a vicious circle: laws exist, but they are not implemented in a way that would actually enable or even motivate drivers to formalize their work. The question whether this is an unintended consequence of the modifications to laws cannot be answered by my research. What is clear, however, is that the current situation gives the authorities a permanent green card to harass the drivers. It does not give the drivers the possibility or the "space" to be legal. Being in this blurry space between legal and illegal keeps tuktuk drivers on the margins without any chance of

---

[37] Interview with driver AL8, Ard el Lewa, August 3, 2015.
[38] Interview with driver AL6, Ard el Lewa, August 3, 2015.
[39] Interview with driver B7, Belqas, October 19, 2016.

getting out. As illustrated in Table 9.1, in February 2010, three mobilizations, in which the drivers demanded they be allowed to license their tuk-tuks or to complete the procedures, were carried out in three different places (Suez, Ismailia, and Cairo), and in different forms (threat of a sit-in, hunger strikes and a protest in front of the parliament). Despite the restrictions regulating collective action after 2013, two mobilizations related to licensing were monitored in 2014. In February 2014, drivers in a city in Gharbeya governorate protested over the high price of licensing. In March 2014, a mobilization asking to be able to license their tuktuks as in the rest of Egypt was monitored in Qena (Upper Egypt). As previously mentioned, due to the lack of information in the newspapers, I was not able to assess the reaction of authorities to these mobilizations. Nonetheless, they show that some drivers in a "specific geography" at a specific moment decided to organize themselves and demand to be made legal, thus attempting to *go out* of the marginal position they are pushed into.

However, these mobilizations came under what Abdelrahman (2012) categorizes as "market-relations based protests"[40]: they are dispersed protests, mostly in rural areas, and are organized by marginalized people who do not want to challenge the state and do not have the power to "access or restructure market relations in their favour." Although they are multiple and dispersed, they do not go beyond their "specific geographies."

> No never a protest happened. Why people will protest. They are satisfied by their work. No definitely I won't participate in any protest.[41]

> They are all helpless, they don't protest. But if they prohibit tuktuk then I won't be silent and other people won't also because this is our source of income and not by violence. But I am sure they won't ever prohibit. It is the profit of big companies in Egypt.[42]

> There are no tuktuk drivers who talk or protest, these things don't exist.[43]

---

[40] In her article, Maha Abdelrahman (2012) identifies three spheres "in which the battle against the regime was waged" in Egypt: the pro-democracy movement, labor struggles, and "market relations-based protests."

[41] Interview with driver AL5, Ard el Lewa, August 3, 2015.

[42] Interview with driver AL11, Ard el Lewa, August 4, 2015.

[43] Interview with tuktuk supplies shop owner, Belqas, October 18, 2016.

There is no "organized" movement of tuktuk drivers against regulations limiting their work and their presence in the streets, such as in the case of Cairo street vendors for instance (Maslin 2015). The mobilizations monitored are localized: they belong to the space and the time they were organized in, and they do not go beyond these. This supports the argument of Bayat that people in disadvantaged areas do not protest unless they are deeply threatened and affected in large numbers (Bayat 2010, pp. 20–21). In other words, when the government started to remove street vendors from their places in downtown Cairo, these people began to be conscious that they were experiencing the same challenge, and the passive networks started to become active (Bayat 2010, pp. 18–19): they started to organize themselves and created an independent syndicate and formulated their claims. (Darwish 2014). By contrast, with the case of tuktuk drivers, none of the regulations directly affected their work in any profound way. Furthermore, the fact that regulations are different from one governorate to another also restricts the "space" of mobilizations to the local level. The change of regulations affects small number of drivers in a limited geographical space. Furthermore, even in a specific and limited geographical space such as Ard el Lewa or Belqas, it is difficult to bring drivers together and organize them into a syndicate because they are different, diverse, and from different places. Most of them regard driving a tuktuk as "temporary" work until they find something else. It is not their real work, which confirms the problem raised by Kaddah (2016) about tuktuk drivers as a categorical label.

However, drivers are still managing to be present and circulating everywhere in Egypt, despite these limitations. They are adopting tactics—within *margins* they are pushed into—for avoiding being caught or surviving being in the streets without being harassed: not passing main streets when they know police officers are there, paying anything that can be paid unless their tuktuk is not bringing in anything, and not entering into direct confrontation with authorities.

> Honestly yes I go out. I transfer customers to the hospital. Many stopped me and they let me talk and sometimes I pay a penalty of E£40 and take a receipt. […] I don't go out in anytime but sometimes when I know they won't be there like now at noon. They are seeing their work and we too are seeing ours.[44]

---

[44] Interview with driver AL8, Ard el Lewa, August 3, 2015.

Fig. 9.3 Picture taken from a tuktuk in Belqas by the researcher, June 22, 2015

In Belqas, drivers who do not license their tuktuk work only during the night because police officers are not present in the streets. The most important thing for drivers is not their rights, but their ability to keep their tuktuk and being able to work every day and earn their living (Fig. 9.3).

This tactic and the discourses of drivers about government are understood within the *infrapolitics* of Scott (1990): "For a social science attuned to the relatively open politics of liberal democracies and to loud, headline-grabbing protests, demonstrations, and rebellions, the circumspect struggle waged daily by subordinate groups is, like infrared rays, beyond the visible end of the spectrum. That it should be invisible, as we have seen, is in large part by design a tactical choice born of a prudent awareness of the balance of power" (Scott 1990, p. 183). Following this reasoning, they do not tend to go into direct and open confrontation with authorities, but they adopt tactics allowing them to do what they want within *margins*, to "see their work," and, at the same time, not be oppressed. In the terms of Scott, this is considered a form of resistance to domination. "In critical reviews of research on everyday life, some scholars have argued that in working around the foundations of domination rather than shaking them, subordinates are merely engaging in survival strategies and are not challenging their domination" (Ismail 2006, p. xxiii). The debate on whether these tactics are resistance or survival ones depends on the context and the positionality of the actors. Both points of view are supported by arguments from the literature and the field, but the result is that the drivers are still in their precarious position and are still under daily permanent threat from the state by different means.

Despite the existence of some protests as monitored in Table 9.1 and analyzed earlier, listening to the stories of drivers in Ard el Lewa and Belqas and how they are always exposed to repression and poor living and working conditions, one question remains: Why don't they unite and reject all these conditions and demand better ones, at least on a local scale?

According to Ismail (2006), "fear and the culture of fear that continuous monitoring, surveillance, humiliation, and abuse have created" (p. 165) are the answers to why poor people in marginalized areas do not organize themselves and participate frequently in contentious acts. The findings of this research which was carried out in 2015–2016 support the findings of Ismail for the 1990s. Drivers do not want to participate in protests because they are afraid: afraid of not having their daily income, afraid of being caught, and afraid of being oppressed. Moreover, and especially after the 2011 revolution, the result of which was that nothing happened to ameliorate their circumstances, they do not believe that any contentious act will be beneficial to them; such acts are useless. Some of them mentioned that this is the position of *well-off* people who are not poor like them. They are conscious of the existing power dynamics related to class, and they are prudent, as Scott explains. Consequently, their way of "resisting" or "surviving" is to avoid direct confrontation and, instead, to create their own *spaces of freedom*, where they can get what they need without being oppressed (Bayat 2010, pp. 25–26).

Piven and Cloward (1977) argued that poor people are led to open confrontation or to protest when there is a transformation both of consciousness and of behavior (Piven and Cloward 1977, p. 3). For them, there are three distinct aspects of the consciousness of poor people that must be changed for protest to occur: they must believe that the regulations and the system put in place by rulers are unjust, start believing that things could be changed and are not inevitable, and finally believe that they have the capacity to change things and are not helpless (Piven and Cloward 1977, pp. 3–4). According to what was mentioned earlier, the drivers who were interviewed believed that the regulations are unjust and could be better, but they still believe that this is inevitable, that they should adapt themselves to what exists, and that they do not have the power to change things, especially through protests. They do not formulate their demands in claims because "no one will hear them," as one of my interview partners said, and they do not have the capacity to change things. It should be done "from above," although they declared several times that the government does not exist.

The position of tuktuk drivers on the margins is not their choice or related to their nature, but it is the result of a process of marginalization, illustrated in this chapter through laws and regulations. At the same time, this position provides space to go beyond legal, social, and cultural norms regulating the *mainstream*. Thus, tuktuks can circulate in most streets and continue to work, although with limitations. However, this does not relieve them of the risks attached to living on the margin: bad working conditions and the threat of being caught. This is why sometimes, according to the specific space and time, they try to protest against this position and demand to be legal, to be part of the mainstream. However, in most cases, they do not succeed, and they continue to survive within the margins out of fear, but also because they do not believe in their capacity to change the dynamics and escape from their marginal position.

9.4 Conclusion

As has been shown in this chapter, tuktuk drivers are caught in a continuous process of marginalization, starting from the date and place of their birth. Understanding their socio-economic conditions (education, work opportunities, and conditions) makes their process of marginalization clearer, and categorizing them as *informal workers* becomes less relevant. Yet, marginalization is not only a matter of structural problems but is reaffirmed by legal, social, and discursive practices.

This chapter focused on the legal practices. It showed that the main conflict between tuktuk drivers and authorities is over the borders, formal and informal, between the margins and the center. It shows that at specific moments and in specific places, some of them protest and express their desire to leave the margins. Their main demand is for access to the *center* by being legal, by being able to circulate in places other than poor areas. However, existing regulations for legalizing and organizing their presence in the streets are not meeting their actual everyday needs. Furthermore, the way authorities are dealing with them in the streets is putting them in a *permanently* vulnerable position. As a result, they end up where they started; on the margins.

Marginalized as shown, the tuktuk drivers studied in this chapter—as is the case with most Egyptians who live in degrading socio-economic conditions—make no systematic and structural effort to escape from their marginal state. They do not believe that they have the capacity to do so, and they cannot afford the costs not only of being mobilized but also of being at the center. Thus, they manage to create specific dynamics in their interactions with the authorities and other actors at the center to survive on the margin: they develop daily tactics for avoiding direct confrontation with authorities. Sometimes some of them try to escape from the margin, but most of them are forced to remain and survive there.

Saad (2012) argues in the case of women from low-status clans in Upper Egypt that the margins could be "a space for experimentation and possibility that is highly responsive to factors of change, including emerging opportunity; a frontier rather than a periphery" (Saad 2012, p. 109). The women of Upper Egypt have managed, using their status of being from a lower and marginalized social class, to actually participate more in the public space and be empowered. That is why the margins for them have become just a space separated from the center by a frontier, just a different space where different social dynamics exist. Although tuktuk drivers are managing to survive, they are still suffering poor living and working conditions. They literally lead a marginal and tenuous existence with few prospects of bettering their circumstances.

References

Abdelrahman, M. (2012). A hierarchy of struggles? The 'economic' and the 'political' in Egypt's revolution. *Review of African Political Economy, 39*(134), 614–628.

Abdelrahman, M. (2013, June 14). Ordering the disorderly? Street vendors and the developmentalist State. *Jadaliyya*.

Abou El Gheit, M. (2016, September 28). Society of the 15%, we present for you: Egypt. *Al Masry Al Youm*.

Adly, A. (2017, May 23). Exploitation or marginalization. *Mada Masr*.
Aswat Masreya (2016, July 27). 27.8 percent of Egyptian population lives below poverty line: CAPMAS. *Egypt Independent*.
Bayat, A. (2010). *Life as politics. How ordinary people change the Middle East*. Amsterdam: Amsterdam University Press.
Bayat, A. (2012). Marginality: Curse or cure? In R. Bush & H. Ayeb (Eds.), *Marginality and exclusion in Egypt* (pp. 14–27). London: ZED Books Ltd.
Boudreau, J.-A., & Davis, D. E. (2017). Introduction: A processual approach to informalization. *Current Sociology, 65*(2), 151–166.
Darwish, P. (2014, July 24). Cairo governorate vs street vendors: A brewing conflict. *Ahram Online*.
Farid, S. (2017, February 8). 'We're very poor,' says Sisi: How did Egyptians react? *Al Arabiya English*.
Hemmings, C. (2012). Affective solidarity: Feminist reflexivity and political transformation. *Feminist Theory, 13*(2), 147–161.
Human Rights Public Library (2014). Traffic law no. 121 for 2008 with its amendments. Retrieved May, 2017, from http://qadaya.net/?p=5379.
Ismail, S. (2006). *Political life in Cairo's new quarters: Encountering the everyday state*. Minneapolis, MN: University of Minnesota Press.
Kaddah, D. (2016). *The tutktuks in Maadi: What is their presence disrupting?* MA Thesis, American University in Cairo: Department of Sociology, Anthropology, Psychology and Egyptology.
Maslin, J. (2015, September 5). Cairo street traders squeezed out in push to make city 'revolution free'. *The Guardian*.
N Gage. (2015). *Tuktuk, an opportunity for development. Presentation of findings*. Cairo: N Gage.
Piven, F., & Cloward, R. (1977). *Poor people's movements. Why they succeed, how they fail*. New York: Pantheon Books.
Rizzo, M. (2011). 'Life is war': Informal transport workers and neoliberalism in Tanzania 1998–2009. *Development and Change, 42*(5), 1179–1205.
Saad, R. (2012). Margins and frontiers. In R. Bush & H. Ayeb (Eds.), *Marginality and exclusion in Egypt* (pp. 97–111). London: ZED Books Ltd.
Schumacher, E. (1973). *Small is beautiful*. New York: Harper & Row.
Scott, J. C. (1990). *Domination and the arts of resistance*. Yale, CT: Yale University Press.
Tastevin, Y. P. (2012). *Autorickshaw: Émergence et recompositions d'une filière entre l'Inde, l'Égypte et le Congo. Milieux, Cultures et Sociétés du Passé et du Présent*. PhD, Université de Paris Ouest Nanterre, Paris.
Zalat, S. (2014, July 7). The essential summary of Sisi's new traffic law. *Mada Masr*.

PART IV

Conclusion

CHAPTER 10

From North Africa to Latin America and Back: Comparative Findings and Theoretical Reflections

Irene Weipert-Fenner and Jonas Wolff

10.1 Introduction

Since the revolutions of 2011, the transformations of the political regimes in Egypt and Tunisia have taken different paths: In Egypt, under President Abdel Fattah el-Sisi, authoritarian rule is being restabilized, while Tunisia has undergone a gradual, yet fragile, institutionalization of democratic rule. Despite these divergent trajectories, some remarkable similarities characterize post-revolutionary developments in the two countries. Until 2013, there was a tremendous increase in polarization between secular and Islamist forces, leading to serious political crises. In this context, issues related to socioeconomic development, social policies and economic reforms were largely marginalized within the political agenda. In both countries, the predominant state response during the first years after the revolutions was marked by pragmatic muddling through that refrained

I. Weipert-Fenner (✉) • J. Wolff
Peace Research Institute Frankfurt, Frankfurt am Main, Hessen, Germany
e-mail: weipert-fenner@hsfk.de; wolff@hsfk.de

© The Author(s) 2020
I. Weipert-Fenner, J. Wolff (eds.), *Socioeconomic Protests in MENA and Latin America*, Middle East Today,
https://doi.org/10.1007/978-3-030-19621-9_10

from pursuing structural and/or redistributive reforms. Post-revolutionary governments in Egypt and Tunisia have been unable and/or unwilling to improve the socioeconomic situation of the general populace, and, as a result, the socioeconomic grievances that were key drivers of the 2010–2011 uprisings have remained unaddressed (see Chap. 2, in this volume; Diwan and Galal 2016; IMF 2014; Kienle 2015; Paciello 2013).

As the studies compiled in this volume document, this overall dynamic of politico-economic development has had complex consequences for those actors that have continued to articulate socioeconomic grievances. But, taking the different case studies together, one general observation stands out: Key agents of socioeconomic contention, including movements by organized labor and the unemployed that were important in the run-up to the uprisings and that saw their political opportunities open up in the immediate aftermath of the revolutions, have since been effectively marginalized as political actors. In this concluding chapter, we reflect on the causes of this weakness of socioeconomic contention by identifying comparative insights that emerge from the contributions to this volume and by situating them in the context of broader comparative and theoretical debates on the relationship between social movements and political change. More specifically, in what follows, we first discuss Egypt's and Tunisia's post-revolutionary trajectories from a comparative perspective. Second, we discuss these comparative findings in the light of experiences in Latin America. Third, drawing again on comparative scholarship on Latin America, we offer a theoretical interpretation of some of the main dynamics observed in Egypt and Tunisia. Fourth and finally, we conclude with some general implications and an outlook.

10.2 Egypt's and Tunisia's Post-revolutionary Trajectories: Comparative Findings

With all the talk about the "revolutions" in Egypt and Tunisia, it is important to start with acknowledging that the uprisings in 2010 and 2011 in the two countries do not even remotely correspond to what the comparative literature usually calls "revolutions."[1] Certainly, the two countries have not experienced *social revolutions*, that is, "rapid, basic transformations of a society's state and class structures" that "are accompanied and in

---

[1] For a comprehensive discussion of the (non-)revolutionary nature of the Arab uprisings, see Bayat (2017).

part carried through by class-based revolts from below" (Skocpol 1979, p. 4). In the terminology used, for instance, in Skocpol's classic study on the topic, the uprisings in Egypt and Tunisia could perhaps be considered *political revolutions*, which "transform state structures but not social structures," and "are not necessarily accomplished through class conflict" (Skocpol 1979, p. 4). But, as Adly and Meddeb (see Chap. 2, in this volume) show, even this categorization overestimates the depth of structural change that followed from the toppling of long-standing dictators. Rather than directly touching upon state structures, the so-called revolutions in Egypt and Tunisia mainly concerned the shape and configuration of political institutions, that is, the political regime.[2] More specifically, what we could observe in the two countries in 2011 were protest-driven, negotiated processes of regime transformation that involved attempts to construct some kind of democratic rule (see Della Porta 2014; Heydemann 2016; Valbjørn 2012).[3] This particular type of politico-institutional transformation, which can still be described as a political revolution based on the more general understanding of the term (Goodwin 2001, p. 4), serves as the "post-revolutionary" context in which the socioeconomic protests unfolded that have been studied in this volume.[4]

This specific characteristic of the revolutions at hand has crucial implications that run through the analyses presented in this volume and, in particular, concern the type of actors and alliances involved in contentious action. Very clearly, the correlations and alliances of actors that shaped the uprisings and their aftermath were not defined by socioeconomic (class) cleavages. Protest movements were decidedly cross-class (Della Porta 2014, Chap. 3; Durac 2015). The terminology of the comparative study of revolutions, again, helps to clarify this point: While, as already mentioned, the results of the uprisings in Egypt and Tunisia can be called political revolutions (in a broad sense), the uprisings themselves were

---

[2] On the distinction between state and political regime, see, for instance, Fishman (1990), Goodwin (2001, pp. 12–13), and O'Donnell (1993).

[3] In terms of the typology of "paths toward democracy" developed by Ruth B. Collier, Egypt and Tunisia roughly correspond to the pattern of "destabilization and extrication," in which protest movements (in Collier's cases, sustained by organized labor, in particular) "destabilized authoritarianism and opened the way for the establishment of a democratically elected government" (Collier 1999, p. 114).

[4] In such a broader sense, Jeff Goodwin (2001, pp. 9–10) defines revolutions as "irregular, extra-constitutional, and sometimes violent changes of political regime and control of state power brought about by popular movements."

hardly driven by a network of actors that might be considered "revolutionary movements," that is, social movements that "attempt to gain control of the state as such" (Goodwin 2001, p. 10).[5] As almost all observers have noted, socioeconomic claims were significant in the emergence and spread of the uprisings, and actors that are defined by socioeconomic cleavages (such as labor organizations or the unemployed) played an important role in the dynamics of mobilization (see Chap. 1, in this volume). And, yet, no relevant sociopolitical force emerged from these protests that would promote anything resembling an agenda for socioeconomic change. This helps understand one key finding of the research compiled in this volume: the apparent paradox that uprisings that (a) have been driven, in particular, by socioeconomic grievances and related demands for social justice and that (b) have had sufficient strength to topple long-standing dictators, have (c) not led to any significant fulfillment of these socioeconomic demands. But what are the implications of this mismatch between the claims and the actual outcomes of the uprisings for the post-revolutionary dynamics of contentious action?

In the immediate aftermath of the uprisings, many observers argued that a decisive question for the future of the ongoing political transformations in Egypt and Tunisia was precisely whether post-revolutionary governments would be able to address "citizen demands for material improvement and social justice" (Burnell 2013, p. 84; see also Schlumberger and Matzke 2012, pp. 107–108). When we started this project, we therefore speculated that a lack of a substantive political response to socioeconomic grievances in Egypt and Tunisia would mean that socioeconomic protests would go on at a continuously high, if not increasing, level. In any case, we expected that the ways in which the emerging political regimes in Egypt and Tunisia "respond to socioeconomic discontent are of crucial importance for [the] political transformation processes" (Weipert-Fenner and Wolff 2015, p. 1). These assumptions have not been disproven by our research, but the findings of this book do suggest a need for differentiation.

As the quantitative protest event analysis conducted by Prisca Jöst and Jan-Philipp Vatthauer shows, socioeconomic protests have not been a continuous phenomenon. The years between 2011 and 2016 in the two

---

[5] Goodwin, here, relies on Charles Tilly's definition of a revolutionary movement as "a social movement 'advancing exclusive competing claims to control of the state, or some segment of it'" (Goodwin 2001, p. 10, citing Tilly 1993, p. 10).

countries have been characterized rather by passing outbursts of discontent, most notably in Egypt in 2013 and in Tunisia in 2016. Since 2013, socioeconomic protests in Egypt have continued, albeit at a low level of intensity. Tunisia, by contrast, has witnessed a massive increase in socioeconomic protests since 2015, which, however, has also taken the form of temporary outbursts. In line with the political opportunity approach in social movement research, these dynamics of socioeconomic contention respond to the evolving political context rather than constituting a relevant driving force of political change. Still, socioeconomic contention has proven relevant for economic policymaking: Arguably in response to protests, including the threat thereof, governments in both Egypt and Tunisia have increased public wages, the size of the public sector and general subsidies (at least in the first years after the revolutions), while refraining from pursuing socioeconomic measures that would have had immediate negative effects on wage earners and self-, under- and unemployed people (see Chap. 2, in this volume; IMF 2014, pp. 8–11; Paciello 2013).

This overall finding is confirmed upon inspection of the key protagonists in socioeconomic protests in the two countries, namely organized and unorganized labor and, in Tunisia, unemployed people. In both countries, while labor organizations were relatively successful in *defending* certain benefits and rights, they were unable to achieve "positive" change. This holds true for both Tunisia, where the unusually strong and united national trade union federation Union Générale Tunisienne du Travail (UGTT) has mainly acted as a mediator, contributing to the contested process of political transition in the country (see Chap. 5, in this volume), and Egypt, where the main trade union federation remains under state control and the independent trade union movement has become increasingly marginalized. Still, even in Egypt, independent trade unions successfully prevented parliament from adopting a new civil service law in early 2016 that included reductions in public sector wages (see Chap. 6, in this volume). The protests by organized and ad hoc groups of unemployed people in Tunisia were also characterized by conservative demands. Actions by the national Union of Unemployed Graduates (UDC) and mobilizations in the Gafsa mining basin—a hotbed of socioeconomic protest in Tunisia—have generally called for a *return of the state* as the guarantor of decent jobs and welfare.[6] Success, therefore, has basically meant

---

[6] A different dynamic, but with similar consequences, could be observed in the case of Egypt's Tuktuk drivers studied in this volume by Abdelrahman Soliman. Here, also, the few

governmental assurances of a certain number of additional public sector jobs for the unemployed (see Chap. 8, in this volume). The case studies also revealed that the fragmentation of societal actors and their low levels of trust in political parties and institutions have contributed to the weakness of socioeconomic protests (see Chaps. 6, 8 and 9 of this volume). The only exception is the Tunisian trade union federation, which has by and large been able to represent the country's organized working class. Given its political role as a mediator guaranteeing Tunisia's transition to democracy, the UGTT has, however, largely refrained from actively making labor-related, socioeconomic demands (see Chap. 5, in this volume). In addition, even if it generally has a leftist profile, the UGTT has presented itself as a nonpartisan, "neutral" actor and, therefore, mostly refrained from forming alliances with political parties.

10.3 Egypt and Tunisia in the Light of Latin American Experiences: Interregional Comparison

As summarized in the two overview chapters by Jonas Wolff (see Chaps. 4 and 7, in this volume), studies on the role and dynamics of social protest and popular mobilization during the processes of democratization in Latin America between the late 1970s and early 1990s have shown how socioeconomic claims, though important for mobilization against authoritarian regimes, were sidelined during actual regime change negotiations.

By and large, democratization in the region meant the establishment of, or return to, a political system with free and fair elections, representative political institutions and constitutionally guaranteed political and civil rights. It did not include any serious attempt to deal with the dramatic socioeconomic inequalities and the systematic disregard of social and economic rights with a view to improving the socioeconomic underpinnings of a more-than-formal democracy. Some observers have explicitly argued that things have to be like this: that in order to get the moderate ("soft") members of the authoritarian regime coalition to support democratization, debates about economic redistribution and structural, socioeconomic change had to be avoided (see O'Donnell and Schmitter 1986, p. 27). Others have rather grudgingly accepted that this

---

protests that took place were characterized by defensive and/or conservative demands on the state, basically aiming at the issue of licensing.

is what happened empirically (see Bermeo 1990, p. 365).[7] Be this as it may, the overall result is undeniable: Political democratization in Latin America succeeded in a context of persisting—if not actually worsening—socioeconomic hardships and inequalities and, thus, did not actually produce socioeconomic benefits for the great majority of the respective population that was, formally, empowered by political change. Recalling the ways in which this general dynamic played out in the region as well as the explanations that have been developed in the comparative literature on Latin American democratization help us better understand the contemporary trajectories of post-revolutionary Egypt and Tunisia as summarized earlier. This, in particular, concerns three key dynamics that can be observed in both contexts.

First, as mentioned earlier, in both sets of cases, we can observe that as soon as the struggle is over, and the negotiation of the shape of the political regime takes center stage, questions concerning the economic order and socioeconomic redistribution are pushed aside in the political agenda. Theoretically, in the case of Latin America, this dynamic can be traced back to (a) the cross-class character of the pro-democracy movements and the relatively privileged status of the Latin American middle classes (including the important segment of organized labor), which made the emergence of a common agenda of socioeconomic change and, more specifically, widely shared claims for socioeconomic redistribution unlikely; (b) the elite-centered and negotiated (non-revolutionary) character of most transitions, which meant that incumbent regime forces and political, military and economic elites, in general, played an important role in shaping political change; and (c) an international context that, by and large, supported this kind of limited, politico-institutional democratization (see O'Donnell and Schmitter 1986; Rueschemeyer et al. 1992, Chap. 5; Wolff 2005, p. 61). The contributions to this volume suggest that these three factors are also relevant in the cases of Egypt and Tunisia. While (a) the cross-class character of the uprising and its consequences for the post-revolutionary dynamics of contention have already been highlighted, the ambivalent

[7] As Nancy Bermeo summarized the findings of the set of volumes on *Transitions to Authoritarian Rule*, the "facts," while dismaying to everyone who, like herself, values "political and economic egalitarianism, "are undeniable": "Virtually none of the surviving transitions to democracy that are discussed in this collection combined a significant redistribution of political *and* economic resources. In every enduring case, dramatic redistributions of property were postponed, circumscribed, or rolled back." (Bermeo 1990, p. 365; see also Karl 1990).

role of organized labor in Egypt and Tunisia also resembles the Latin American experiences. As the chapters by Abdalla and Karray (see Chaps. 5 and 6, in this volume) show, key trade union organizations in both countries have been much more active in defending their (privileged) position than in trying to articulate a progressive socioeconomic agenda in the name of the broader popular sectors. In the case of Tunisia, this attitude is directly reflected in the tensions between the UGTT (at the national level) and the mobilization of unemployed people (see Chap. 8, in this volume). Even if these dimensions have not been studied in detail in this volume, it is also clear that (b) incumbent regime forces and elites, in general, were also key actors in the contested negotiations of political change in the two North African cases (see Boubekeur 2016; Roll 2016), and that (c) the international context—while certainly heterogeneous in terms of its political implications—tended to support austerity policies and neoliberal reforms and, in any case, did not favor any kind of progressive socioeconomic reform agenda (see Hinnebusch 2015; Paciello 2013; Teti 2012).

Second, in the "historic" context of politico-institutional change with socioeconomic continuity in Latin America, popular-sector organizations that had originally voiced socioeconomic demands either (a) joined the trend and likewise started to focus on politico-institutional issues, (b) tried to continue pushing for a broader socioeconomic agenda but faced increasing fragmentation and marginalization from the political debate or (c) turned inward and/or to the local area and focused on survival strategies and self-help activities. The case studies included in this volume certainly do not cover (not nearly) the broad range of popular-sector organizations in Egypt and Tunisia, but the available evidence—again—reveals comparable dynamics. In terms of (a), in the two post-revolutionary contexts, the Tunisian UGTT stands out as a labor organization that can be considered a relevant—and, indeed, quite powerful—political actor. But, as Karray's chapter (see Chap. 5, in this volume) demonstrates, the UGTT's role has been strong precisely as a participant in the politico-institutional transition process—at the expense of a socioeconomic agenda that, for instance, would have worked toward meeting specific workers' demands. The issue of fragmentation and marginalization (b), which also showed up in the quantitative protest event analysis, has already been mentioned as a general feature in both countries, and it was particularly pronounced in the case of Egypt's independent labor movement and the different types of unemployed mobilization in Tunisia. Finally (c), in different ways and forms, the case studies of the Egyptian Tuktuk drivers and the protests in

Tunisia's Gafsa mining region revealed patterns of (partially contentious) interactions with the state that follow a rather "unpolitical"—localized and self-help-oriented—logic (see Chaps. 8 and 9 in this volume).

This last observation points to the third dynamic: the political consequences of these patterns of contentious action. As already suggested, the overall phenomenon in both sets of cases is that socioeconomic grievances that contributed to motivating popular resistance to authoritarian regimes in the first place were not addressed and, correspondingly, socioeconomic contention continued—but it did (or does) so taking localized and/or fragmented, actor- and/or issue-specific forms that have a significant impact at the macropolitical level. As research on contentious action in Latin America's post-transition democracies shows, the combination of persisting socioeconomic grievances with the opening of political opportunities in this region—surprisingly[8]—did not lead to ever-more escalating popular protest. Rather, what scholars have described is an overall process of "demobilization of the popular sectors" (Oxhorn 1998, p. 208) characterized by an "angry atomization of society" (O'Donnell 1993, p. 1365) and erratic, short-lived expressions of discontent at the national level (Portes and Hoffman 2003, pp. 76–77), as well as new territorialized forms of popular-sector mobilization at the local level (Rossi 2017, pp. 13–15). Thus, the relative absence, or reduction, in popular protests, making socioeconomic claims at the national level did *not* imply satisfaction, but rather reflected politico-economic dynamics that concern both the internal mechanisms of organization and mobilization among the popular sectors and their relationship with the broader political, economic and international context (see the two overview chapters on Latin America, Chaps. 4 and 7, in this volume). This is, in general terms, what we also find in post-revolutionary Egypt and Tunisia. More specifically, the case studies of Egypt's independent labor movement and Tunisia's unemployed movement emphasized the internal weakness of existing popular-sector organizations, the lack of reliable and relevant sociopolitical allies and a political context that severely limited (Egypt) or limited to a relative degree (Tunisia) meaningful access to the political system.

[8] In her 1989 book on *Power and Popular Protest*, Susan Eckstein (1989, p. 41) still speculated that, in particular, in the context of open and thus protest-prone democratic regimes, the combination of increasing socioeconomic hardships due to region-wide economic crises and reduced state capacity for diffusing potential unrest with "patronage and subsidies" due to the austerity programs might lead to increasing levels of popular protest. See also O'Donnell and Schmitter (1986, pp. 52–53).

As an overall result, it has been argued, with regard to Latin America, that in the end the *non-responsivity* to social grievances of the post-transition regimes proved instrumental for the stability of the post-transition regimes, as it helped avoid elite resistance to the "risks" that democratization posed for their privileges in terms of power and wealth (see Chaps. 4 and 7, in this volume). Although this was not studied in this volume, it is at least plausible to argue that democratization in Tunisia has benefited from a similar dynamic: In a context of significant mobilization around (class-based) socioeconomic cleavages, it certainly would have been hard to establish the kind of alliances that were key elements in the negotiated transition to democracy, such as the National Dialogue Quartet that united the UGTT and the Tunisian Confederation of Industry, Trade and Handicrafts (UTICA) or the different party coalitions that brought together an Islamist party with social-democratic parties or with a conservative party alliance, respectively.

To be sure, these overall dynamics represent general patterns only. In the case of Latin America, in the 1980s and early 1990s, several countries saw quite important waves of socioeconomic contention. But these protests were, on the one hand, defensive reactions to austerity policies and neoliberal reforms rather than proactive moves demanding socioeconomic change—again something we can also observe in protest dynamics in Egypt and Tunisia. On the other hand, while governments in post-transition Latin America did frequently respond with repression, the ultimate failure of these protests to prevent the kinds of (neoliberal and/or austerity) policies they were fighting was not due to overwhelming state repression (see the two overview chapters on Latin America, Chaps. 4 and 7, in this volume).[9] In the case of Egypt—which has (for the time being) seen the re-establishment of authoritarian rule, with levels of restrictions on civil society organizations that even exceed the pre-revolutionary situation—the political repression of (potentially) contentious actors is clearly a factor also evident in the low numbers of overall protests since the coup against Morsi (see Chap. 3, in this volume). Tunisia, for obvious reasons, much more closely resembles Latin America's post-transition experiences in this regard.

---

[9] As Eckstein (1989, p. 47) noted in the late 1980s, "Latin American governments do not have the material capability of employing force on a large scale unless financed from abroad, and the democratic countries in the region cannot, for ideological reasons, rely on prolonged and extensive use of force to rule." Repression, under these conditions, tended to strengthen, rather than weaken, movements (Eckstein 1989, p. 46).

10.4 Contentious Politics in Times of Incorporation Crises: Theoretical Reflections

Comparing Egypt and Tunisia brings a remarkable pattern of similarities and differences to the fore. First, as we have seen, there is a quite high level of convergence between the two countries when it comes to the very characteristics of the uprisings that culminated in the toppling of long-standing dictators in early 2011. Second, however, the trajectories of political transformation after the revolutions are pointed in opposite directions. Third, these diverging political contexts notwithstanding, post-revolutionary Egypt and Tunisia again display quite similar patterns in economic policy-making and, in general terms, in their respective lack of general structural economic change. Fourth, quantitative trends in socioeconomic protests are very different (clearly reflecting the differences in political opportunity structures rather than socioeconomic similarities). But, fifth, key qualitative characteristics of these socioeconomic protests are again fairly similar (fragmented, territorialized, issue-specific, etc.), and this common weakness is, sixth, reflected in the (limited and mainly status quo-oriented) consequences of these protests, which do not significantly reflect the dramatically different degrees of access to the political system that would be expected, given the diverging politico-institutional contexts.

In a nutshell, this pattern suggests that the politico-institutional context significantly shapes the quantity and intensity of (socioeconomic) protests (as predicted by the contentious political approach), but that the qualitative characteristics of the socioeconomic protests, which have more immediate consequences in macropolitical terms, are shaped by *different* conditions. In order to make theoretical sense of this observation, it is again helpful to turn to an academic literature that has emerged in the comparative study of Latin American politics, namely the debate on the question of incorporation.

In a landmark study first published in 1991, Ruth and David Collier analyzed the historical processes through which the labor movement was initially incorporated into the political system during the first half of the twentieth century. Studying and comparing the cases of Argentina, Brazil, Chile, Colombia, Mexico, Peru, Uruguay, and Venezuela, they identified different strategies and types of labor incorporation, which led to varying patterns of conflict and accommodation and produced long-lasting legacies in terms of party system development and political regime dynamics

(Collier and Collier 2002).[10] Recently, scholars have revived the concept of incorporation arguing that, since the 1990s, Latin America has been experiencing a new incorporation crisis that, with the so-called left turn, has given way to a "second historical process of mass political incorporation" (Roberts 2008, p. 300; see Luna and Filgueira 2009; Rossi 2015, 2017; Silva 2017). In contrast to the first period of incorporation, the new period of incorporation involves a much more heterogeneous set of social groups that, in the Latin American debate, is usually called "the popular sectors."[11] Generally speaking, their incorporation has two dimensions: a political dimension that concerns the inclusion of popular-sector claims and interests into the political agenda as well as "the concrete mechanisms that link popular sector organizations to the political arena and policymaking" (Silva 2017, p. 95; see also Rossi 2017, p. xi) and a socioeconomic dimension that refers to the substantive efforts at socioeconomic inclusion through the strengthening of socioeconomic rights and/or corresponding social and economic policies (Luna and Filgueira 2009, p. 375).

The recent wave of popular-sector struggles across Latin America, which in the first decade of the twenty-first century led to the election of a whole series of leftist and center-left governments, followed from the consequences of neoliberal reforms in two regards: On the one hand, the broken promise of neoliberal incorporation[12] was a key driving force in the

---

[10] Studying the emergence of organized labor movements in Latin America as well as the varying responses of the state to this new phenomenon, Collier and Collier identified different types and patterns of what they call the "initial incorporation" of the labor movement. As a critical juncture, the shape of this incorporation, then, was shown to have long-term effects on party systems and regime dynamics in the respective countries. Most notably, they distinguish between two different types of incorporation: In cases of state incorporation, "the legal and bureaucratic apparatus of the state" was the key agency of incorporation, "and the principal goal of the leaders who initiated incorporation was the control and depoliticization of the labor movement"; in cases of party incorporation, by contrast, "a central agency of incorporation was a political party or political movement that later became a party, and a fundamental goal of political leaders, in addition to control, was the mobilization of working class support through this party of movement" (Collier and Collier 2002, p. 8).

[11] Eduardo Silva defines the popular sectors as "poor subaltern social sectors," including both "urban poor social groups in the formal and informal labor sectors" and "peasants, indigenous peoples, and other peoples of color in urban and rural spaces organized on socio-territorial bases" (2017, p. 116, note 1).

[12] Luna and Filgueira characterize Latin America's pattern of (failed) incorporation in the 1990s as "electoral incorporation in the context of faulty democracies and segmented market incorporation" and argue that "[n]eoliberalism did not fail simply because of its inability in most Latin American settings to achieve stable growth, wealth redistribution or market

upsurge of social (protest) movements that many Latin American countries have experienced since the late 1990s (see Roberts 2008). On the other hand, neoliberal reforms generally meant a process of "disincorporation" of organized labor, which saw itself dramatically weakened both in socioeconomic and in political terms (Rossi 2017, pp. 15–17); in general, the "fragmented, heterogeneous popular sector landscape," from which new dynamics of contentious mobilization have emerged since the late 1990s, were very much the socio-structural result of neoliberalism (Silva 2017, p. 95).[13] These popular sectors, while formally empowered by the establishment of democratic regimes during the long 1980s, were de facto marginalized in both political and socioeconomic terms in the context of democratization-cum-neoliberal reforms (see Kurtz 2004; Oxhorn 1998; Wolff 2005, pp. 62–67, 2007, pp. 10–13).

The election of left and center-left governments across the region as well as the series of socioeconomic and politico-institutional changes that this left turn has brought about can, therefore, be understood "as both the outcomes of, and a set of alternative solutions to, a 'second incorporation crisis'" (Luna and Filgueira 2009, p. 372). Important differences between the left and center-left governments that came to power in many Latin American countries in the early 2000s notwithstanding, their overall agenda has combined (a) a turn to post-neoliberal social and economic policies that aimed at socioeconomic incorporation of the popular sectors (basically, by reducing poverty and income inequality) and (b) varying attempts to politically incorporate the popular sectors (via popular-sector organizations such as labor unions or social movement organizations representing, for instance, indigenous or unemployed people; via leftist and/or movement-type political parties; via new mechanisms of participatory and/or plebiscitary democracy).

In the context of this concluding chapter, it is impossible to discuss the specific patterns and actual outcomes of incorporation in Latin America (see Rossi 2017; Silva and Rossi 2018; Wolff 2018). Suffice it to say that progress in terms of both socioeconomic and political inclusion was diverse but real. Yet, it remained relative only and its sustainability doubtful, given

incorporation, but also because it was unable to structure political incorporation by providing legitimate representation (i.e., by delivering policies and outcomes that were able to synchronise collective expectations and individual needs)" (2009, p. 376).

[13] To be sure, neoliberal structural adjustment in this regard combined with austerity policies, monetary stabilization measures, the effects of the severe economic crisis of the 1980s, as well as with the consequences of the military dictatorships.

that socioeconomic inclusion depended to an important extent on high commodity prices, while political inclusion frequently depended on informal mechanisms. In sum, therefore, the crisis of incorporation which has underlain Latin America's "leftist turn" is, thus, far from resolved. What is relevant for our purposes, however, is the overall idea of incorporation periods—incorporation crises and attempted solutions of such crises—which result from basic socio-structural changes (but, to be sure, have to be activated through processes of social mobilization). As we will suggest in the following, considering them as expressions of a fundamental crisis of incorporation helps to make sense of the empirical observations collected in this volume.

In fact, the Arab uprisings have already been interpreted as resulting from the breakdown of an "authoritarian social contract" that had sustained the autocratic regimes in the region for many decades (see Achy 2015; Guazzone and Pioppi 2012; Zorob 2013). Generally speaking, this social contract (in Egypt and Tunisia but also elsewhere in the region) involved key mechanisms of incorporation: In political terms, state corporatism was a key feature which basically connected organized labor with the political arena through a state-controlled and co-opted labor movement (other mechanisms of political incorporation included, for instance, parliaments that, in the same way, served to connect key constituencies to the political regime, see Weipert-Fenner 2015). In socioeconomic terms, research has particularly highlighted the material benefits offered by the authoritarian regimes (jobs in the public sector, social security, social subsidies, etc.). With neoliberal structural adjustment, this authoritarian social contract gradually lost its material basis, while (partially related) changes in the social and economic structures of the countries meant that corporatist arrangements reached a decreasing share of the popular sectors. The resulting crisis of incorporation has become manifest with the rise of an independent labor movement in Egypt since 2006, the 2008 protests in Tunisia's Gafsa region and, finally, with the uprisings of 2010–2011.

As our analysis of post-revolutionary dynamics in Egypt and Tunisia shows, these old mechanisms of incorporation still exist. Furthermore, key ideological elements of the authoritarian social contract continue to shape the popular discourses and agendas of key actors (as exemplified by Tunisia's unemployed protests and their primary demand to be hired by the state). Yet, a persisting crisis of incorporation is hard to deny. Post-revolutionary developments have, therefore, not meant a re-establishment of the earlier scheme of incorporation. The extremely repressive turn in the Egyptian government's relationship with civil society actors, on the one hand, and the extent of public discontent as well as the recent outbursts of socioeconomic protests in Tunisia, on the other hand, clearly suggest that existing ("old") mechanisms of incorporation reach only a limited (privileged) part of the popular sectors, and they do so in increasingly precarious ways. The extent and reach of socioeconomic incorporation—through, for instance, socioeconomic measures (public sector jobs, subsidies)—is clearly insufficient. The same holds true for the politico-institutional dimension, where, for instance, the corporatist inclusion of organized labor is not only highly exclusive and state-controlled but is also largely formal, without enabling any kind of substantive influence on policymaking.

At the same time, however, new mechanisms of incorporation—which might enable a new social contract—have yet to emerge. Rather, as in Latin America in the 1980s and 1990s, current dynamics in Egypt and Tunisia fluctuate between (or combine) neoliberal approaches that emphasize inclusion "by and through the market" and fairly traditional state-centered and state-corporatist approaches. In the case of Tunisia, the idea of a "social dialogue," which has been promoted by the UGTT and which basically represents an attempt to revise corporatist incorporation in the new context, cautiously points in a more innovative direction. But, generally, our case studies document little to no new dynamics of incorporation. In different ways and gradations, this lack of any institutional articulation with the political arena can be observed in the case of the unemployed protests in Gafsa and the Tuktuk drivers in Egypt, that is, in the informal sectors of the countries but also in the labor activism in Egypt that is continuing despite the banning of independent labor unions and the renewed co-optation of the official labor union (Hamzawy 2017). Clearly, those large parts of the population that are outside the formal labor market are entirely excluded from existing mechanisms of incorporation but also important groups of formally employed people are not or are only indirectly or ephemerally part of corporatist interest intermediation.

To what extent does this interpretation of the post-revolutionary setting—as an incorporation crisis that openly broke out with the uprisings and has yet to be addressed—help understand the puzzling similarities and differences between Egypt and Tunisia? First, the notion of a persisting crisis of incorporation points to a common feature that characterizes political developments in the two countries. While the development of the political regimes in a narrow sense has taken divergent trajectories, the ways in which these emerging regimes incorporate (or do not incorporate) the popular sectors and their organizations reveal some important similarities. In democratic Tunisia, as in authoritarian Egypt, institutionalized access of popular-sector organizations to the political arena is as limited as the political responsiveness to their concerns. This similarity across different political regimes is hardly surprising when the Latin American experience is taken into account: The establishment of representative democracy does not automatically imply a process of popular-sector incorporation. In their comparison of Egypt and Tunisia, Adly and Meddeb (see Chap. 2, in this volume) therefore basically confirm what research on Latin America's post-transition democracies has established: That changes in the set-up of political institutions and the formal granting of universal political and civil rights as implied by democratization can perfectly coexist with far-reaching continuities in social power relations, which will, then, most probably also be reflected in the overall characteristics of social and economic policies (see Kurtz 2004; Oxhorn 1998; Wolff 2005).

Second, the dynamics of socioeconomic protests and their political relevance are also shaped by the underlying crisis of incorporation that particularly concerns the heterogeneous set of social groups that make up the popular sectors. Expressing the ongoing struggles for incorporation, protests continue with ebbs and flows in both countries and, in the much more open Tunisian context, with fairly dramatic outbursts of discontent. But, given the heterogeneity of the social groups and the fragmentation of the popular-sector organizations involved, these protests neither force authorities to respond with offers of meaningful incorporation nor do they accumulate into broader waves of contention that would (once again) challenge the political regimes. The different *quantitative* dynamics of socioeconomic protests in Egypt and Tunisia thus reflect the differences in the political opportunity structures, but the similar *quality*—and hence a similarly low degree of political relevance— of the protests is arguably related to the socio-structural and organizational set-up of the popular sectors. As in the Latin American 1990s, these characteristics of popular-sector mobilization reflect the combined legacies of decades of authoritarian rule and neoliberal structural adjustment. In sum, therefore, recognizing the unaddressed crisis of popular-sector incorporation helps explain key dynamics in contentious politics in Egypt and Tunisia.

10.5 Outlook

At the end of the 1980s, a volume on *Power and Popular Protest* in Latin America started with the observation that "Latin Americans have been more defiant than the available literature would lead us to believe, even if less so than we might expect, given existing injustices and inequities" (Eckstein 1989, p. 3). The same kind of statement could well have started our analysis of socioeconomic protest in Egypt and Tunisia: The Arab uprisings of 2010–2011 and what has happened ever since clearly show that the people in the region are more defiant than previous assessments of Arab exceptionalism and authoritarian persistence suggested, even if less defiant than we might expect, given persisting injustices and inequities. In Latin America, it took roughly two decades until the failure of post-transitional (democratic) regimes to do anything about the persisting (if not aggravating) injustices and inequities led to a renewed wave of popular mobilization that placed the social question back on the agenda. In the early 2000s, this new upsurge in sociopolitical mobilization in Latin America ushered in a period of remarkable political and socioeconomic change in which left and center-left governments adopted more inclusive and redistributive ("post-neoliberal") social and economic policies and, contradictions and limitations notwithstanding, achieved significant reductions in poverty and inequality (see Huber and Stephens 2012; Levitsky and Roberts 2011; Rossi 2017; Silva and Rossi 2018).

In this concluding chapter, we have argued that Egypt and Tunisia—and plausibly broader parts of the Middle East and North Africa (MENA) region as well—are currently confronting a crisis of popular-sector incorporation that is fairly similar to the one Latin America has been facing since the 1980s (and which is still far from resolved in that region). Large parts of the population—namely those representing the lower strata of society—do not have access to effective mechanisms that link them with the political arena, give them an institutional voice in the political process and/or make policymaking responsive to their interests and values. With the popular uprisings of 2010–2011, this lack of incorporation, which reflects the breakdown of the previous scheme of incorporation (the "authoritarian social contract"), turned into a full-fledged crisis. In both post-revolutionary contexts studied in this volume, governments have been unwilling to establish new processes for incorporating organizations representing the popular sectors, while the latter have been mostly unable to apply pressure for their incorporation from below. This dynamic is remarkably similar in

Egypt and Tunisia, despite the different political regimes that have taken shape in the two countries. This observation reinforces our argument that we are confronted here with underlying social (sociopolitical and politico-economic) dynamics that shape contentious politics and are relatively independent of changes at the level of the political system.

What are we to make of this overall assessment? The idea behind the interregional comparative perspective is definitely *not* that Latin America, as a somewhat more advanced region, serves to demonstrate to North Africa or the Arab world "the image of its own future," to paraphrase Karl Marx. This story is neither about late developers repeating the experiences of others, nor about models that might be exported. But, by being capitalist societies with a peripheral place in the global political economy in times of neoliberal globalization, Latin America and North Africa are part of global processes of social change and, at the same time, are experiencing processes of domestic social change that can be expected to exhibit certain common features. It is in this sense that it is promising to speculate that Egypt and Tunisia are undergoing a period of contested incorporation that is structurally similar to the one that Latin America has been experiencing since the 1990s. This analogy, in addition to helping us make sense of the empirical phenomena studied in this volume, raises three important questions that might be crucial for the future of Egypt and Tunisia (and the Arab world, more generally speaking), and with which we want to conclude this book.

First, with a view to future academic research, it seems promising to systematically address the question of incorporation (periods, crises and attempts) from an interregional comparative perspective. Informed by what we know from Latin America about mechanisms and patterns, demands and struggles, outcomes and problems of popular-sector incorporation, such a research agenda would study in detail the shifts and continuities in the ways in which different segments of the popular sectors in the MENA region create or use links with the political arena to make their demands heard and in which, stated the other way round, states and political parties use, establish or adapt links with the popular sectors. From an interregional comparative perspective, one key question is whether we can identify new dynamics of popular-sector incorporation in the MENA region that might offer (competing, more or less promising) solutions to the incorporation crisis. Such new dynamics in the MENA region may emerge from below, from the very place where popular-sector groups organize and act collectively or from above, as political responses to challenges from below. In the end, however, they will result from contentious politics dynamics in which social agency from below interacts with macropolitical dynamics from above. In any case, the dynamics that may already be underway in the MENA region will most certainly be very different from the ones observed in the context of Latin America's "left turn." But, as we have suggested in this concluding chapter, they respond to fairly similar social and political challenges and will, therefore, probably be characterized by structural similarities and/or functional equivalents.

Going beyond such a descriptive research agenda, a second—and related—question obviously concerns the conditions and factors that might enable or activate new dynamics of popular-sector incorporation in the MENA region in general, and in Egypt and Tunisia in particular. Again, Latin American experiences do not offer a direct answer to this question, but still might be worth considering. As briefly summarized in the second overview chapter by Jonas Wolff (see Chap. 7, in this volume), scholars have explained the recent re-emergence of strong popular-sector movements in Latin America, which prepared the ground for the "left turn," by emphasizing the necessary combination of macro- and micro-conditions. To recap: The *opportunity* and the *motive* to mobilize were constituted by the overall political space offered by democracy as well as by the mobilizing threats implied by neoliberal reforms and austerity policies. Yet, in terms of the *capacity* to organize and act collectively, associational spaces and pre-existing societal networks at the local level as well as horizontal networks and communication across different local settings were crucial in enabling popular-sector groups to effectively seize the opportunities and respond to the threats (see Silva 2009; Wolff 2007; Yashar 2005).

Third, the question of incorporation is far from a purely academic issue. As the comparative scholarship on the different periods of mass incorporation in Latin America demonstrates, the patterns and dynamics of incorporation are of the utmost political importance. The ways in which the popular sectors are or are not incorporated have immediate and long-term consequences for party system development and political regime dynamics as well as for political stability and societal peace. This means that it is not only *generally* important to search for ways in which, say, unemployed people in Tunisia or shantytown dwellers in Egypt can gain an institutionalized voice in the political arena, it will also be crucial for political developments in these countries *how* they might eventually do so: whether by means of relatively autonomous social movements or the expansion of existing (labor) organizations, or through old or new, leftist, Islamist or whatever-kind-of parties or through state institutions and agencies. Recognizing the manifold experiences from Latin America in this regard may enable academics, politicians and activists to identify promising attempts to facilitate popular-sector incorporation that emerge in Egypt, Tunisia and beyond, as well as ways of promoting innovation in popular-sector incorporation from the outside at an early stage. To mention only one specific lesson from Latin America, promising experiments in popular-sector incorporation might particularly emerge in local settings, at the municipal level, where it is easier for social movements to establish direct and organic links with the political arena (see Goldfrank 2011; Van Cott 2008). In terms of political reforms, this raises the issue of decentralization and the question how to enable or deepen political participation at the local level.

All this is not to say that it is irrelevant whether representative democracy exists, whether individual human rights are respected or whether civil society actors in general can act autonomously and have access to the political arena. All this is certainly of crucial importance in many regards.[14] But, as the focus on socioeconomic protests shows all too well, the structural inequalities that characterize societies in the Arab world as in Latin America (or, for that matter, Europe) *also* demand a perspective that takes social class and power relations seriously. As Ruth Collier concluded in her study on the role of the working class during democratization processes in Western Europe and Latin America, in times of political transformation, it is not "transition games but political economy [that] becomes crucially important" (Collier 1999, p. 197). In normative terms, such a perspective should specifically zoom in on those sectors of society that are struggling for survival, political empowerment and social justice from a disadvantaged position—and whose success is, therefore, of particular relevance when it comes to constructing societies that are both politically more democratic and socially more just.

---

[14] In fact, as mentioned above, scholars have emphasized the relevance of the overall political space offered by representative democracy—even if this opportunity structure was, obviously, only an enabling condition (see Levitsky and Roberts 2011; Wolff 2007; Yashar 2005).

References

Achy, L. (2015). Breakdown of the authoritarian 'social contract' and emergence of new social actors: An ongoing process? In L. Sadiki (Ed.), *Routledge handbook of the Arab spring: Rethinking democratization* (pp. 303–318). London: Routledge.

Bayat, A. (2017). *Revolution without revolutionaries. Making sense of the Arab spring*. Stanford, CA: Stanford University Press.

Bermeo, N. (1990). Review article: Rethinking regime change. *Comparative Politics, 22*(3), 359–377.

Boubekeur, A. (2016). Islamists, secularists and old regime elites in Tunisia: Bargained competition. *Mediterranean Politics, 21*(1), 107–127.

Burnell, P. (2013). Democratisation in the Middle East and North Africa: Perspectives from democracy support. *Third World Quarterly, 34*(5), 838–855.

Collier, R. (1999). *Paths toward democracy. The working class and elites in Western Europe and South America*. Cambridge: Cambridge University Press.

Collier, R., & Collier, D. (2002). *Shaping the political arena. Critical junctures, the labor movement, and regime dynamics in Latin America*. Notre Dame, IN: University of Notre Dame Press.

Della Porta, D. (2014). *Mobilizing for democracy. Comparing 1989 and 2011*. Oxford: Oxford University Press.

Diwan, I., & Galal, A. (2016). *The Middle East economies in times of transition*. London: Palgrave Macmillan UK.

Durac, V. (2015). Social movements, protest movements and cross-ideological coalitions: The Arab uprisings re-appraised. *Democratization, 22*(2), 239–258.

Eckstein, S. (1989). *Power and popular protest. Latin American social movements*. Berkeley, CA: University of California Press.

Fishman, R. (1990). Rethinking state and regime: Southern Europe's transition to democracy. *World Politics, 42*(3), 422–440.

Goldfrank, B. (2011). The left and participatory democracy: Brazil, Uruguay, and Venezuela. In S. Levitsky & K. Roberts (Eds.), *The resurgence of the Latin American left* (pp. 162–183). Baltimore, MD: The Johns Hopkins University Press.

Goodwin, J. (2001). *No other way out. States and revolutionary movements, 1945–1991*. Cambridge: Cambridge University Press.

Guazzone, L., & Pioppi, D. (2012). *The Arab state and neoliberal globalization. The restructuring of state power in the Middle East*. Reading: Ithaca Press.

Hamzawy, A. (2017). *Egypt's resilient and evolving social activism*. Washington, DC: Carnegie Endowment for International Peace.

Heydemann, S. (2016). Explaining the Arab uprisings: Transformations in comparative perspective. *Mediterranean Politics, 21*(1), 192–204.

Hinnebusch, R. (2015). Globalization, democratization, and the Arab uprising: The international factor in MENA's failed democratization. *Democratization, 22*(2), 335–357.

Huber, E., & Stephens, J. (2012). *Democracy and the left. social policy and inequality in Latin America.* Chicago, IL: The University of Chicago Press.

IMF (International Monetary Fund). (2014). *Toward new horizons: Arab economic transformation amid political transitions.* Washington, DC.

Karl, T. (1990). Dilemmas of democratization in Latin America. *Comparative Politics, 23*(1), 1–21.

Kienle, E. (2015). *Changed regimes, changed priorities? Economic and social policies after the 2011 elections in Tunisia and Egypt.* Economic research forum working paper 928. Retrieved October 25, 2018, from http://erf.org.eg/wp-content/uploads/2015/12/928.pdf.

Kurtz, M. (2004). The dilemmas of democracy in the open economy. Lessons from Latin America. *World Politics, 56*(1), 262–302.

Levitsky, S., & Roberts, K. (2011). *The resurgence of the Latin American left.* Baltimore, MD: The Johns Hopkins University Press.

Luna, J. P., & Filgueira, F. (2009). The left turns as multiple paradigmatic crises. *Third World Quarterly, 30*(2), 371–395.

O'Donnell, G. (1993). On the state, democratization and some conceptual problems: A Latin American view with glances at some postcommunist countries. *World Development, 21*(8), 1355–1369.

O'Donnell, G., & Schmitter, P. C. (1986). *Transitions from authoritarian rule. Tentative conclusions about uncertain democracies.* Baltimore, MD: The Johns Hopkins University Press.

Oxhorn, P. (1998). Is the century of corporatism over? Neoliberalism and the rise of neopluralism. In P. Oxhorn & G. Ducatenzeiler (Eds.), *What kind of democracy? What kind of market? Latin America in the age of neoliberalism* (pp. 195–217). University Park, PA: The Pennsylvania State University Press.

Paciello, M. C. (2013). Delivering the revolution? Post-uprising socio-economics in Tunisia and Egypt. *The International Spectator, 48*(4), 7–29.

Portes, A., & Hoffman, K. (2003). Latin American class structures: Their composition and change during the neoliberal era. *Latin American Research Review, 38*(1), 41–82.

Roberts, K. (2008). The mobilization of opposition to economic liberalization. *Annual Review of Political Science, 11*, 327–349.

Roll, S. (2016). Managing change: How Egypt's military leadership shaped the transformation. *Mediterranean Politics, 21*(1), 23–43.

Rossi, F. (2015). The second wave of incorporation in Latin America: A conceptualization of the quest for inclusion applied to Argentina. *Latin American Politics and Society, 57*(1), 1–28.

Rossi, F. (2017). *The poor's struggle for political incorporation. The Piquetero movement in Argentina.* Cambridge: Cambridge University Press.

Rueschemeyer, D., Huber Stephen, E., & Stephens, J. (1992). *Capitalist development and democracy*. Cambridge: Polity Press.

Schlumberger, O., & Matzke, T. (2012). Path toward democracy? The role of economic development. *Swiss Political Science Review, 18*(1), 105–109.

Silva, E. (2009). *Challenging neoliberalism in Latin America*. Cambridge: Cambridge University Press.

Silva, E. (2017). Reorganizing popular sector incorporation: Propositions from Bolivia, Ecuador, and Venezuela. *Politics & Society, 45*(1), 91–122.

Silva, E., & Rossi, F. M. (2018). *Reshaping the political arena in Latin America: From resisting neoliberalism to the second incorporation*. Pittsburgh, PA: University of Pittsburgh Press. forthcoming.

Skocpol, T. (1979). *States and social revolutions. A comparative analysis of France, Russia, and China*. Cambridge: Cambridge University Press.

Teti, A. (2012). The EU's first response to the 'Arab spring': A critical discourse analysis of the partnership for democracy and shared prosperity. *Mediterranean Politics, 17*(3), 266–284.

Tilly, C. (1993). *European revolutions, 1492–1992*. Oxford: Blackwell.

Valbjørn, M. (2012). Upgrading post-democratization studies: Examining a re-politicized Arab world in a transition to somewhere. *Middle East Critique, 21*(1), 25–35.

Van Cott, D. L. (2008). *Radical democracy in the Andes*. Cambridge: Cambridge University Press.

Weipert-Fenner, I. (2015). Making the crisis visible: A reassessment of the parliament in the Mubarak regime. In L. Sadiki (Ed.), *Routledge handbook of the Arab spring: Rethinking democratization* (pp. 215–226). London: Routledge.

Weipert-Fenner, I., & Wolff, J. (2015). *Socioeconomic contention and post-revolutionary political change in Egypt and Tunisia: A research agenda*. PRIF working papers 24. Retrieved October 25, 2018, from http://www.hsfk.de/fileadmin/HSFK/hsfk_downloads/PRIF_WP_24.pdf.

Wolff, J. (2005). Ambivalent consequences of social exclusion for real-existing democracy in Latin America: The example of the argentine crisis. *Journal of International Relations and Development, 8*(1), 58–87.

Wolff, J. (2007). (De-)mobilising the marginalised. a comparison of the argentine Piqueteros and Ecuador's indigenous movement. *Journal of Latin American Studies, 39*(1), 1–29.

Wolff, J. (2018). Political incorporation in measures of democracy: A missing dimension (and the case of Bolivia). *Democratization, 25*(4), 692–708.

Yashar, D. J. (2005). *Contesting citizenship in Latin America. The rise of indigenous movements and the postliberal challenge*. Cambridge: Cambridge University Press.

Zorob, A. (2013). Der Zusammenbruch des autoritären Gesellschaftsvertrags. Sozio-ökonomische Hintergründe der arabischen Proteste. In A. Jünemann & A. Zorob (Eds.), *Arabellions. Zur Vielfalt von protest und Revolte im Nahen Osten und Nordafrika* (pp. 229–256). Wiesbaden: Springer.

Open Access This chapter is distributed under the terms of the Creative Commons Attribution 4.0 International License (http://creativecommons.org/licenses/by/4.0/), which permits use, duplication, adaptation, distribution and reproduction in any medium or format, as long as you give appropriate credit to the original author(s) and the source, a link is provided to the Creative Commons license and any changes made are indicated.

The images or other third party material in this chapter are included in the work's Creative Commons license, unless indicated otherwise in the credit line; if such material is not included in the work's Creative Commons license and the respective action is not permitted by statutory regulation, users will need to obtain permission from the license holder to duplicate, adapt or reproduce the material.

Printed in the United States
By Bookmasters